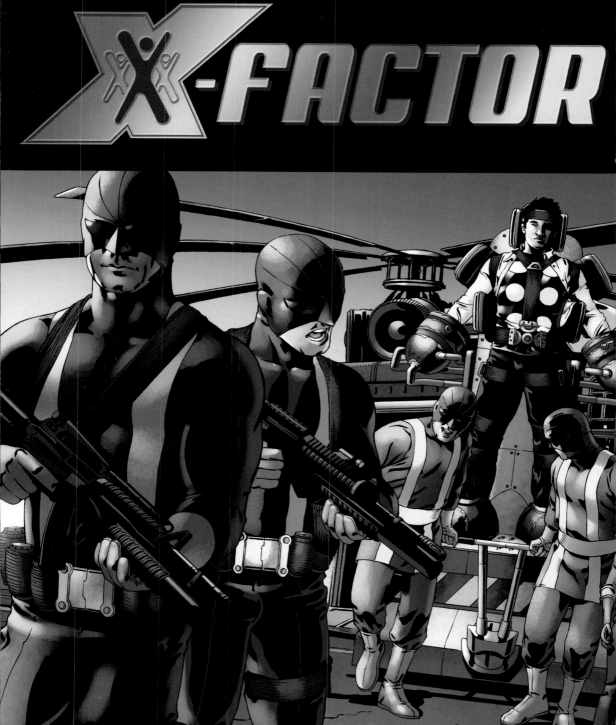

X-FACTOR

MANY LIVES OF MADROX

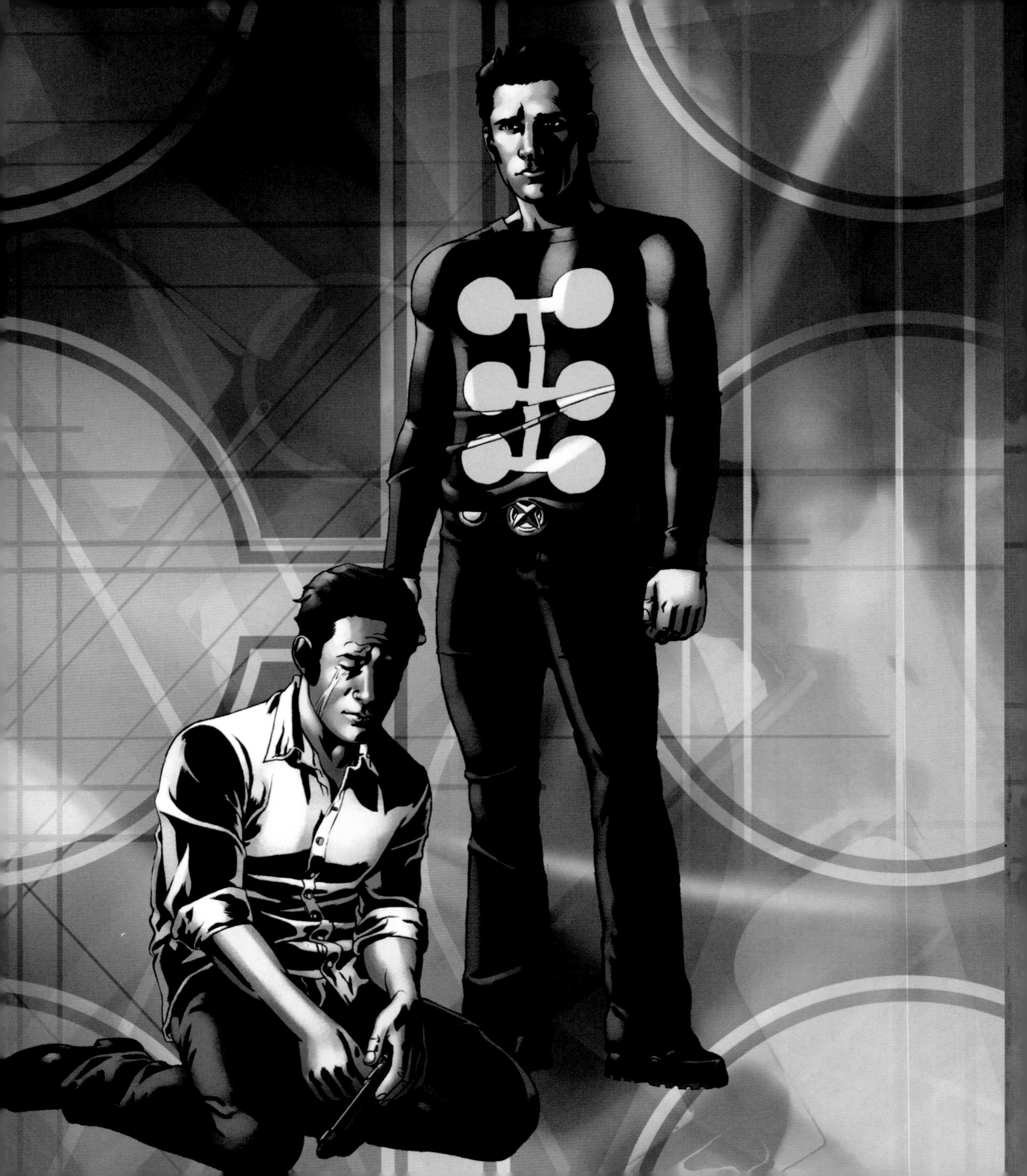

MANY LIVES OF MADROX

Writer: **PETER DAVID**
Art: **PABLO RAIMONDI WITH KHOI PHAM**
& SANDU FLORIA (ISSUE #17)
Colors: **BRIAN REBER**
Letterer: **VIRTUAL CALLIGRAPHY'S CORY PETIT**
Cover Art: **PABLO RAIMONDI & JOE QUESADA (ISSUE #13 VARIANT)**
Assistant Editor: **SEAN RYAN**
Editor: **ANDY SCHMIDT**

Collection Editor: **JENNIFER GRÜNWALD**
Assistant Editors: **MICHAEL SHORT & CORY LEVINE**
Associate Editor: **MARK D. BEAZLEY**
Senior Editor, Special Projects: **JEFF YOUNGQUIST**
Senior Vice President of Sales: **DAVID GABRIEL**
Production: **JERRON QUALITY COLOR & JERRY KALINOWSKI**
Vice President of Creative: **TOM MARVELLI**

Editor in Chief: **JOE QUESADA**
Publisher: **DAN BUCKLEY**

X-FACTOR: MANY LIVES OF MADROX. Contains material originally published in magazine form as X-FACTOR #13-17. First printing 2007. ISBN# 0-7851-2805-0. Published by MARVEL PUBLISHING, INC., a subsidiary of MARVEL ENTERTAINMENT, INC. OFFICE OF PUBLICATION: 417 5th Avenue, New York, NY 10016. Copyright © 2006 and 2007 Marvel Characters, Inc. All rights reserved. $19.99 per copy in the U.S. and $32.00 in Canada (GST #R127032852); Canadian Agreement #40668537. All characters featured in this issue and the distinctive names and likenesses thereof, and all related indicia are trademarks of Marvel Characters, Inc. No similarity between any of the names, characters, persons, and/or institutions in this magazine with those of any living or dead person or institution is intended, and any such similarity which may exist is purely coincidental. **Printed in the U.S.A.** ALAN FINE, CEO Marvel Toys & Publishing Divisions and CMO Marvel Entertainment, Inc.; DAVID GABRIEL, Senior VP of Publishing Sales & Circulation; DAVID BOGART, VP of Business Affairs & Editorial Operations; JIM BOYLE, VP of Publishing Operations; DAN CARR, Executive Director of Publishing Technology; JUSTIN F. GABRIE, Managing Editor; SUSAN CRESPI, Production Manager; STAN LEE, Chairman Emeritus. For information regarding advertising in Marvel Comics or on Marvel.com, please contact Joe Maimone, Advertising Director, at jmaimone@marvel.com or 212-576-8534.

10 9 8 7 6 5 4 3 2 1

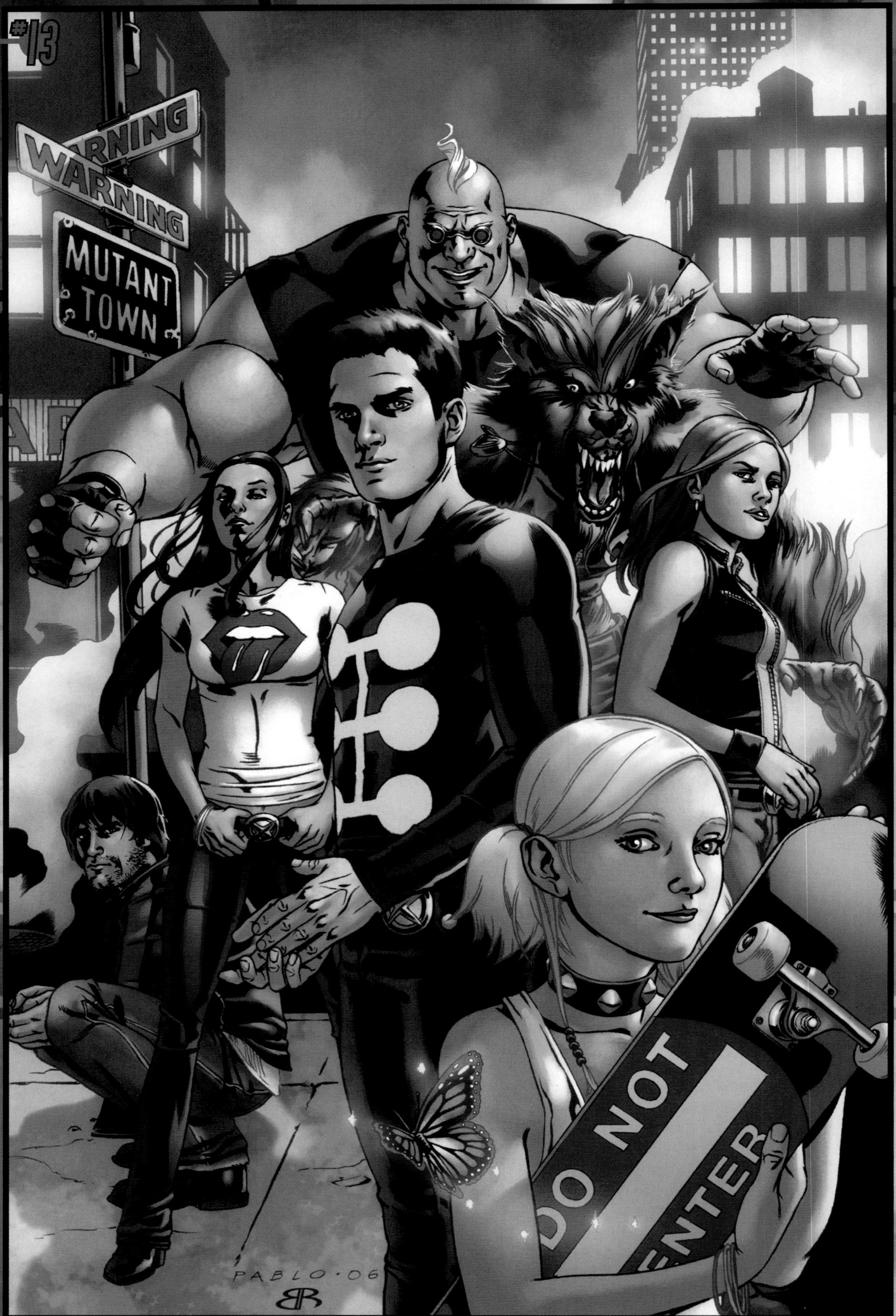
#13
WARNING
WARNING
WARNING
MUTANT TOWN
DO NOT ENTER
PABLO·06

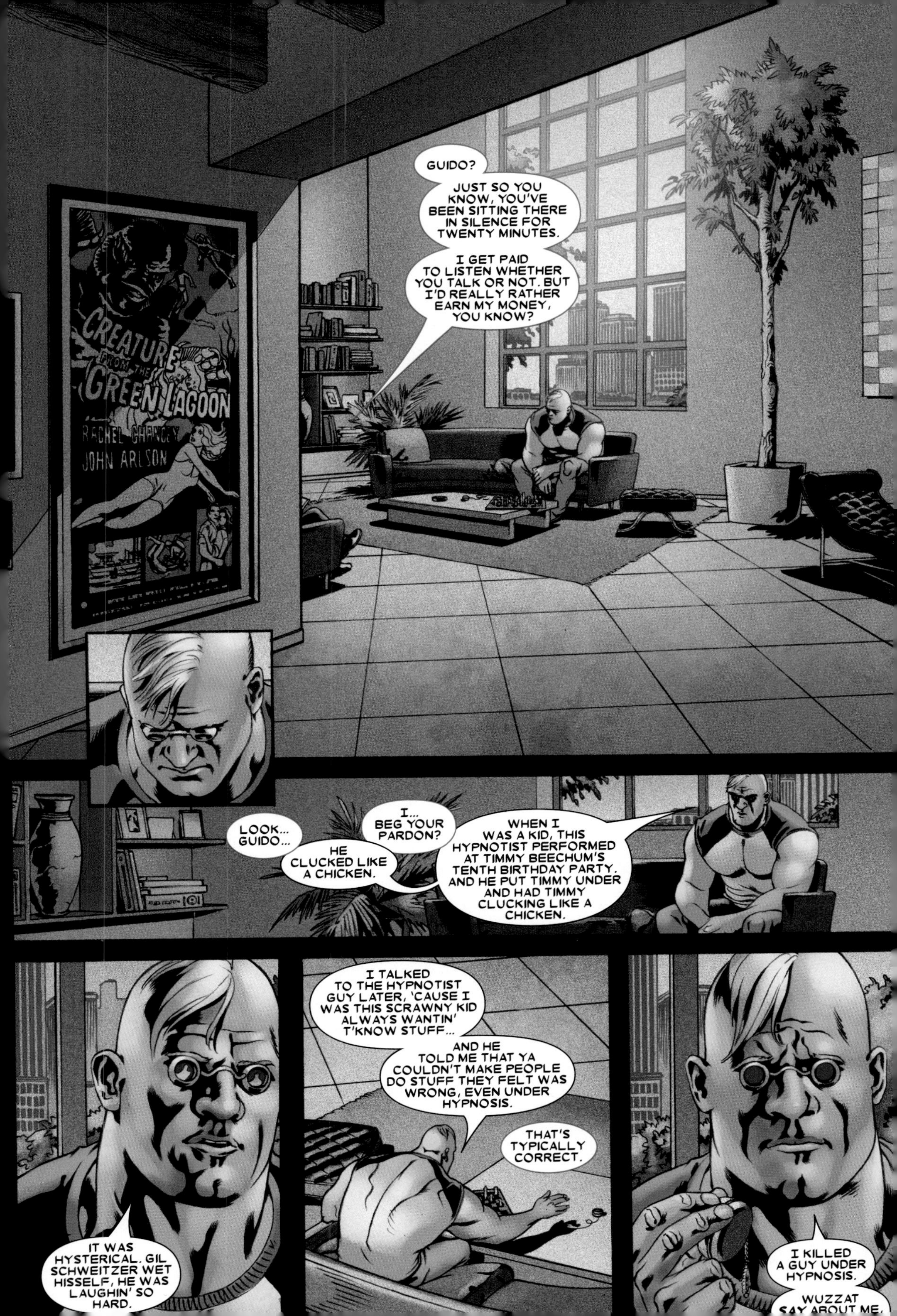
CREATURE FROM THE GREEN LAGOON
RACHEL CHANCEY
JOHN ARLSON
GUIDO?
JUST SO YOU KNOW, YOU'VE BEEN SITTING THERE IN SILENCE FOR TWENTY MINUTES.
I GET PAID TO LISTEN WHETHER YOU TALK OR NOT. BUT I'D REALLY RATHER EARN MY MONEY, YOU KNOW?
WHEN I WAS A KID, THIS HYPNOTIST PERFORMED AT TIMMY BEECHUM'S TENTH BIRTHDAY PARTY. AND HE PUT TIMMY UNDER AND HAD TIMMY CLUCKING LIKE A CHICKEN.
HE CLUCKED LIKE A CHICKEN.
LOOK... GUIDO...
I... BEG YOUR PARDON?
IT WAS HYSTERICAL. GIL SCHWEITZER WET HISSELF, HE WAS LAUGHIN' SO HARD.
I TALKED TO THE HYPNOTIST GUY LATER, 'CAUSE I WAS THIS SCRAWNY KID ALWAYS WANTIN' T'KNOW STUFF...
AND HE TOLD ME THAT YA COULDN'T MAKE PEOPLE DO STUFF THEY FELT WAS WRONG, EVEN UNDER HYPNOSIS.
THAT'S TYPICALLY CORRECT.
I KILLED A GUY UNDER HYPNOSIS.
WUZZAT SAY ABOUT ME.

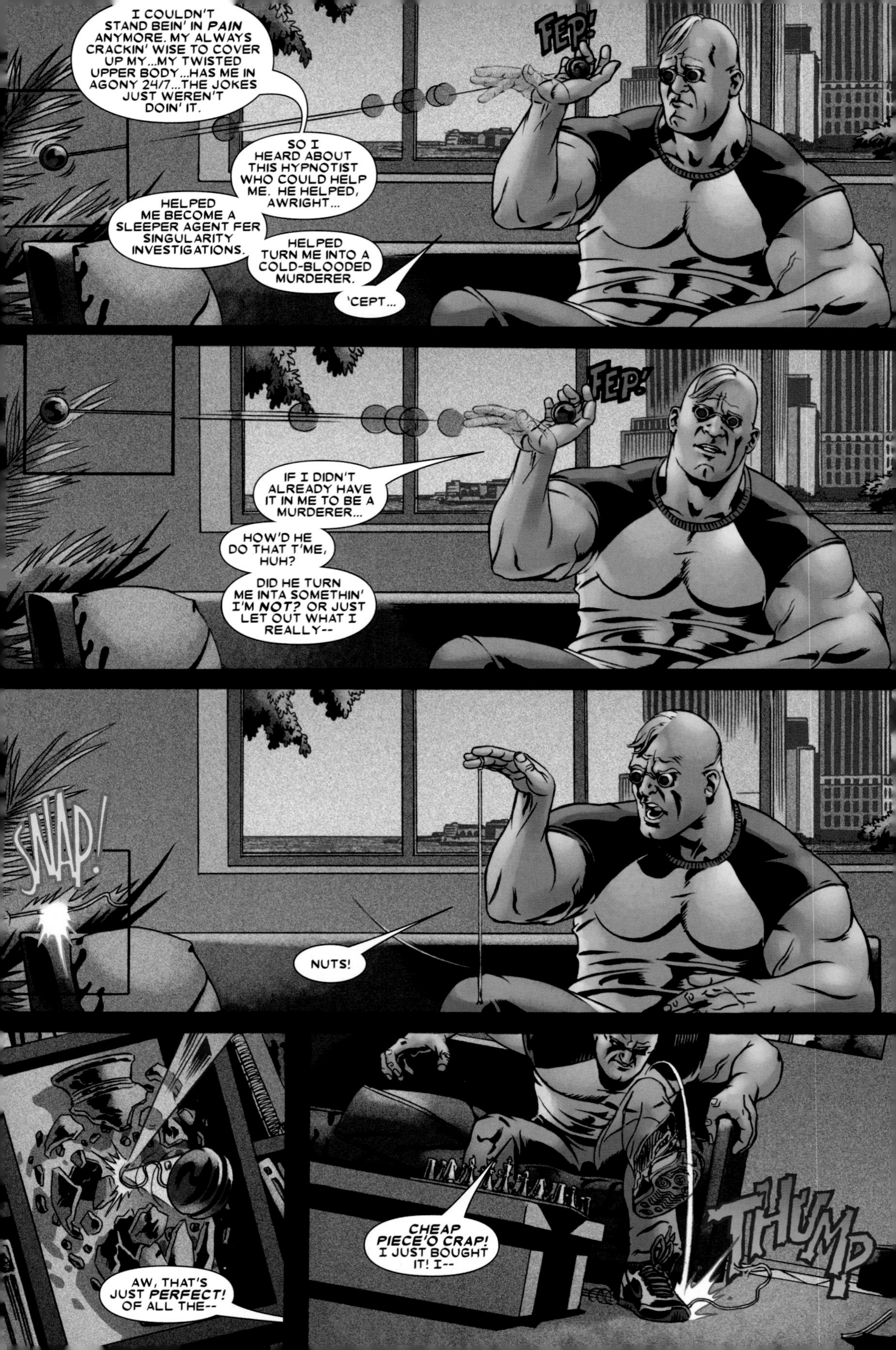
I COULDN'T STAND BEIN' IN PAIN ANYMORE. MY ALWAYS CRACKIN' WISE TO COVER UP MY...MY TWISTED UPPER BODY...HAS ME IN AGONY 24/7...THE JOKES JUST WEREN'T DOIN' IT.
FEP!
SO I HEARD ABOUT THIS HYPNOTIST WHO COULD HELP ME. HE HELPED, AWRIGHT...
HELPED ME BECOME A SLEEPER AGENT FER SINGULARITY INVESTIGATIONS.
HELPED TURN ME INTO A COLD-BLOODED MURDERER.
'CEPT...
FEP!
IF I DIDN'T ALREADY HAVE IT IN ME TO BE A MURDERER...
HOW'D HE DO THAT T'ME, HUH?
DID HE TURN ME INTA SOMETHIN' I'M NOT? OR JUST LET OUT WHAT I REALLY--
SNAP!
NUTS!
AW, THAT'S JUST PERFECT! OF ALL THE--
CHEAP PIECE'O CRAP! I JUST BOUGHT IT! I--
THUMP

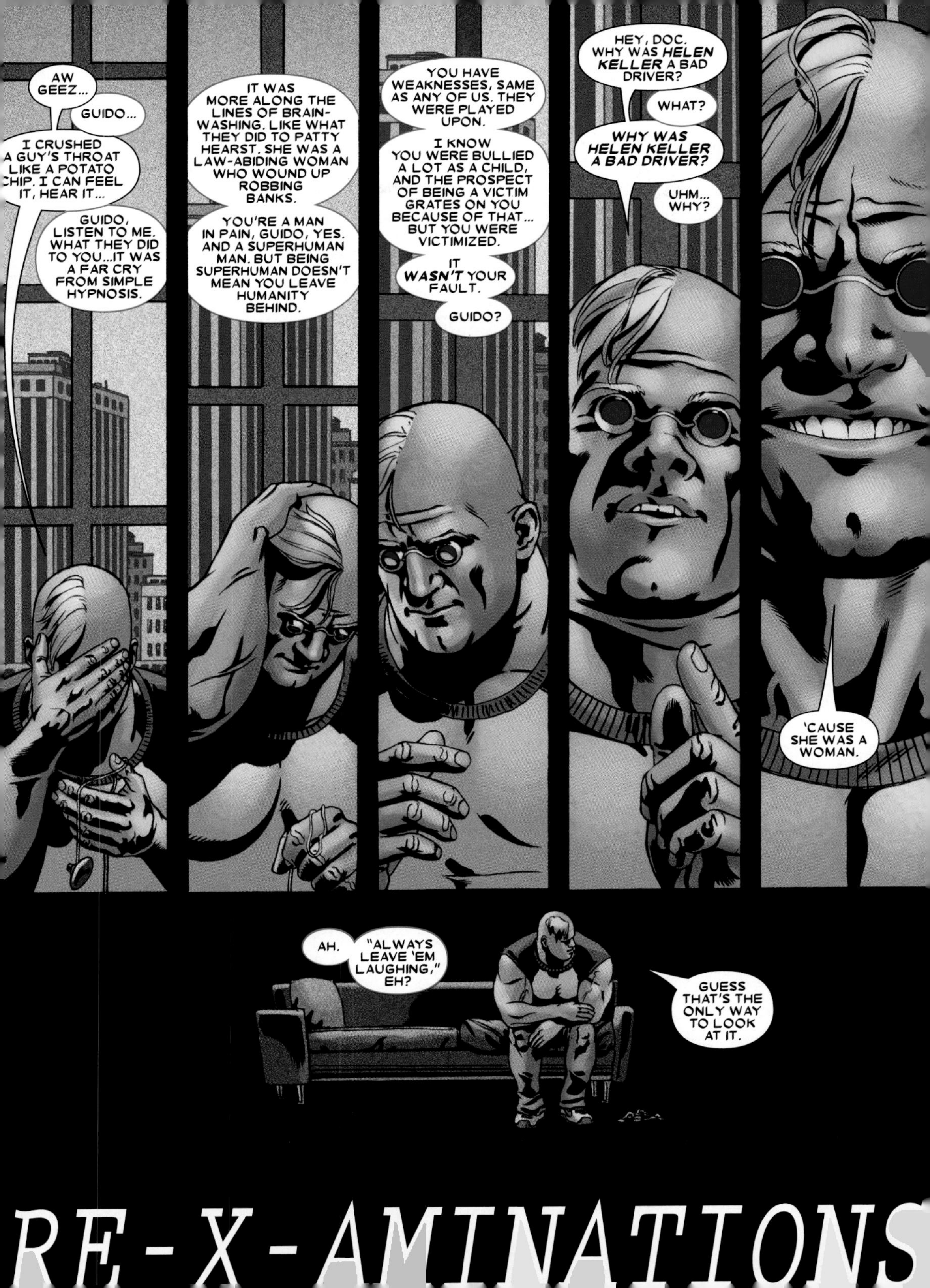

AW GEEZ...
GUIDO...
I CRUSHED A GUY'S THROAT LIKE A POTATO CHIP. I CAN FEEL IT, HEAR IT...
GUIDO, LISTEN TO ME. WHAT THEY DID TO YOU...IT WAS A FAR CRY FROM SIMPLE HYPNOSIS.
IT WAS MORE ALONG THE LINES OF BRAIN-WASHING. LIKE WHAT THEY DID TO PATTY HEARST. SHE WAS A LAW-ABIDING WOMAN WHO WOUND UP ROBBING BANKS.
YOU'RE A MAN IN PAIN, GUIDO, YES. AND A SUPERHUMAN MAN. BUT BEING SUPERHUMAN DOESN'T MEAN YOU LEAVE HUMANITY BEHIND.
YOU HAVE WEAKNESSES, SAME AS ANY OF US. THEY WERE PLAYED UPON.
I KNOW YOU WERE BULLIED A LOT AS A CHILD, AND THE PROSPECT OF BEING A VICTIM GRATES ON YOU BECAUSE OF THAT... BUT YOU WERE VICTIMIZED.
IT WASN'T YOUR FAULT.
GUIDO?
HEY, DOC. WHY WAS HELEN KELLER A BAD DRIVER?
WHAT?
WHY WAS HELEN KELLER A BAD DRIVER?
UHM... WHY?
'CAUSE SHE WAS A WOMAN.
AH.
"ALWAYS LEAVE 'EM LAUGHING," EH?
GUESS THAT'S THE ONLY WAY TO LOOK AT IT.
RE-X-AMINATIONS

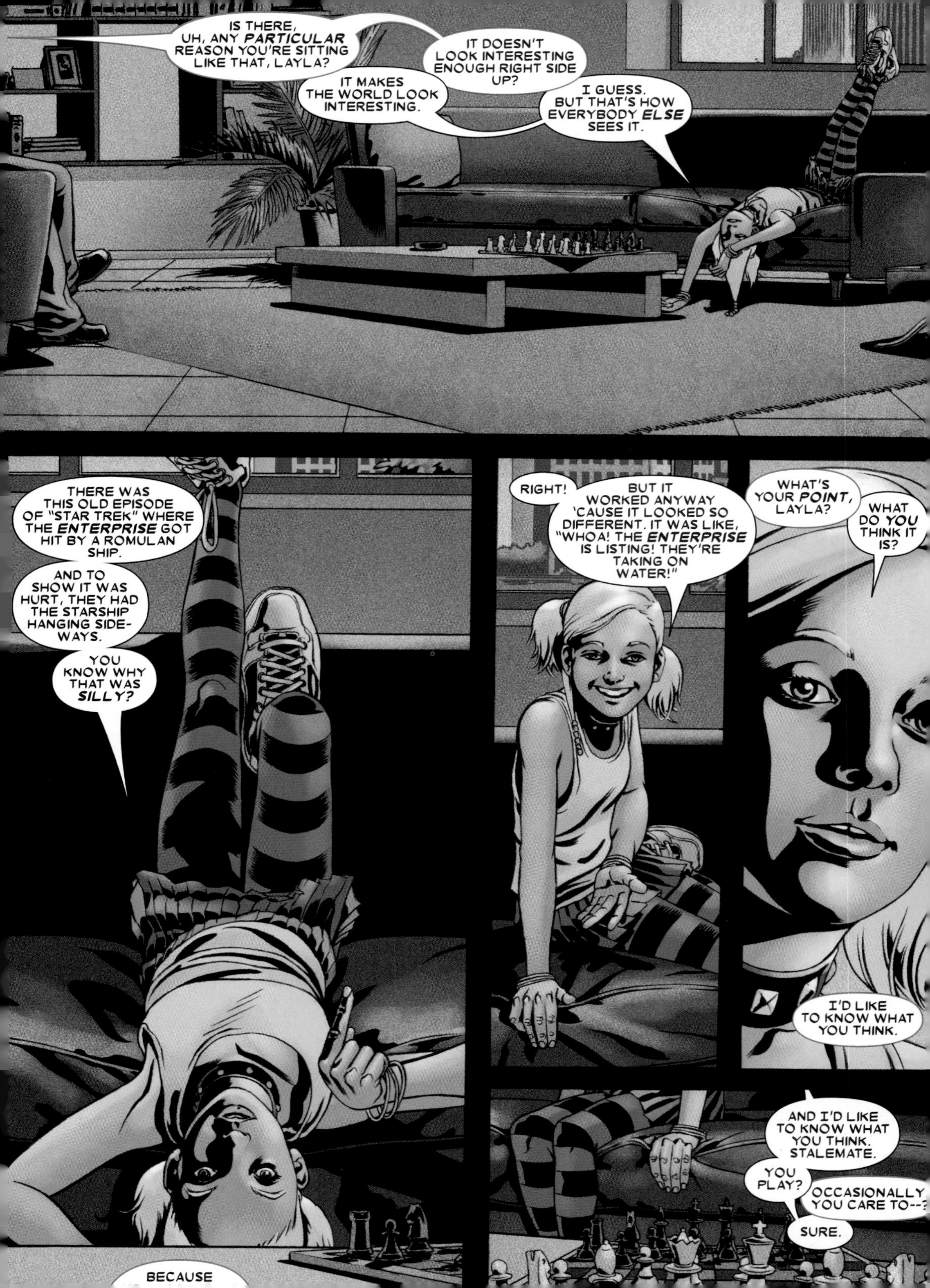
IS THERE, UH, ANY PARTICULAR REASON YOU'RE SITTING LIKE THAT, LAYLA?
IT MAKES THE WORLD LOOK INTERESTING.
IT DOESN'T LOOK INTERESTING ENOUGH RIGHT SIDE UP?
I GUESS. BUT THAT'S HOW EVERYBODY ELSE SEES IT.
THERE WAS THIS OLD EPISODE OF "STAR TREK" WHERE THE ENTERPRISE GOT HIT BY A ROMULAN SHIP.
AND TO SHOW IT WAS HURT, THEY HAD THE STARSHIP HANGING SIDE-WAYS.
YOU KNOW WHY THAT WAS SILLY?
BECAUSE
RIGHT!
BUT IT WORKED ANYWAY 'CAUSE IT LOOKED SO DIFFERENT. IT WAS LIKE, "WHOA! THE ENTERPRISE IS LISTING! THEY'RE TAKING ON WATER!"
WHAT'S YOUR POINT, LAYLA?
WHAT DO YOU THINK IT IS?
I'D LIKE TO KNOW WHAT YOU THINK.
AND I'D LIKE TO KNOW WHAT YOU THINK. STALEMATE.
YOU PLAY?
OCCASIONALLY. YOU CARE TO--?
SURE.

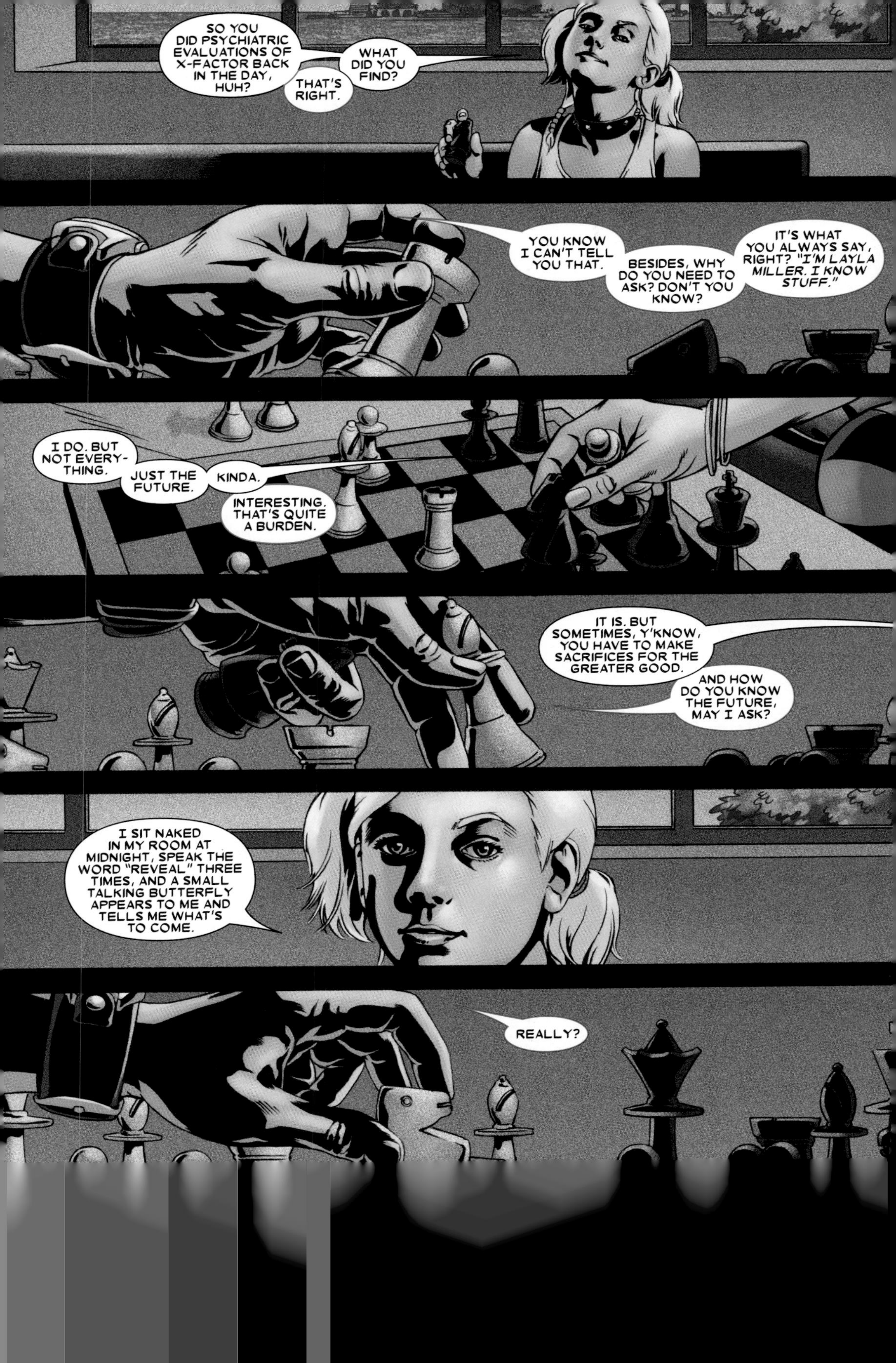
SO YOU DID PSYCHIATRIC EVALUATIONS OF X-FACTOR BACK IN THE DAY, HUH?
THAT'S RIGHT.
WHAT DID YOU FIND?
YOU KNOW I CAN'T TELL YOU THAT.
BESIDES, WHY DO YOU NEED TO ASK? DON'T YOU KNOW?
IT'S WHAT YOU ALWAYS SAY, RIGHT? "I'M LAYLA MILLER. I KNOW STUFF."
I DO. BUT NOT EVERYTHING.
JUST THE FUTURE.
KINDA.
INTERESTING. THAT'S QUITE A BURDEN.
IT IS. BUT SOMETIMES, Y'KNOW, YOU HAVE TO MAKE SACRIFICES FOR THE GREATER GOOD.
AND HOW DO YOU KNOW THE FUTURE, MAY I ASK?
I SIT NAKED IN MY ROOM AT MIDNIGHT, SPEAK THE WORD "REVEAL" THREE TIMES, AND A SMALL TALKING BUTTERFLY APPEARS TO ME AND TELLS ME WHAT'S TO COME.
REALLY?

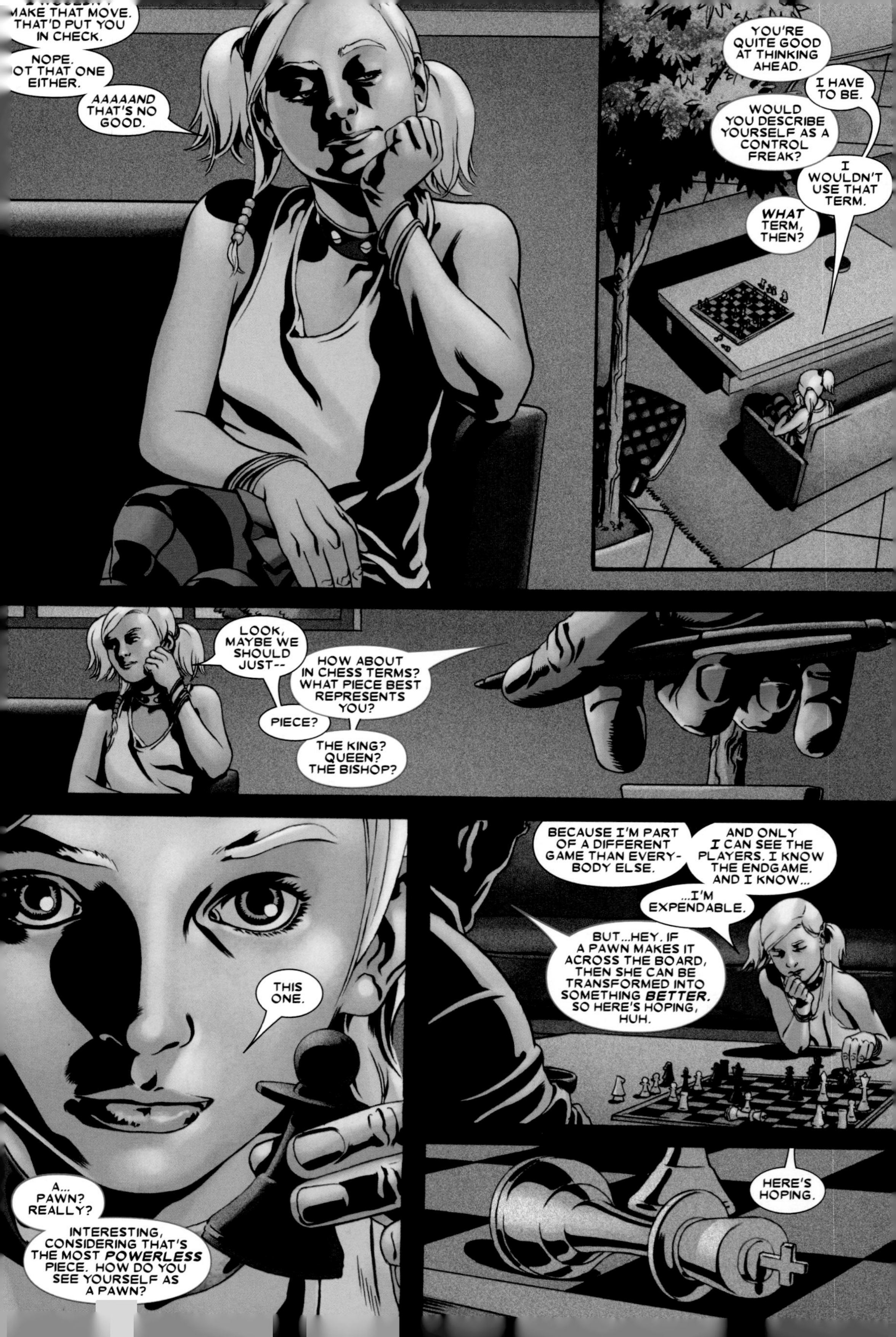

MAKE THAT MOVE. THAT'D PUT YOU IN CHECK.
NOPE. OT THAT ONE EITHER.
AAAAAND THAT'S NO GOOD.
YOU'RE QUITE GOOD AT THINKING AHEAD.
I HAVE TO BE.
WOULD YOU DESCRIBE YOURSELF AS A CONTROL FREAK?
I WOULDN'T USE THAT TERM.
WHAT TERM, THEN?
LOOK, MAYBE WE SHOULD JUST--
HOW ABOUT IN CHESS TERMS? WHAT PIECE BEST REPRESENTS YOU?
PIECE?
THE KING? QUEEN? THE BISHOP?
THIS ONE.
A... PAWN? REALLY?
INTERESTING, CONSIDERING THAT'S THE MOST POWERLESS PIECE. HOW DO YOU SEE YOURSELF AS A PAWN?
BECAUSE I'M PART OF A DIFFERENT GAME THAN EVERY-BODY ELSE.
AND ONLY I CAN SEE THE PLAYERS. I KNOW THE ENDGAME. AND I KNOW...
...I'M EXPENDABLE.
BUT...HEY. IF A PAWN MAKES IT ACROSS THE BOARD, THEN SHE CAN BE TRANSFORMED INTO SOMETHING BETTER. SO HERE'S HOPING, HUH.
HERE'S HOPING.

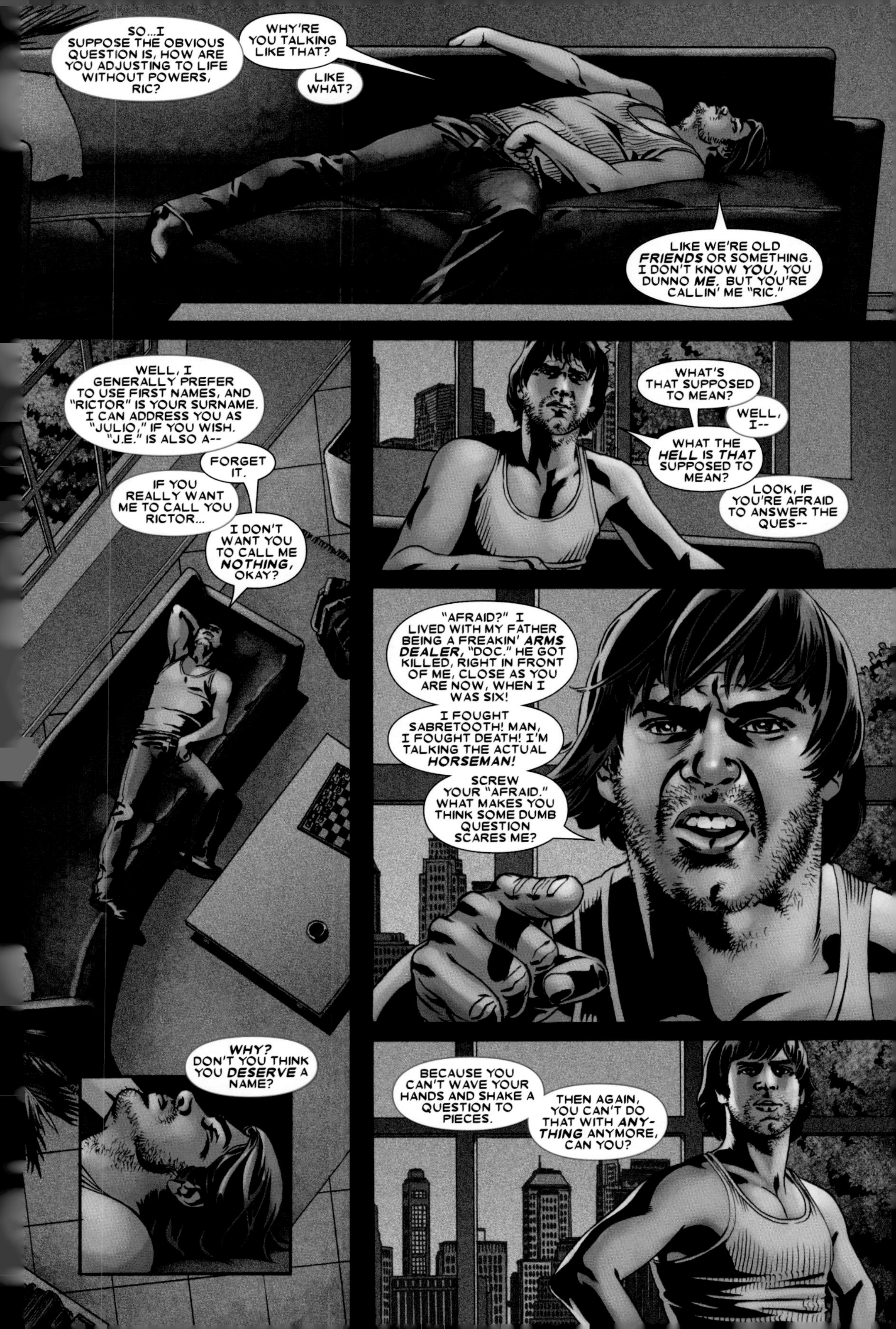
SO...I SUPPOSE THE OBVIOUS QUESTION IS, HOW ARE YOU ADJUSTING TO LIFE WITHOUT POWERS, RIC?
WHY'RE YOU TALKING LIKE THAT?
LIKE WHAT?
LIKE WE'RE OLD FRIENDS OR SOMETHING. I DON'T KNOW YOU, YOU DUNNO ME. BUT YOU'RE CALLIN' ME "RIC."
WELL, I GENERALLY PREFER TO USE FIRST NAMES, AND "RICTOR" IS YOUR SURNAME. I CAN ADDRESS YOU AS "JULIO," IF YOU WISH. "J.E." IS ALSO A--
FORGET IT.
IF YOU REALLY WANT ME TO CALL YOU RICTOR...
I DON'T WANT YOU TO CALL ME NOTHING, OKAY?
WHAT'S THAT SUPPOSED TO MEAN?
WELL, I--
WHAT THE HELL IS THAT SUPPOSED TO MEAN?
LOOK, IF YOU'RE AFRAID TO ANSWER THE QUES--
"AFRAID?" I LIVED WITH MY FATHER BEING A FREAKIN' ARMS DEALER, "DOC." HE GOT KILLED, RIGHT IN FRONT OF ME, CLOSE AS YOU ARE NOW, WHEN I WAS SIX!
I FOUGHT SABRETOOTH! MAN, I FOUGHT DEATH! I'M TALKING THE ACTUAL HORSEMAN!
SCREW YOUR "AFRAID." WHAT MAKES YOU THINK SOME DUMB QUESTION SCARES ME?
WHY? DON'T YOU THINK YOU DESERVE A NAME?
BECAUSE YOU CAN'T WAVE YOUR HANDS AND SHAKE A QUESTION TO PIECES.
THEN AGAIN, YOU CAN'T DO THAT WITH ANYTHING ANYMORE, CAN YOU?

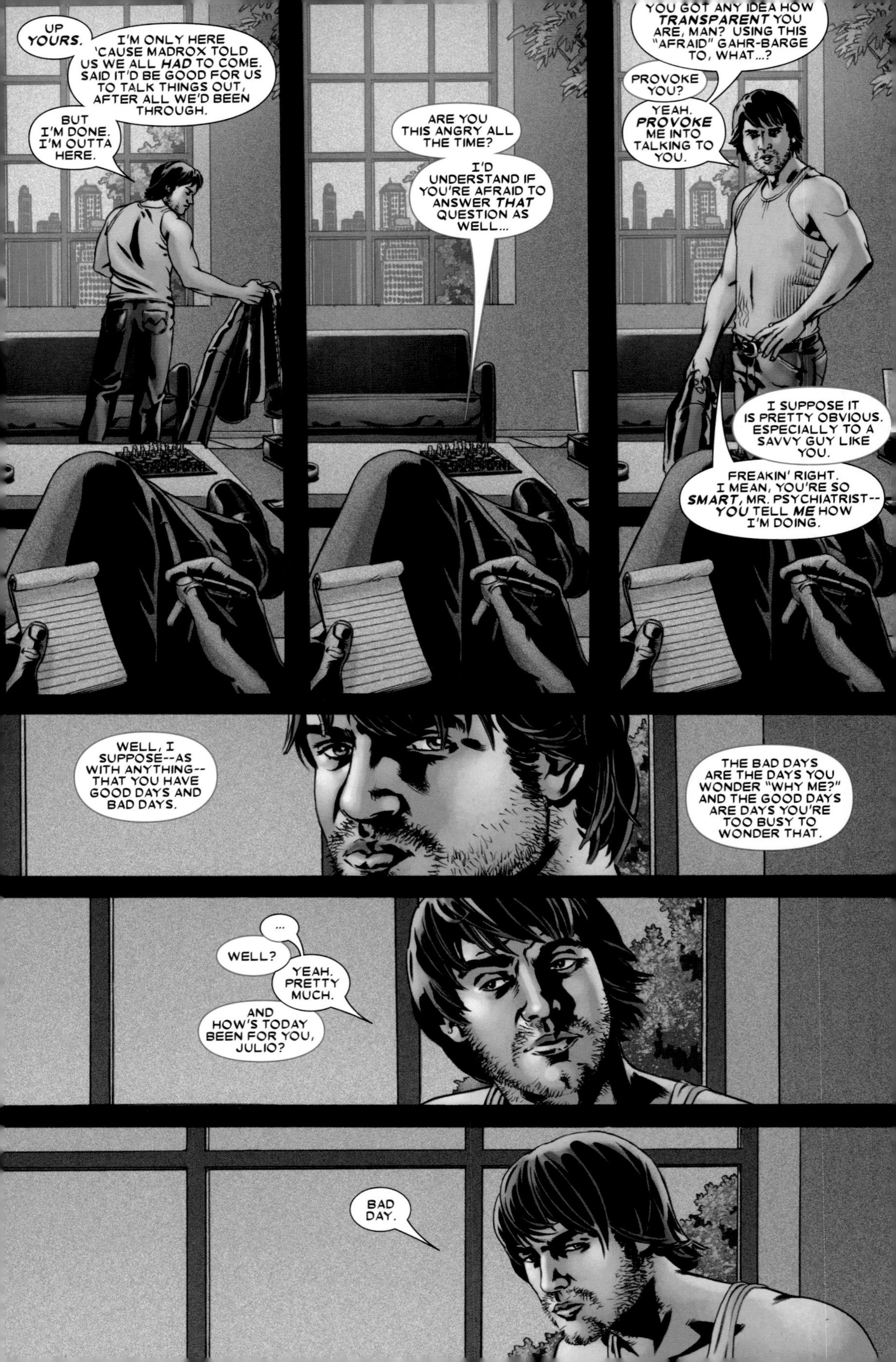

UP YOURS.
I'M ONLY HERE 'CAUSE MADROX TOLD US WE ALL HAD TO COME. SAID IT'D BE GOOD FOR US TO TALK THINGS OUT, AFTER ALL WE'D BEEN THROUGH.
BUT I'M DONE. I'M OUTTA HERE.
ARE YOU THIS ANGRY ALL THE TIME?
I'D UNDERSTAND IF YOU'RE AFRAID TO ANSWER THAT QUESTION AS WELL...
YOU GOT ANY IDEA HOW TRANSPARENT YOU ARE, MAN? USING THIS "AFRAID" GAHR-BARGE TO, WHAT...?
PROVOKE YOU?
YEAH. PROVOKE ME INTO TALKING TO YOU.
I SUPPOSE IT IS PRETTY OBVIOUS. ESPECIALLY TO A SAVVY GUY LIKE YOU.
FREAKIN' RIGHT. I MEAN, YOU'RE SO SMART, MR. PSYCHIATRIST--YOU TELL ME HOW I'M DOING.
WELL, I SUPPOSE--AS WITH ANYTHING--THAT YOU HAVE GOOD DAYS AND BAD DAYS.
THE BAD DAYS ARE THE DAYS YOU WONDER "WHY ME?" AND THE GOOD DAYS ARE DAYS YOU'RE TOO BUSY TO WONDER THAT.
...
WELL?
YEAH. PRETTY MUCH.
AND HOW'S TODAY BEEN FOR YOU, JULIO?
BAD DAY.

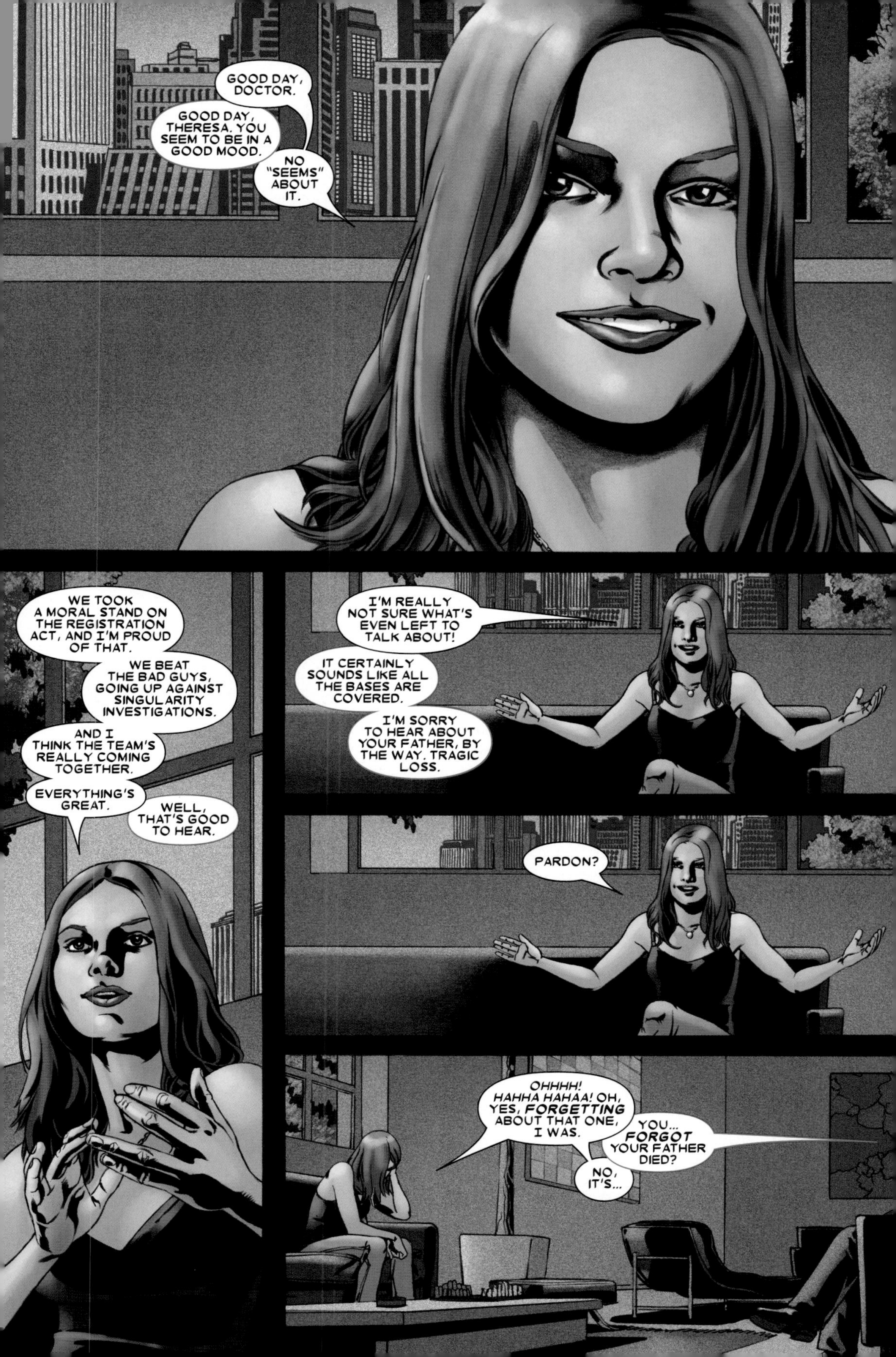
GOOD DAY, DOCTOR.
GOOD DAY, THERESA. YOU SEEM TO BE IN A GOOD MOOD.
NO "SEEMS" ABOUT IT.
WE TOOK A MORAL STAND ON THE REGISTRATION ACT, AND I'M PROUD OF THAT.
WE BEAT THE BAD GUYS, GOING UP AGAINST SINGULARITY INVESTIGATIONS.
AND I THINK THE TEAM'S REALLY COMING TOGETHER.
EVERYTHING'S GREAT.
WELL, THAT'S GOOD TO HEAR.
I'M REALLY NOT SURE WHAT'S EVEN LEFT TO TALK ABOUT!
IT CERTAINLY SOUNDS LIKE ALL THE BASES ARE COVERED.
I'M SORRY TO HEAR ABOUT YOUR FATHER, BY THE WAY. TRAGIC LOSS.
PARDON?
OHHHH! HAHHA HAHAA! OH, YES, FORGETTING ABOUT THAT ONE, I WAS.
YOU... FORGOT YOUR FATHER DIED?
NO, IT'S...

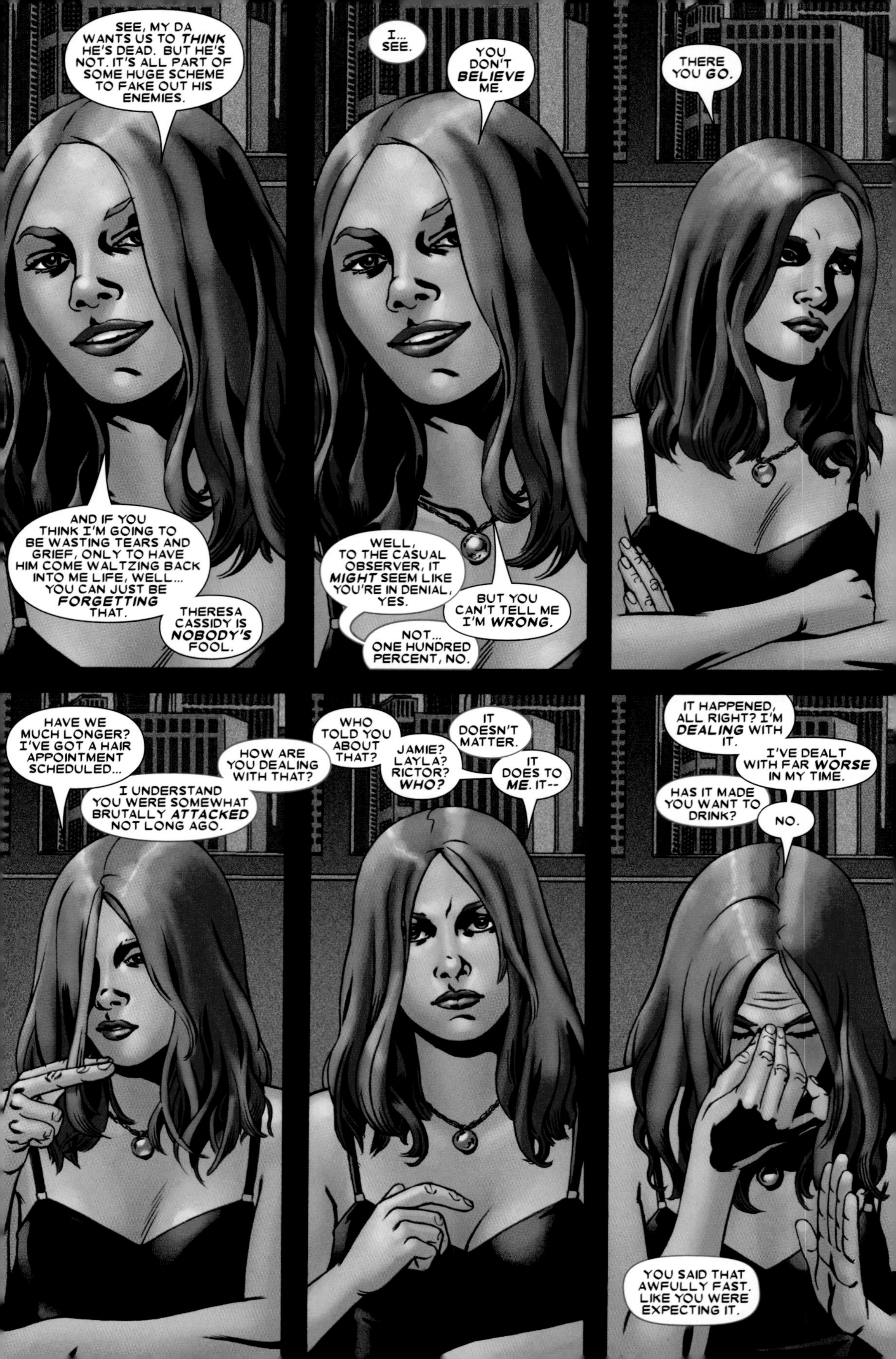
SEE, MY DA WANTS US TO THINK HE'S DEAD. BUT HE'S NOT. IT'S ALL PART OF SOME HUGE SCHEME TO FAKE OUT HIS ENEMIES.
AND IF YOU THINK I'M GOING TO BE WASTING TEARS AND GRIEF, ONLY TO HAVE HIM COME WALTZING BACK INTO ME LIFE, WELL... YOU CAN JUST BE FORGETTING THAT.
THERESA CASSIDY IS NOBODY'S FOOL.
I... SEE.
YOU DON'T BELIEVE ME.
WELL, TO THE CASUAL OBSERVER, IT MIGHT SEEM LIKE YOU'RE IN DENIAL, YES.
BUT YOU CAN'T TELL ME I'M WRONG.
NOT... ONE HUNDRED PERCENT, NO.
THERE YOU GO.
HAVE WE MUCH LONGER? I'VE GOT A HAIR APPOINTMENT SCHEDULED...
I UNDERSTAND YOU WERE SOMEWHAT BRUTALLY ATTACKED NOT LONG AGO.
HOW ARE YOU DEALING WITH THAT?
WHO TOLD YOU ABOUT THAT?
JAMIE? LAYLA? RICTOR? WHO?
IT DOESN'T MATTER.
IT DOES TO ME. IT--
IT HAPPENED, ALL RIGHT? I'M DEALING WITH IT.
I'VE DEALT WITH FAR WORSE IN MY TIME.
HAS IT MADE YOU WANT TO DRINK?
NO.
YOU SAID THAT AWFULLY FAST. LIKE YOU WERE EXPECTING IT.

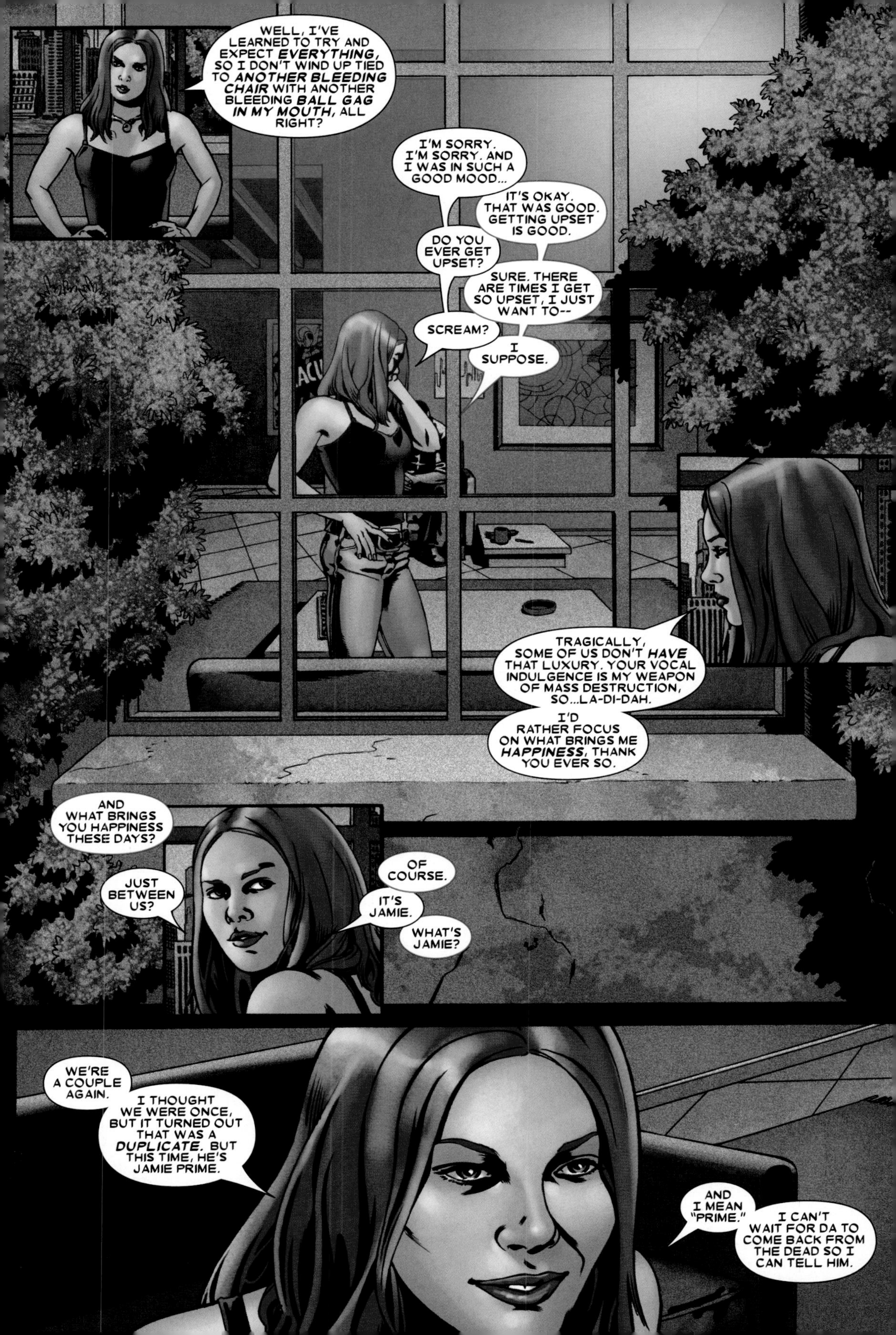

WELL, I'VE LEARNED TO TRY AND EXPECT EVERYTHING, SO I DON'T WIND UP TIED TO ANOTHER BLEEDING CHAIR WITH ANOTHER BLEEDING BALL GAG IN MY MOUTH, ALL RIGHT?
I'M SORRY. I'M SORRY. AND I WAS IN SUCH A GOOD MOOD...
IT'S OKAY. THAT WAS GOOD. GETTING UPSET IS GOOD.
DO YOU EVER GET UPSET?
SURE. THERE ARE TIMES I GET SO UPSET, I JUST WANT TO--
SCREAM?
I SUPPOSE.
TRAGICALLY, SOME OF US DON'T HAVE THAT LUXURY. YOUR VOCAL INDULGENCE IS MY WEAPON OF MASS DESTRUCTION, SO...LA-DI-DAH.
I'D RATHER FOCUS ON WHAT BRINGS ME HAPPINESS, THANK YOU EVER SO.
AND WHAT BRINGS YOU HAPPINESS THESE DAYS?
JUST BETWEEN US?
OF COURSE.
IT'S JAMIE.
WHAT'S JAMIE?
WE'RE A COUPLE AGAIN.
I THOUGHT WE WERE ONCE, BUT IT TURNED OUT THAT WAS A DUPLICATE. BUT THIS TIME, HE'S JAMIE PRIME.
AND I MEAN "PRIME."
I CAN'T WAIT FOR DA TO COME BACK FROM THE DEAD SO I CAN TELL HIM.

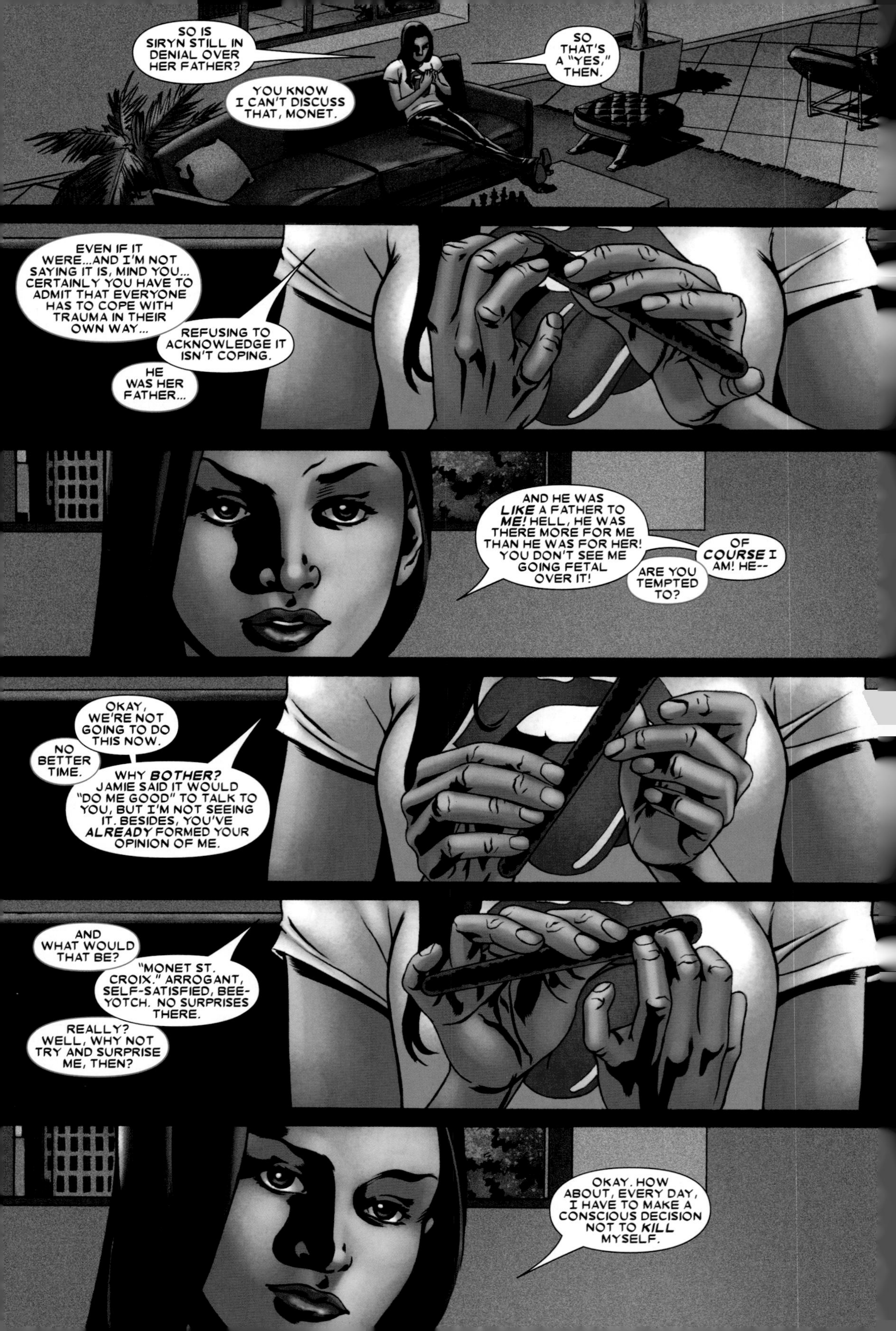
SO IS SIRYN STILL IN DENIAL OVER HER FATHER?
YOU KNOW I CAN'T DISCUSS THAT, MONET.
SO THAT'S A "YES," THEN.
EVEN IF IT WERE...AND I'M NOT SAYING IT IS, MIND YOU... CERTAINLY YOU HAVE TO ADMIT THAT EVERYONE HAS TO COPE WITH TRAUMA IN THEIR OWN WAY...
REFUSING TO ACKNOWLEDGE IT ISN'T COPING.
HE WAS HER FATHER...
AND HE WAS LIKE A FATHER TO ME! HELL, HE WAS THERE MORE FOR ME THAN HE WAS FOR HER! YOU DON'T SEE ME GOING FETAL OVER IT!
ARE YOU TEMPTED TO?
OF COURSE I AM! HE--
OKAY, WE'RE NOT GOING TO DO THIS NOW.
NO BETTER TIME.
WHY BOTHER? JAMIE SAID IT WOULD "DO ME GOOD" TO TALK TO YOU, BUT I'M NOT SEEING IT. BESIDES, YOU'VE ALREADY FORMED YOUR OPINION OF ME.
AND WHAT WOULD THAT BE?
"MONET ST. CROIX." ARROGANT, SELF-SATISFIED, BEE-YOTCH. NO SURPRISES THERE.
REALLY? WELL, WHY NOT TRY AND SURPRISE ME, THEN?
OKAY. HOW ABOUT, EVERY DAY, I HAVE TO MAKE A CONSCIOUS DECISION NOT TO KILL MYSELF.

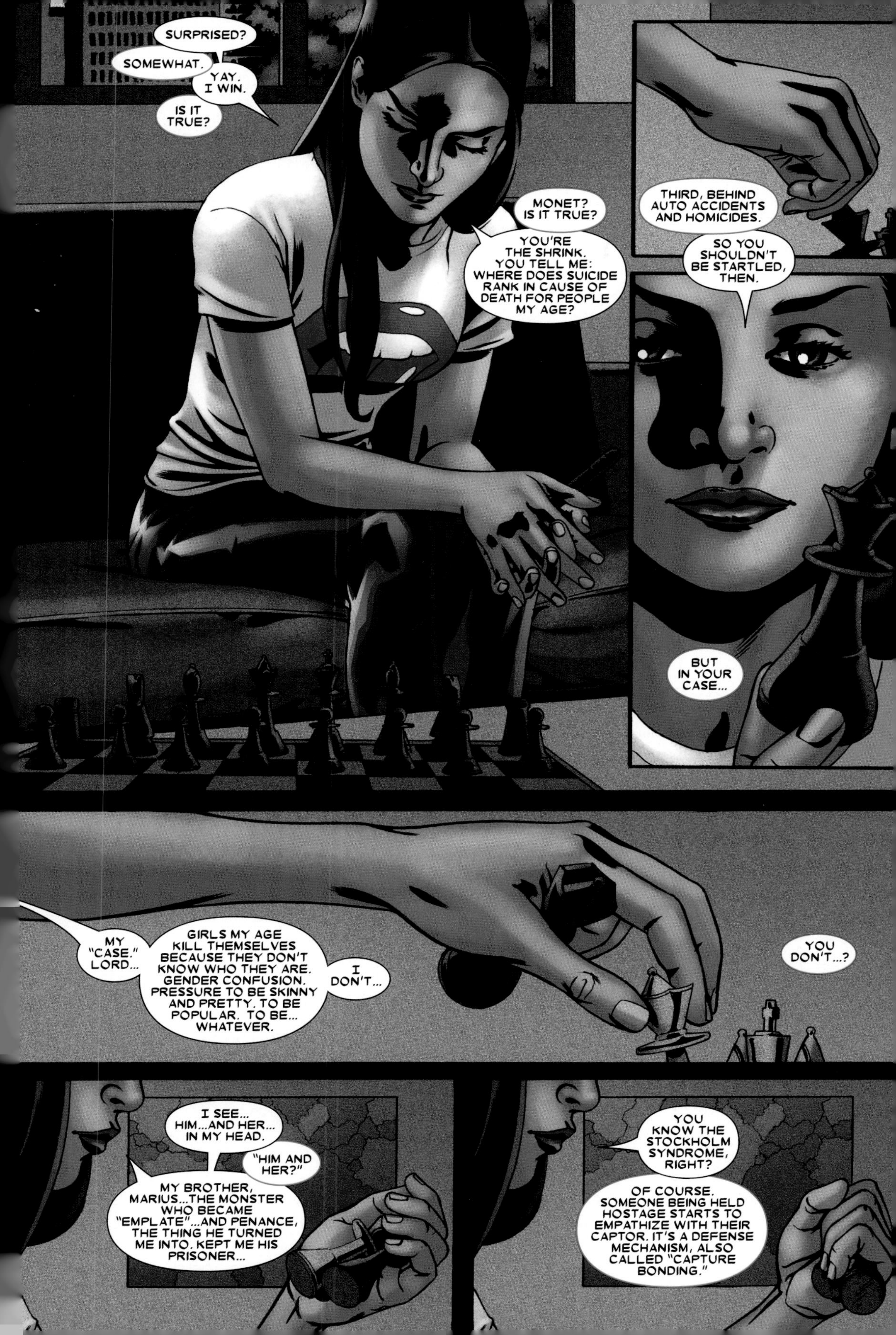
SURPRISED?
SOMEWHAT.
YAY. I WIN.
IS IT TRUE?
MONET? IS IT TRUE?
YOU'RE THE SHRINK. YOU TELL ME: WHERE DOES SUICIDE RANK IN CAUSE OF DEATH FOR PEOPLE MY AGE?
THIRD, BEHIND AUTO ACCIDENTS AND HOMICIDES.
SO YOU SHOULDN'T BE STARTLED, THEN.
BUT IN YOUR CASE...
MY "CASE." LORD...
GIRLS MY AGE KILL THEMSELVES BECAUSE THEY DON'T KNOW WHO THEY ARE. GENDER CONFUSION. PRESSURE TO BE SKINNY AND PRETTY. TO BE POPULAR. TO BE... WHATEVER.
I DON'T...
YOU DON'T...?
I SEE... HIM...AND HER... IN MY HEAD.
"HIM AND HER?"
MY BROTHER, MARIUS...THE MONSTER WHO BECAME "EMPLATE"...AND PENANCE, THE THING HE TURNED ME INTO. KEPT ME HIS PRISONER...
YOU KNOW THE STOCKHOLM SYNDROME, RIGHT?
OF COURSE. SOMEONE BEING HELD HOSTAGE STARTS TO EMPATHIZE WITH THEIR CAPTOR. IT'S A DEFENSE MECHANISM, ALSO CALLED "CAPTURE BONDING."

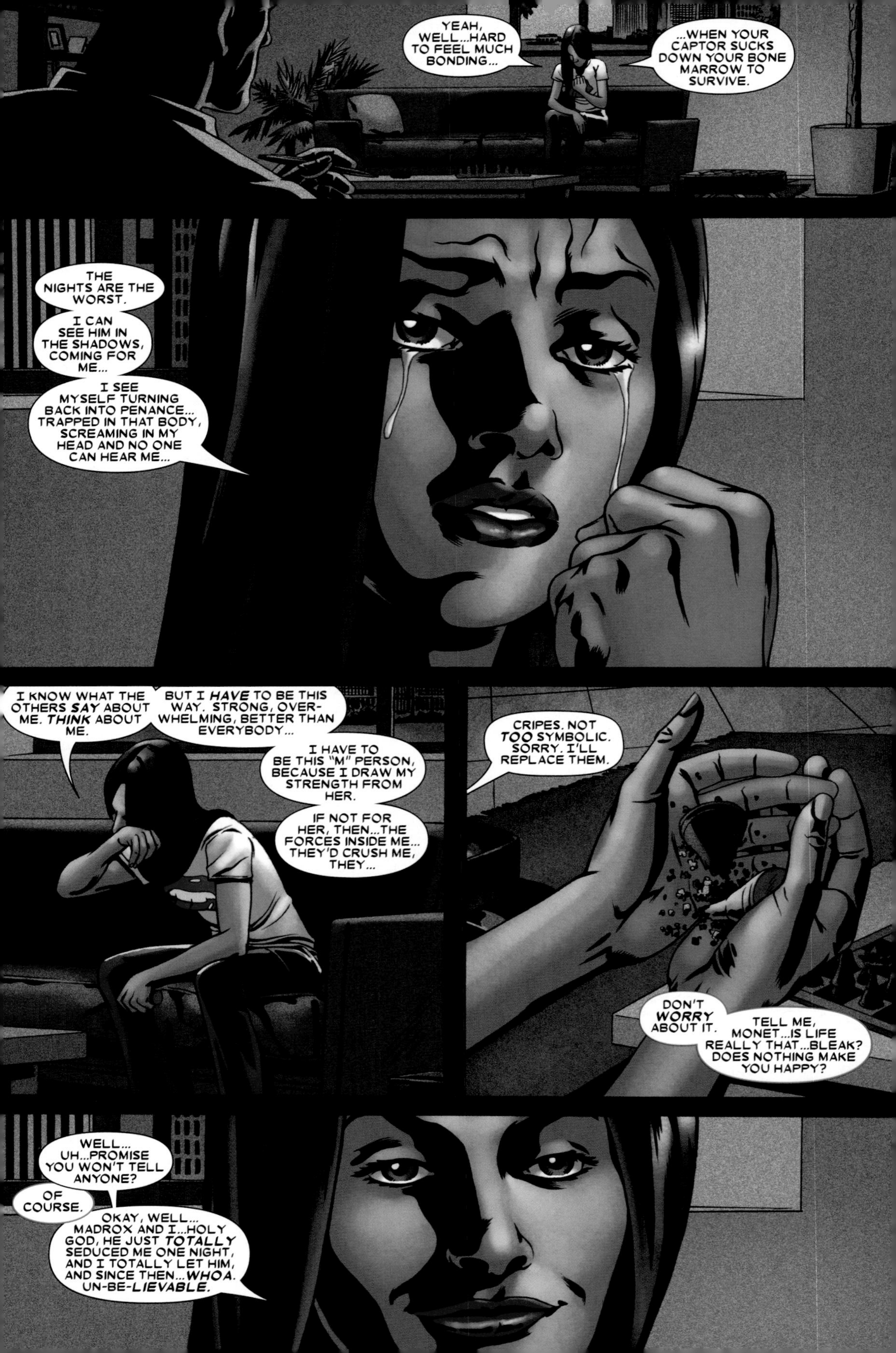
YEAH, WELL...HARD TO FEEL MUCH BONDING...
...WHEN YOUR CAPTOR SUCKS DOWN YOUR BONE MARROW TO SURVIVE.
THE NIGHTS ARE THE WORST.
I CAN SEE HIM IN THE SHADOWS, COMING FOR ME...
I SEE MYSELF TURNING BACK INTO PENANCE... TRAPPED IN THAT BODY, SCREAMING IN MY HEAD AND NO ONE CAN HEAR ME...
I KNOW WHAT THE OTHERS SAY ABOUT ME. THINK ABOUT ME.
BUT I HAVE TO BE THIS WAY. STRONG, OVER-WHELMING, BETTER THAN EVERYBODY...
I HAVE TO BE THIS "M" PERSON, BECAUSE I DRAW MY STRENGTH FROM HER.
IF NOT FOR HER, THEN...THE FORCES INSIDE ME... THEY'D CRUSH ME, THEY...
CRIPES. NOT TOO SYMBOLIC. SORRY. I'LL REPLACE THEM.
DON'T WORRY ABOUT IT.
TELL ME, MONET...IS LIFE REALLY THAT...BLEAK? DOES NOTHING MAKE YOU HAPPY?
WELL... UH...PROMISE YOU WON'T TELL ANYONE?
OF COURSE.
OKAY, WELL... MADROX AND I...HOLY GOD, HE JUST TOTALLY SEDUCED ME ONE NIGHT, AND I TOTALLY LET HIM, AND SINCE THEN...WHOA. UN-BE-LIEVABLE.

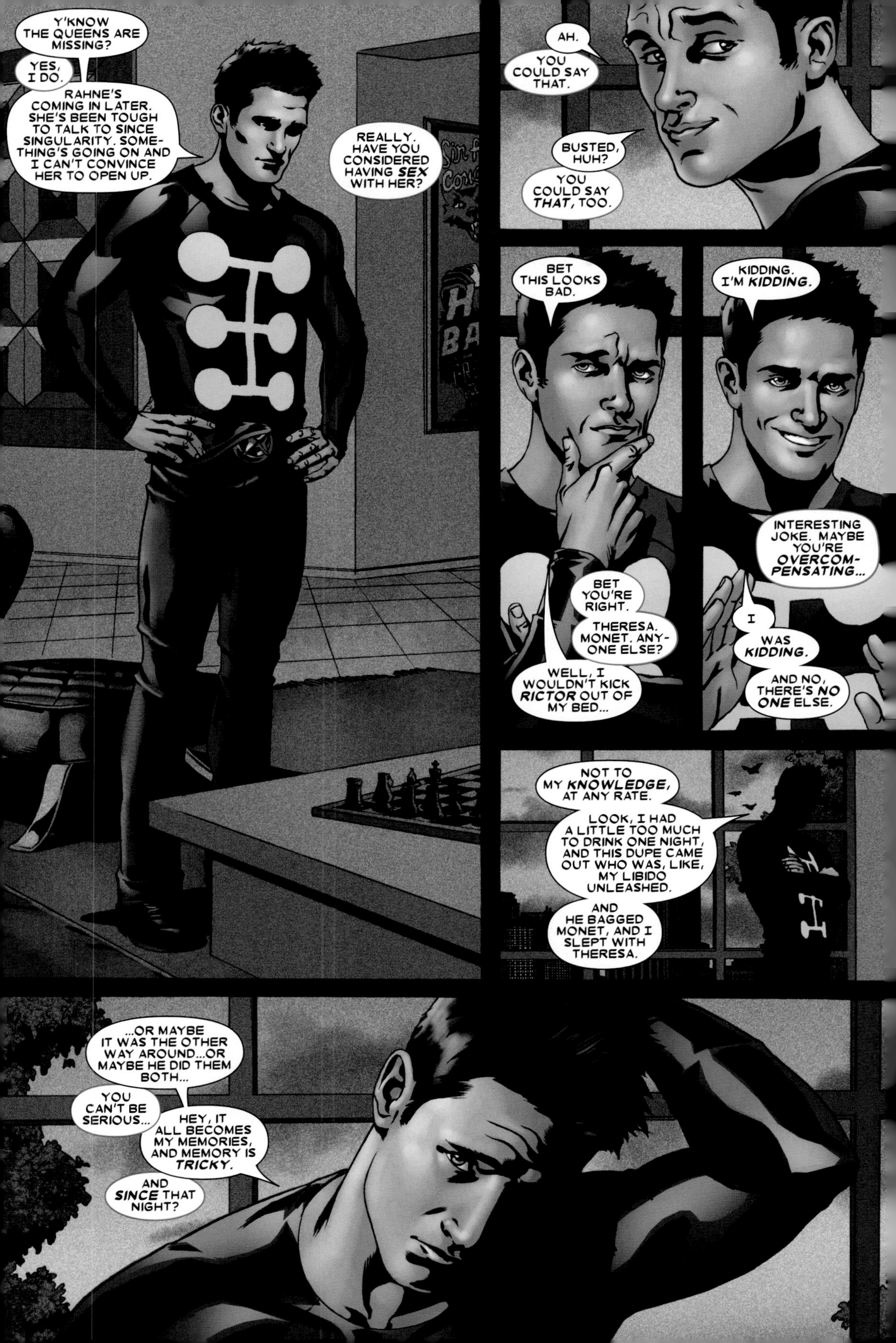
Y'KNOW THE QUEENS ARE MISSING?
YES, I DO.
RAHNE'S COMING IN LATER. SHE'S BEEN TOUGH TO TALK TO SINCE SINGULARITY. SOME-THING'S GOING ON AND I CAN'T CONVINCE HER TO OPEN UP.
REALLY. HAVE YOU CONSIDERED HAVING *SEX* WITH HER?
AH.
YOU COULD SAY THAT.
BUSTED, HUH?
YOU COULD SAY *THAT*, TOO.
BET THIS LOOKS BAD.
BET YOU'RE RIGHT.
THERESA. MONET. ANY-ONE ELSE?
WELL, I WOULDN'T KICK *RICTOR* OUT OF MY BED...
KIDDING. I'M *KIDDING.*
INTERESTING JOKE. MAYBE YOU'RE *OVERCOM-PENSATING...*
I
WAS *KIDDING.*
AND NO, THERE'S *NO ONE* ELSE.
NOT TO MY *KNOWLEDGE,* AT ANY RATE.
LOOK, I HAD A LITTLE TOO MUCH TO DRINK ONE NIGHT, AND THIS DUPE CAME OUT WHO WAS, LIKE, MY LIBIDO UNLEASHED.
AND HE BAGGED MONET, AND I SLEPT WITH THERESA.
...OR MAYBE IT WAS THE OTHER WAY AROUND...OR MAYBE HE DID THEM BOTH...
YOU CAN'T BE SERIOUS...
HEY, IT ALL BECOMES MY MEMORIES, AND MEMORY IS *TRICKY.*
AND *SINCE* THAT NIGHT?

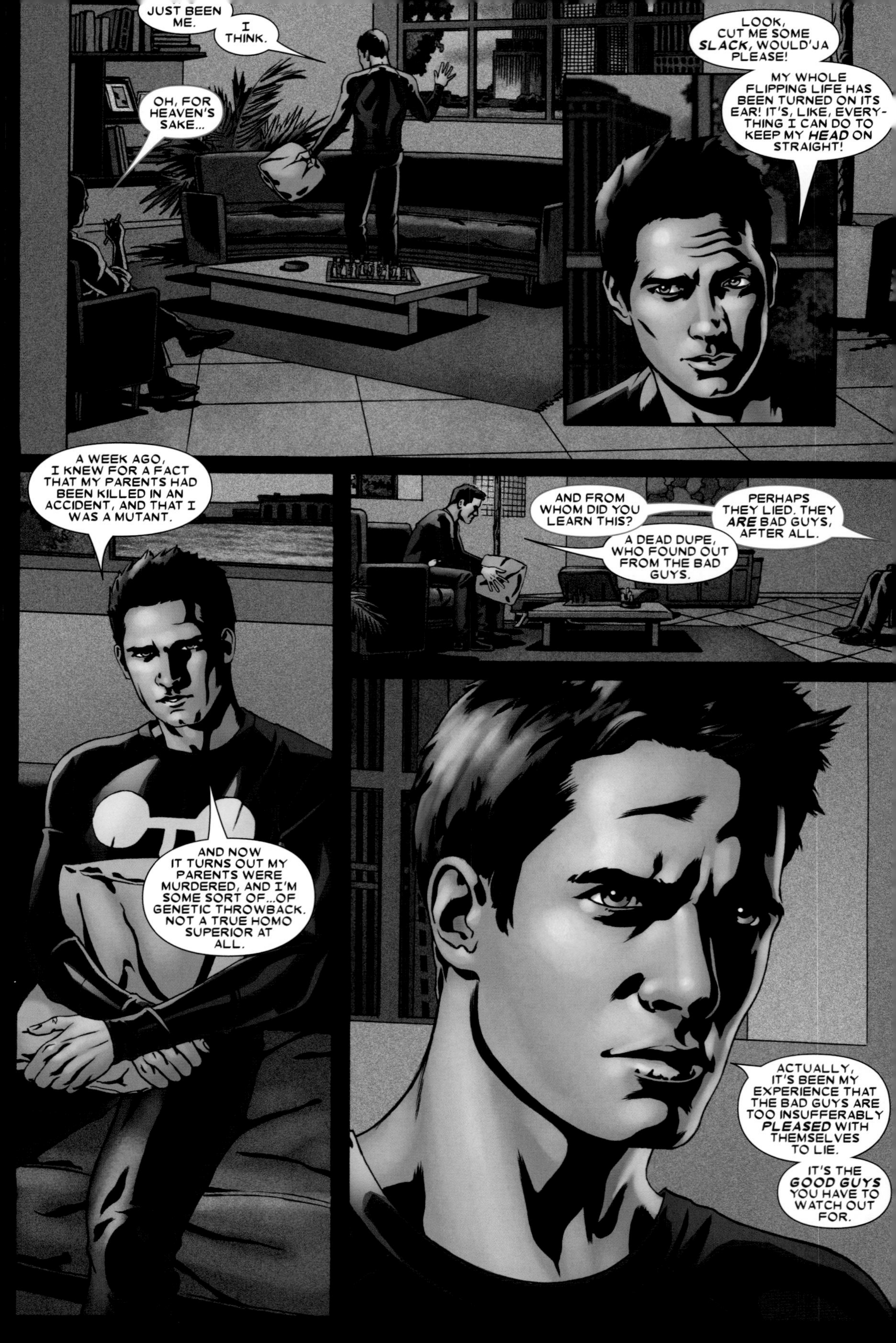
JUST BEEN ME.
I THINK.
OH, FOR HEAVEN'S SAKE...
LOOK, CUT ME SOME SLACK, WOULD'JA PLEASE!
MY WHOLE FLIPPING LIFE HAS BEEN TURNED ON ITS EAR! IT'S, LIKE, EVERYTHING I CAN DO TO KEEP MY HEAD ON STRAIGHT!
A WEEK AGO, I KNEW FOR A FACT THAT MY PARENTS HAD BEEN KILLED IN AN ACCIDENT, AND THAT I WAS A MUTANT.
AND NOW IT TURNS OUT MY PARENTS WERE MURDERED, AND I'M SOME SORT OF...OF GENETIC THROWBACK. NOT A TRUE HOMO SUPERIOR AT ALL.
AND FROM WHOM DID YOU LEARN THIS?
A DEAD DUPE, WHO FOUND OUT FROM THE BAD GUYS.
PERHAPS THEY LIED. THEY ARE BAD GUYS, AFTER ALL.
ACTUALLY, IT'S BEEN MY EXPERIENCE THAT THE BAD GUYS ARE TOO INSUFFERABLY PLEASED WITH THEMSELVES TO LIE.
IT'S THE GOOD GUYS YOU HAVE TO WATCH OUT FOR.

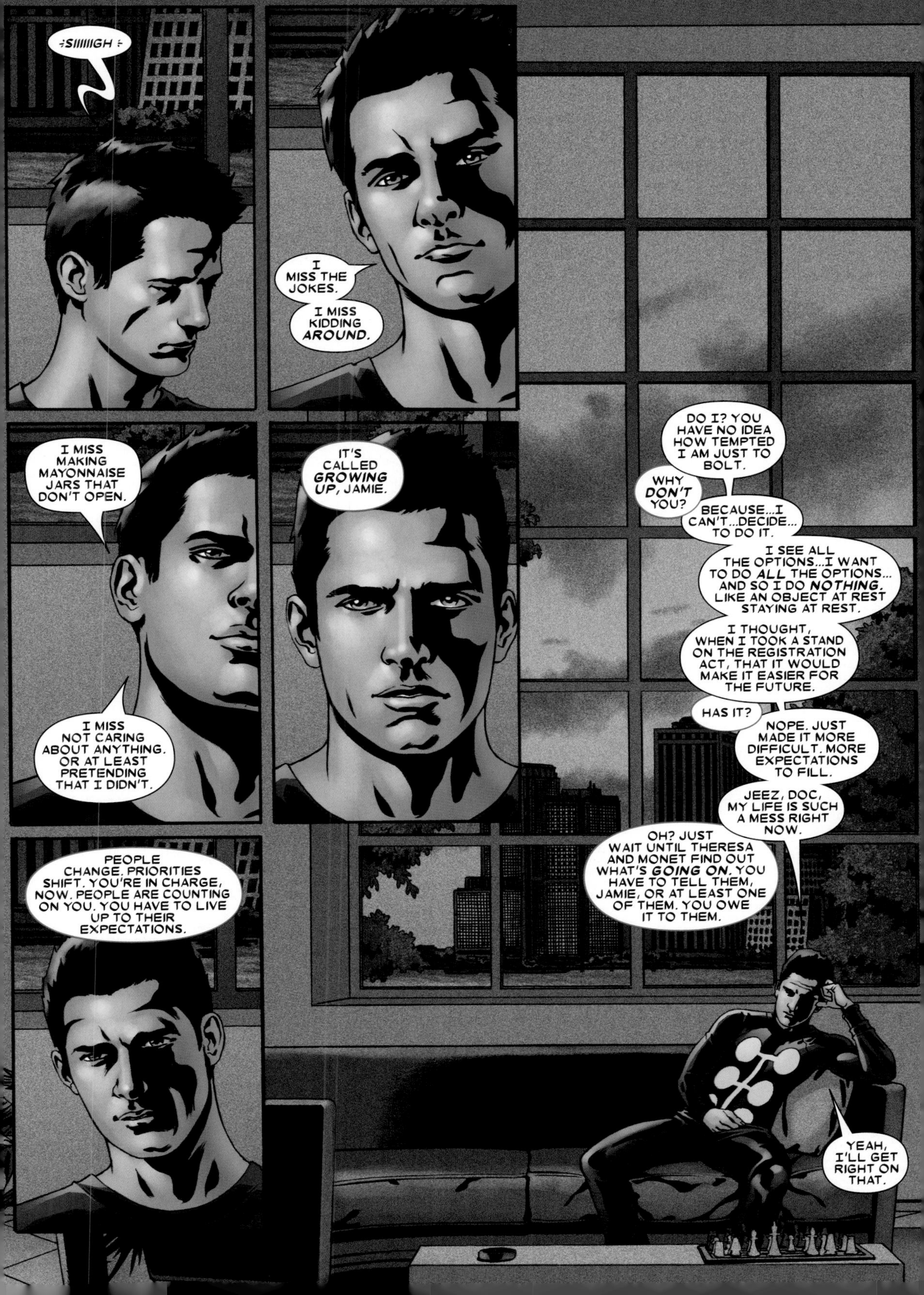

=SIIIIIGH=
I MISS THE JOKES.
I MISS KIDDING AROUND.
I MISS MAKING MAYONNAISE JARS THAT DON'T OPEN.
I MISS NOT CARING ABOUT ANYTHING. OR AT LEAST PRETENDING THAT I DIDN'T.
IT'S CALLED GROWING UP, JAMIE.
PEOPLE CHANGE. PRIORITIES SHIFT. YOU'RE IN CHARGE, NOW. PEOPLE ARE COUNTING ON YOU. YOU HAVE TO LIVE UP TO THEIR EXPECTATIONS.
DO I? YOU HAVE NO IDEA HOW TEMPTED I AM JUST TO BOLT.
WHY DON'T YOU?
BECAUSE...I CAN'T...DECIDE... TO DO IT.
I SEE ALL THE OPTIONS...I WANT TO DO ALL THE OPTIONS... AND SO I DO NOTHING. LIKE AN OBJECT AT REST STAYING AT REST.
I THOUGHT, WHEN I TOOK A STAND ON THE REGISTRATION ACT, THAT IT WOULD MAKE IT EASIER FOR THE FUTURE.
HAS IT?
NOPE. JUST MADE IT MORE DIFFICULT. MORE EXPECTATIONS TO FILL.
JEEZ, DOC, MY LIFE IS SUCH A MESS RIGHT NOW.
OH? JUST WAIT UNTIL THERESA AND MONET FIND OUT WHAT'S GOING ON. YOU HAVE TO TELL THEM, JAMIE, OR AT LEAST ONE OF THEM. YOU OWE IT TO THEM.
YEAH, I'LL GET RIGHT ON THAT.

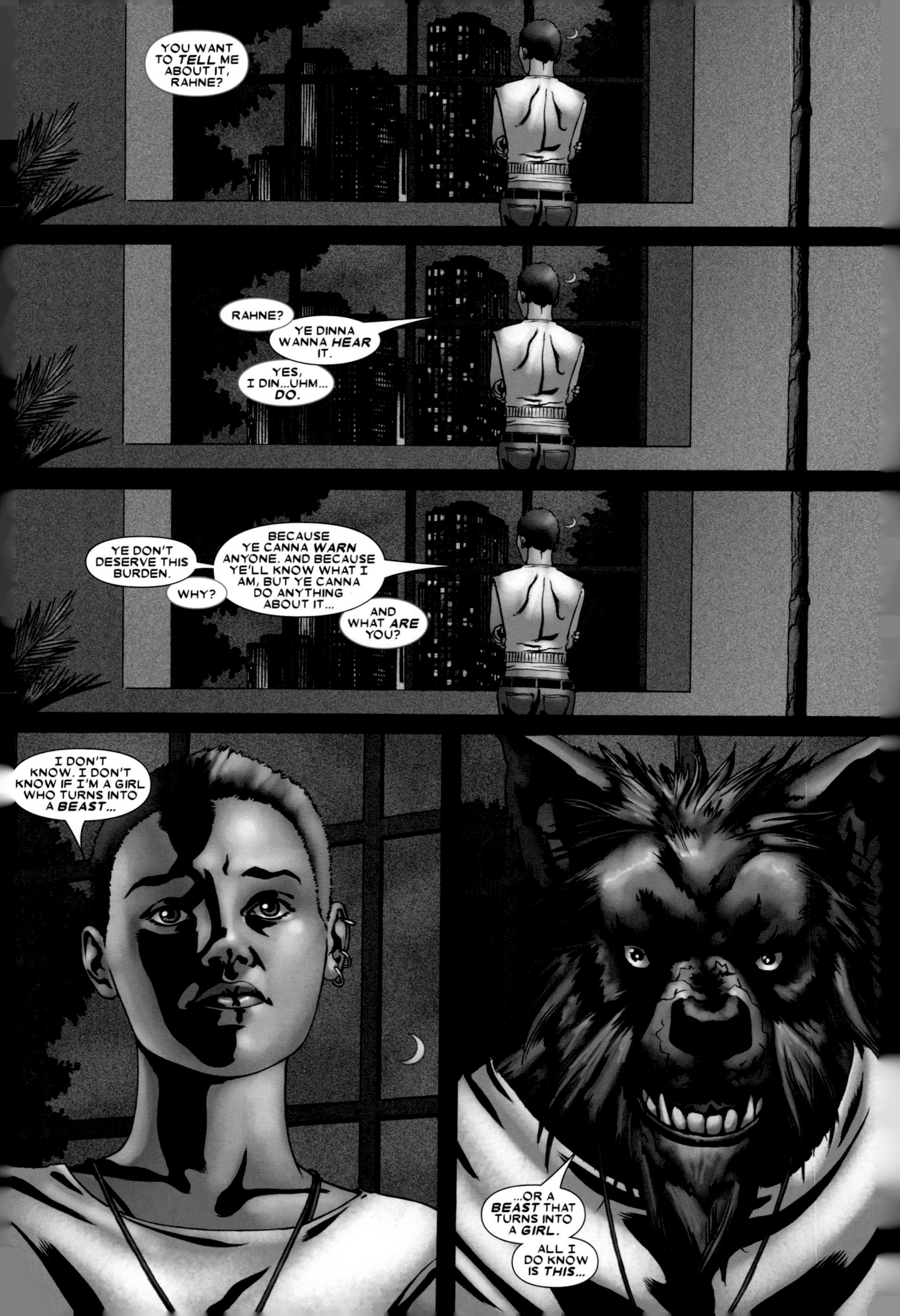
YOU WANT TO *TELL* ME ABOUT IT, RAHNE?
RAHNE?
YE DINNA WANNA *HEAR* IT.
YES, I DIN...UHM... *DO.*
YE DON'T DESERVE THIS BURDEN.
WHY?
BECAUSE YE CANNA *WARN* ANYONE. AND BECAUSE YE'LL KNOW WHAT I AM, BUT YE CANNA DO ANYTHING ABOUT IT...
AND WHAT *ARE* YOU?
I DON'T KNOW. I DON'T KNOW IF I'M A GIRL WHO TURNS INTO A *BEAST*...
...OR A *BEAST* THAT TURNS INTO A *GIRL*.
ALL I DO KNOW IS *THIS*...

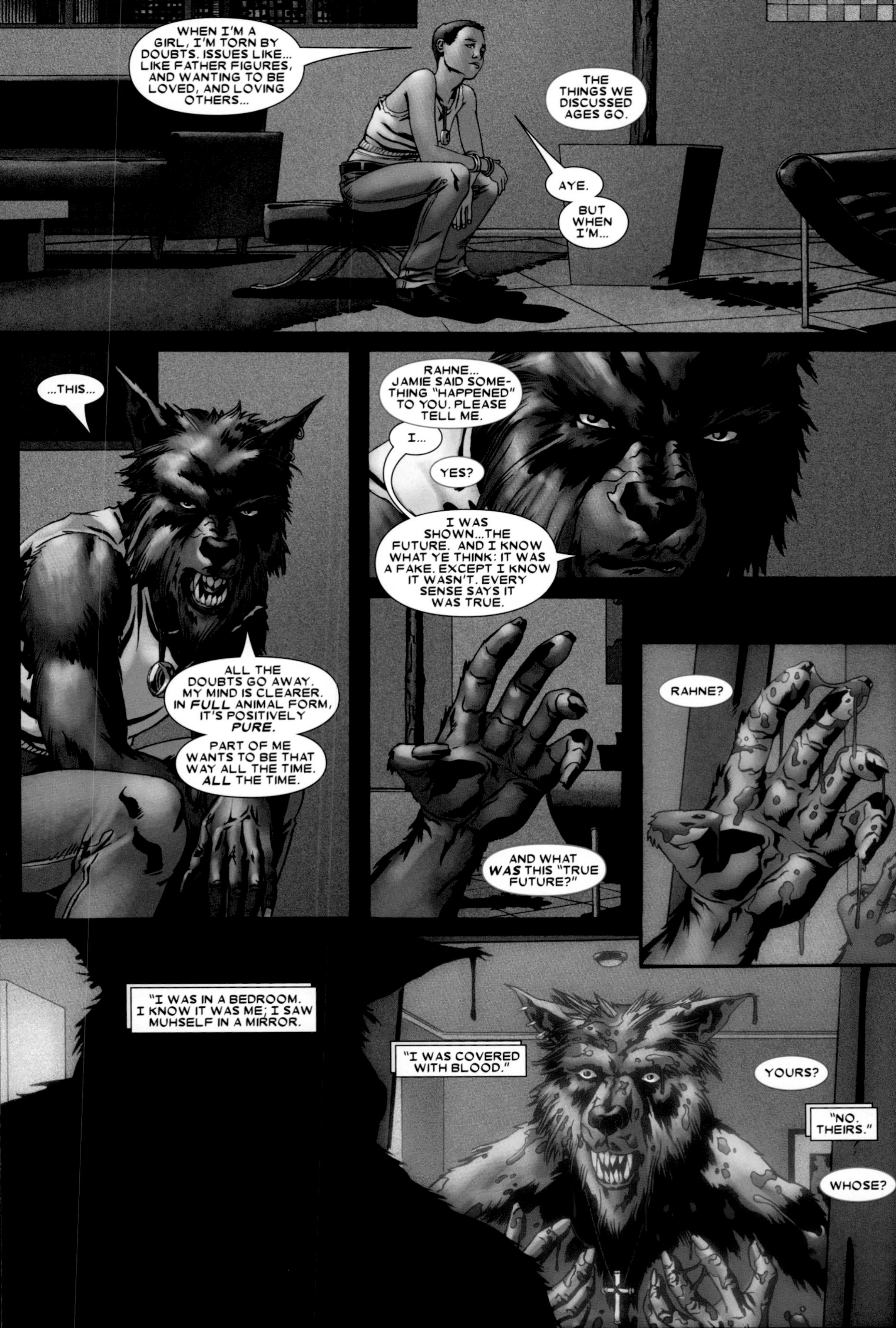
WHEN I'M A GIRL, I'M TORN BY DOUBTS. ISSUES LIKE... LIKE FATHER FIGURES, AND WANTING TO BE LOVED, AND LOVING OTHERS...
THE THINGS WE DISCUSSED AGES GO.
AYE.
BUT WHEN I'M...
...THIS...
ALL THE DOUBTS GO AWAY. MY MIND IS CLEARER. IN FULL ANIMAL FORM, IT'S POSITIVELY PURE.
PART OF ME WANTS TO BE THAT WAY ALL THE TIME. ALL THE TIME.
RAHNE... JAMIE SAID SOME-THING "HAPPENED" TO YOU. PLEASE TELL ME.
I...
YES?
I WAS SHOWN...THE FUTURE. AND I KNOW WHAT YE THINK: IT WAS A FAKE. EXCEPT I KNOW IT WASN'T. EVERY SENSE SAYS IT WAS TRUE.
AND WHAT WAS THIS "TRUE FUTURE?"
RAHNE?
"I WAS IN A BEDROOM. I KNOW IT WAS ME; I SAW MUHSELF IN A MIRROR.
"I WAS COVERED WITH BLOOD."
YOURS?
"NO. THEIRS."
WHOSE?

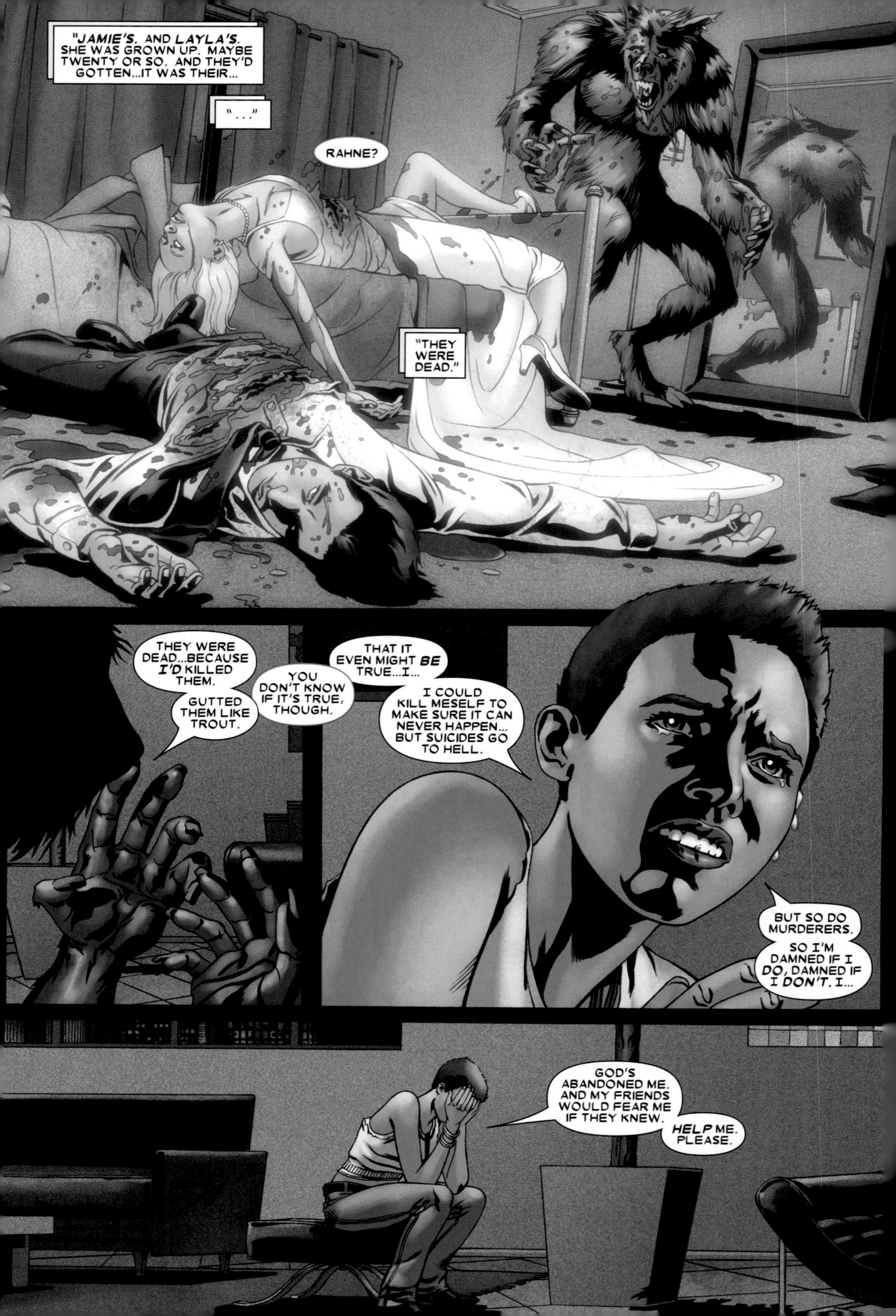

"JAMIE'S. AND LAYLA'S. SHE WAS GROWN UP. MAYBE TWENTY OR SO. AND THEY'D GOTTEN...IT WAS THEIR...
"..."
RAHNE?
"THEY WERE DEAD."
THEY WERE DEAD...BECAUSE I'D KILLED THEM.
GUTTED THEM LIKE TROUT.
YOU DON'T KNOW IF IT'S TRUE, THOUGH.
THAT IT EVEN MIGHT BE TRUE...I...
I COULD KILL MESELF TO MAKE SURE IT CAN NEVER HAPPEN... BUT SUICIDES GO TO HELL.
BUT SO DO MURDERERS.
SO I'M DAMNED IF I DO, DAMNED IF I DON'T. I...
GOD'S ABANDONED ME. AND MY FRIENDS WOULD FEAR ME IF THEY KNEW.
HELP ME. PLEASE.

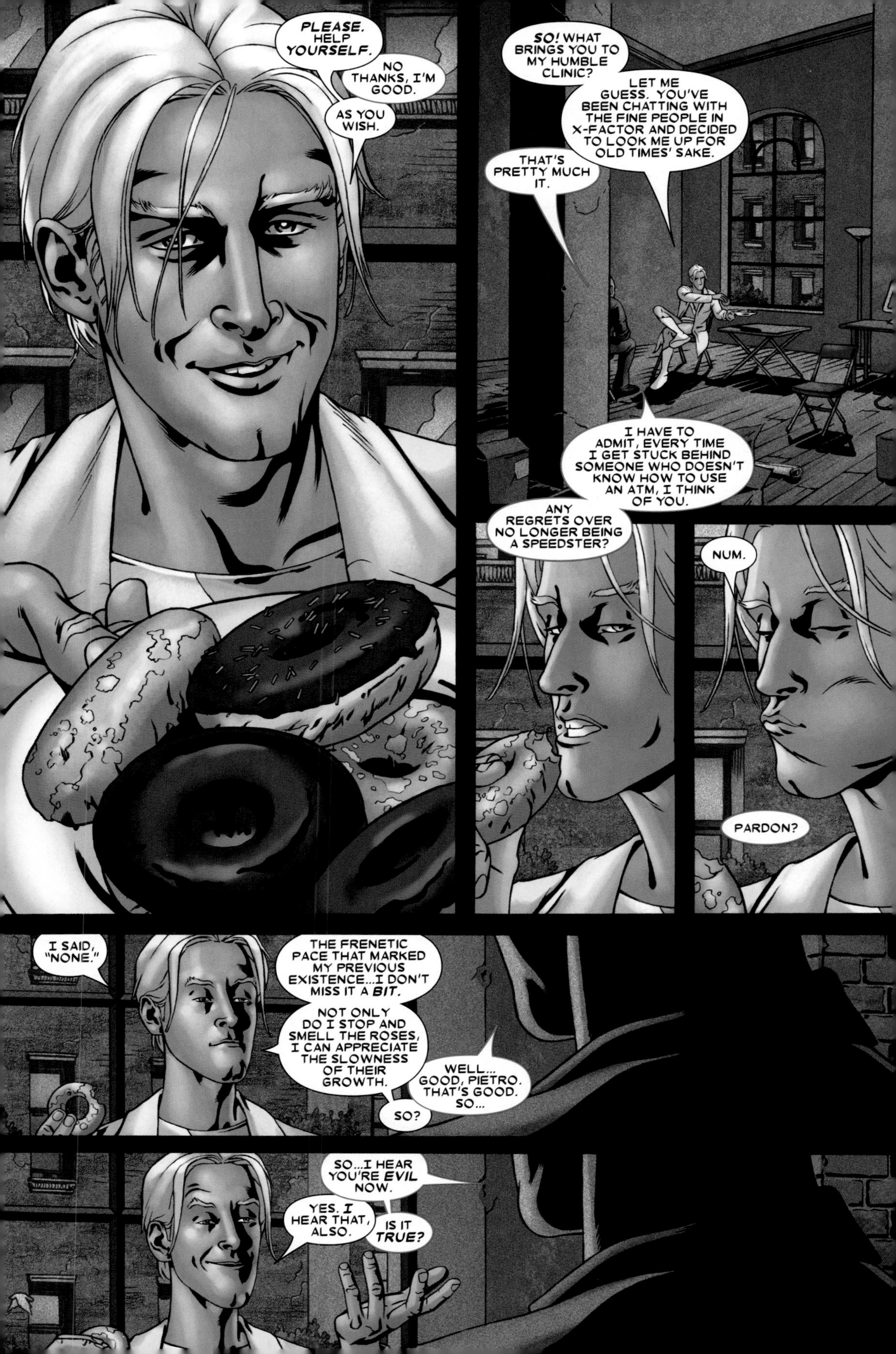
PLEASE. HELP YOURSELF.
NO THANKS, I'M GOOD.
AS YOU WISH.
SO! WHAT BRINGS YOU TO MY HUMBLE CLINIC?
LET ME GUESS. YOU'VE BEEN CHATTING WITH THE FINE PEOPLE IN X-FACTOR AND DECIDED TO LOOK ME UP FOR OLD TIMES' SAKE.
THAT'S PRETTY MUCH IT.
I HAVE TO ADMIT, EVERY TIME I GET STUCK BEHIND SOMEONE WHO DOESN'T KNOW HOW TO USE AN ATM, I THINK OF YOU.
ANY REGRETS OVER NO LONGER BEING A SPEEDSTER?
NUM.
PARDON?
I SAID, "NONE."
THE FRENETIC PACE THAT MARKED MY PREVIOUS EXISTENCE...I DON'T MISS IT A BIT.
NOT ONLY DO I STOP AND SMELL THE ROSES, I CAN APPRECIATE THE SLOWNESS OF THEIR GROWTH.
SO?
WELL... GOOD, PIETRO. THAT'S GOOD. SO...
SO...I HEAR YOU'RE EVIL NOW.
YES. I HEAR THAT, ALSO.
IS IT TRUE?

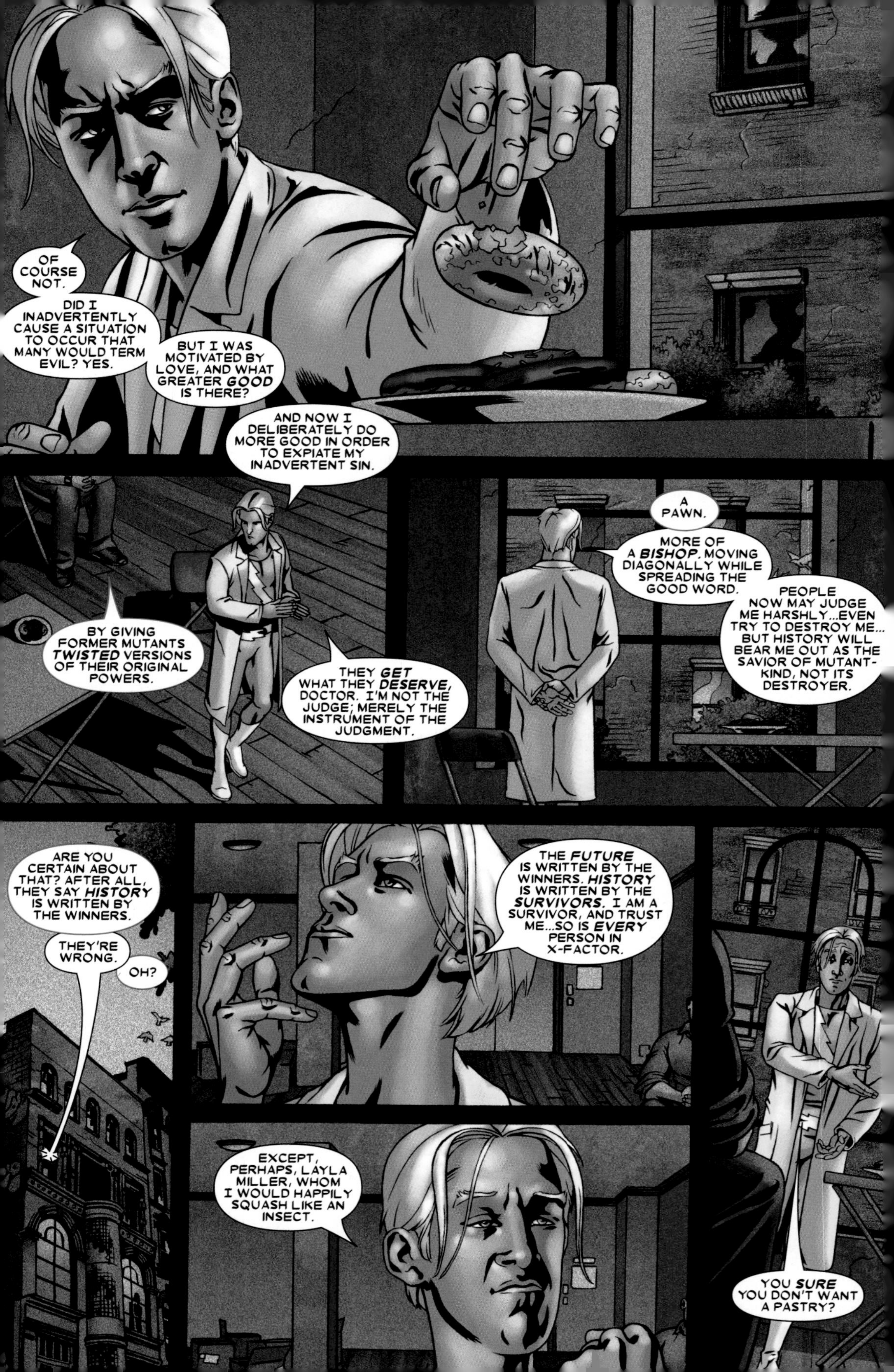
OF COURSE NOT.
DID I INADVERTENTLY CAUSE A SITUATION TO OCCUR THAT MANY WOULD TERM EVIL? YES.
BUT I WAS MOTIVATED BY LOVE, AND WHAT GREATER GOOD IS THERE?
AND NOW I DELIBERATELY DO MORE GOOD IN ORDER TO EXPIATE MY INADVERTENT SIN.
BY GIVING FORMER MUTANTS TWISTED VERSIONS OF THEIR ORIGINAL POWERS.
THEY GET WHAT THEY DESERVE, DOCTOR. I'M NOT THE JUDGE; MERELY THE INSTRUMENT OF THE JUDGMENT.
A PAWN.
MORE OF A BISHOP. MOVING DIAGONALLY WHILE SPREADING THE GOOD WORD.
PEOPLE NOW MAY JUDGE ME HARSHLY...EVEN TRY TO DESTROY ME... BUT HISTORY WILL BEAR ME OUT AS THE SAVIOR OF MUTANT-KIND, NOT ITS DESTROYER.
ARE YOU CERTAIN ABOUT THAT? AFTER ALL, THEY SAY HISTORY IS WRITTEN BY THE WINNERS.
THEY'RE WRONG.
OH?
THE FUTURE IS WRITTEN BY THE WINNERS. HISTORY IS WRITTEN BY THE SURVIVORS. I AM A SURVIVOR, AND TRUST ME...SO IS EVERY PERSON IN X-FACTOR.
EXCEPT, PERHAPS, LAYLA MILLER, WHOM I WOULD HAPPILY SQUASH LIKE AN INSECT.
YOU SURE YOU DON'T WANT A PASTRY?

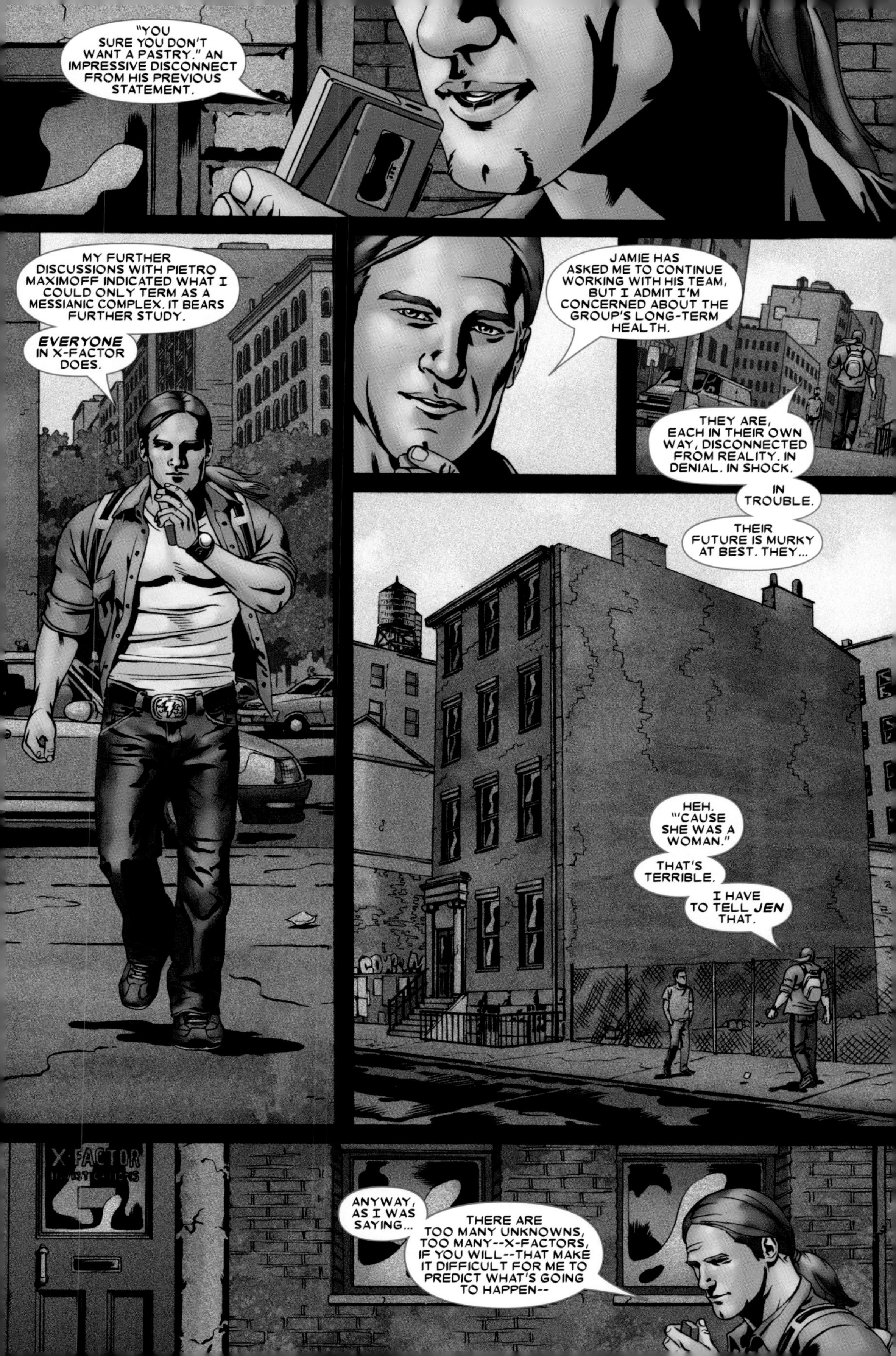
"YOU SURE YOU DON'T WANT A PASTRY." AN IMPRESSIVE DISCONNECT FROM HIS PREVIOUS STATEMENT.
MY FURTHER DISCUSSIONS WITH PIETRO MAXIMOFF INDICATED WHAT I COULD ONLY TERM AS A MESSIANIC COMPLEX. IT BEARS FURTHER STUDY.
EVERYONE IN X-FACTOR DOES.
JAMIE HAS ASKED ME TO CONTINUE WORKING WITH HIS TEAM, BUT I ADMIT I'M CONCERNED ABOUT THE GROUP'S LONG-TERM HEALTH.
THEY ARE, EACH IN THEIR OWN WAY, DISCONNECTED FROM REALITY. IN DENIAL. IN SHOCK.
IN TROUBLE.
THEIR FUTURE IS MURKY AT BEST. THEY...
HEH. "'CAUSE SHE WAS A WOMAN."
THAT'S TERRIBLE.
I HAVE TO TELL JEN THAT.
X-FACTOR
ANYWAY, AS I WAS SAYING...
THERE ARE TOO MANY UNKNOWNS, TOO MANY--X-FACTORS, IF YOU WILL--THAT MAKE IT DIFFICULT FOR ME TO PREDICT WHAT'S GOING TO HAPPEN--

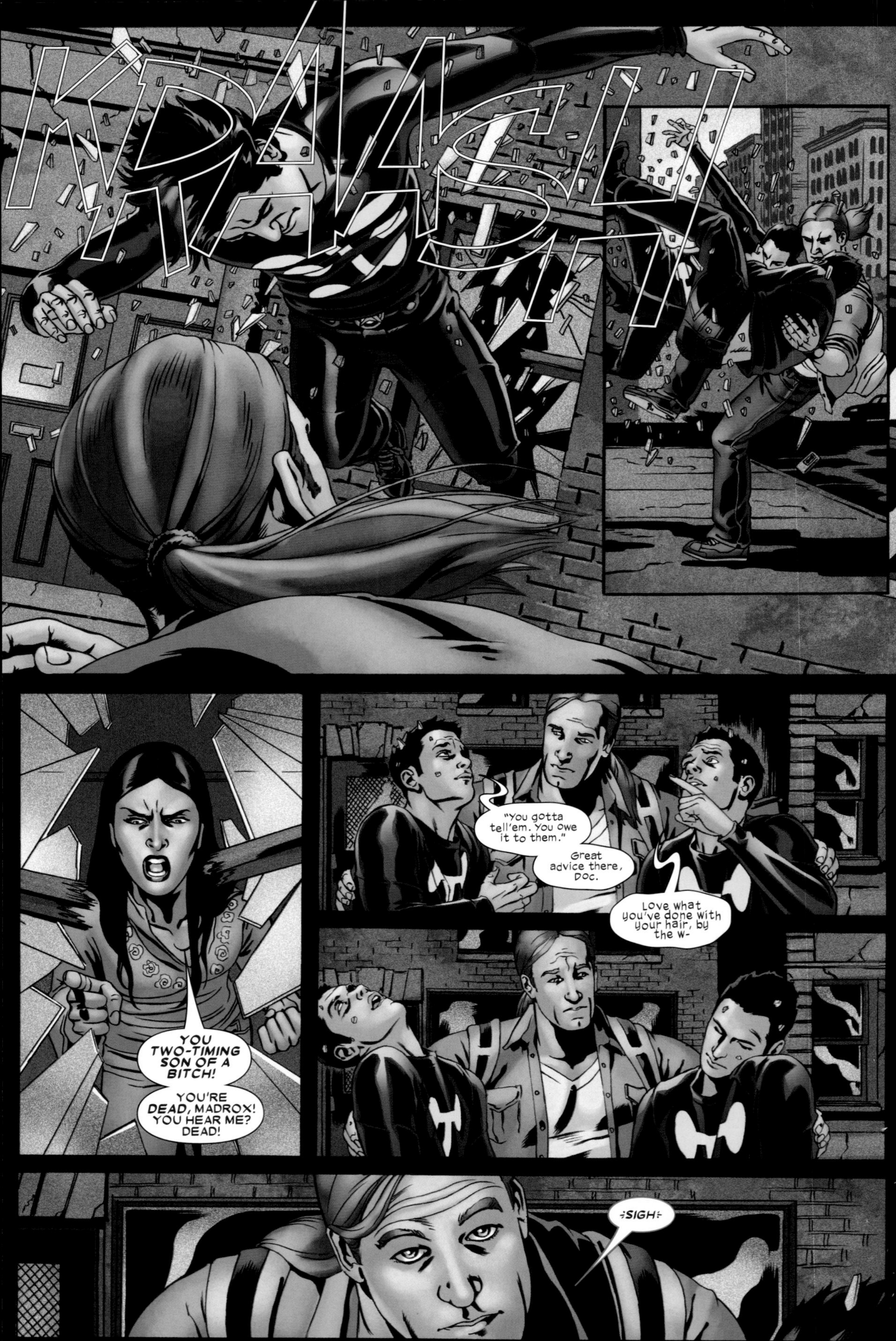
KRAASH
"You gotta tell'em. You owe it to them."
Great advice there, Doc.
Love what you've done with your hair, by the w-
YOU TWO-TIMING SON OF A BITCH!
YOU'RE DEAD, MADROX! YOU HEAR ME? DEAD!
SIGH

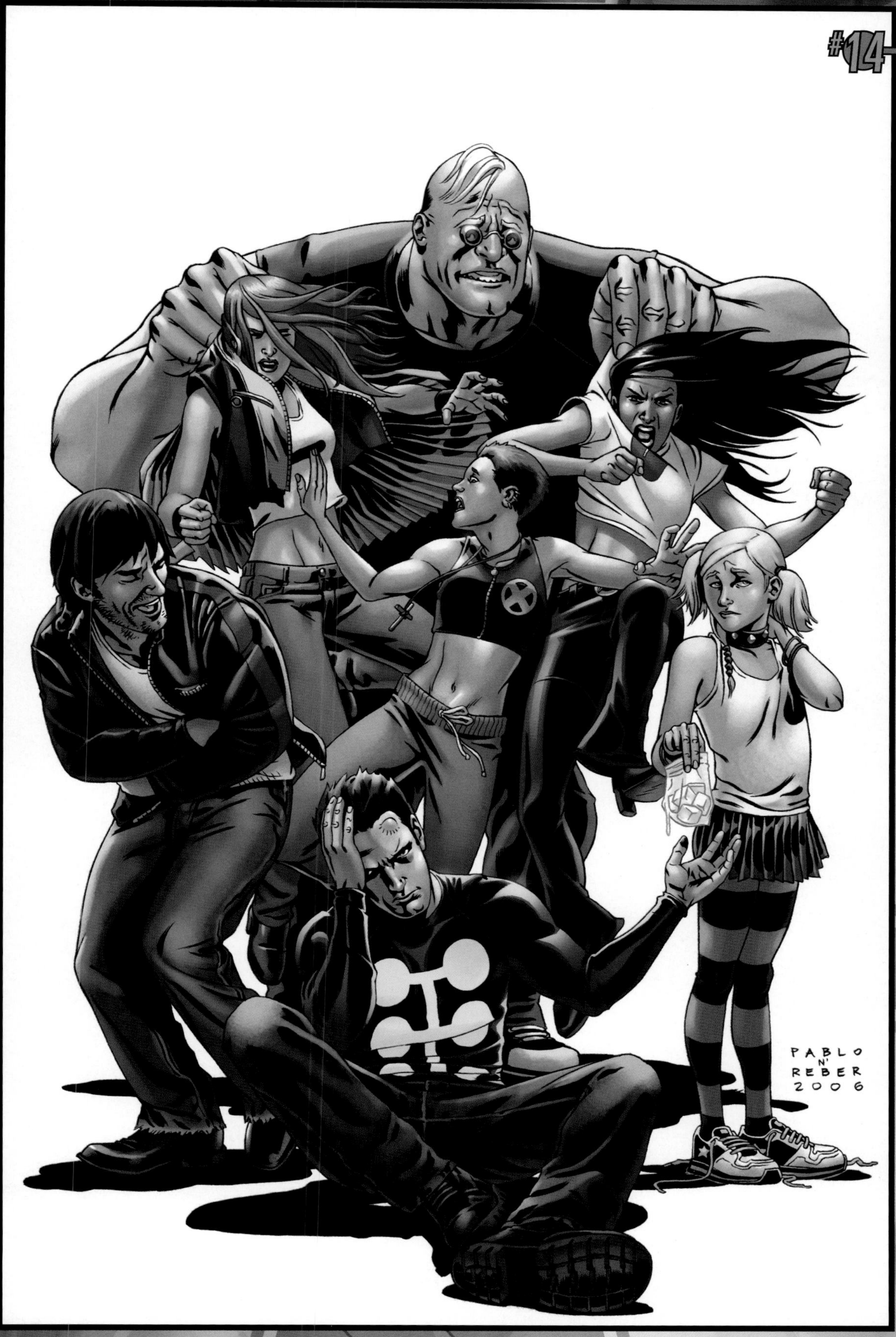
#14
PABLO
N'
REBER
2006

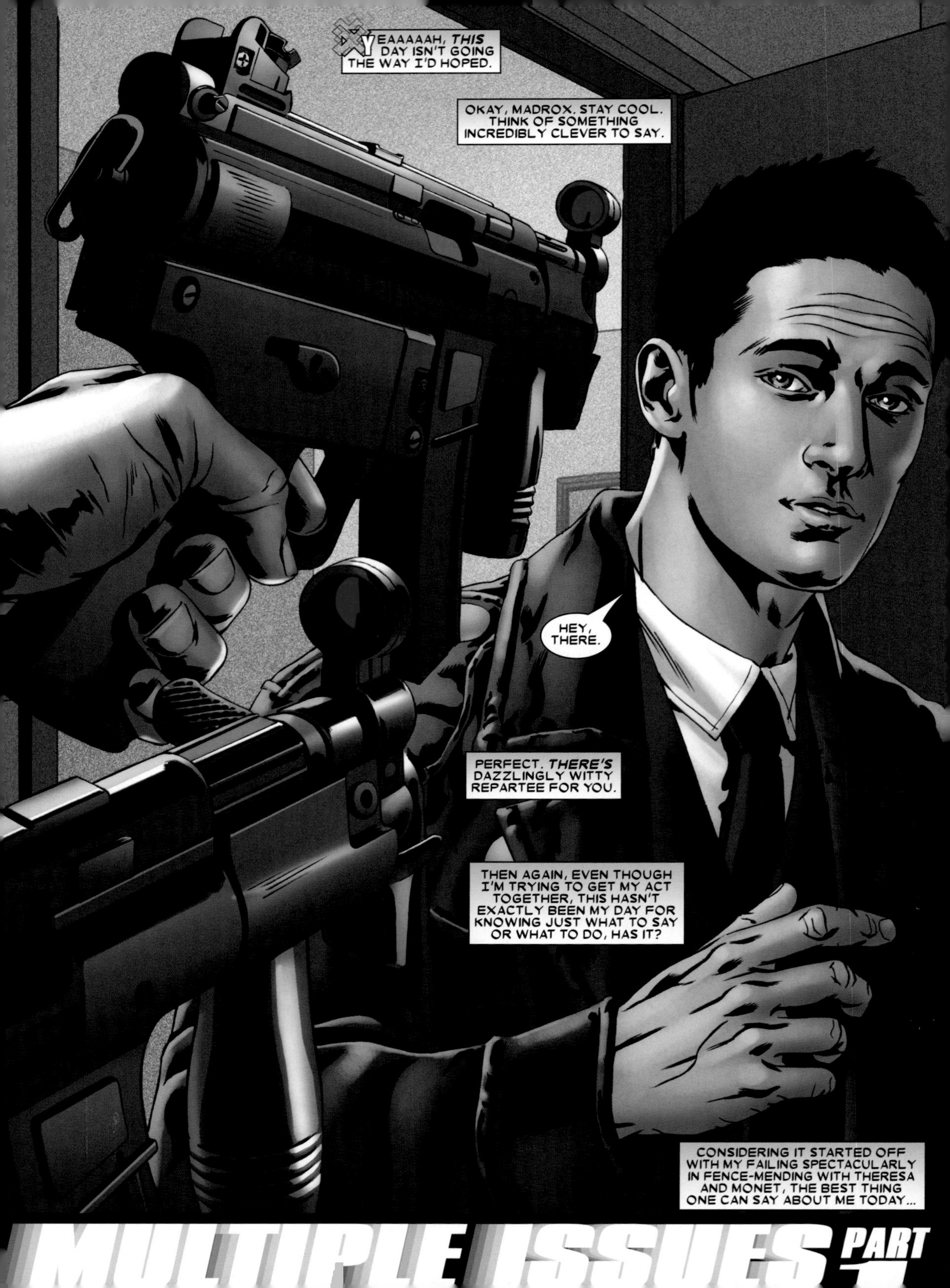
YEAAAAAH, THIS DAY ISN'T GOING THE WAY I'D HOPED.
OKAY, MADROX. STAY COOL. THINK OF SOMETHING INCREDIBLY CLEVER TO SAY.
HEY, THERE.
PERFECT. THERE'S DAZZLINGLY WITTY REPARTEE FOR YOU.
THEN AGAIN, EVEN THOUGH I'M TRYING TO GET MY ACT TOGETHER, THIS HASN'T EXACTLY BEEN MY DAY FOR KNOWING JUST WHAT TO SAY OR WHAT TO DO, HAS IT?
CONSIDERING IT STARTED OFF WITH MY FAILING SPECTACULARLY IN FENCE-MENDING WITH THERESA AND MONET, THE BEST THING ONE CAN SAY ABOUT ME TODAY...
MULTIPLE ISSUES PART 1

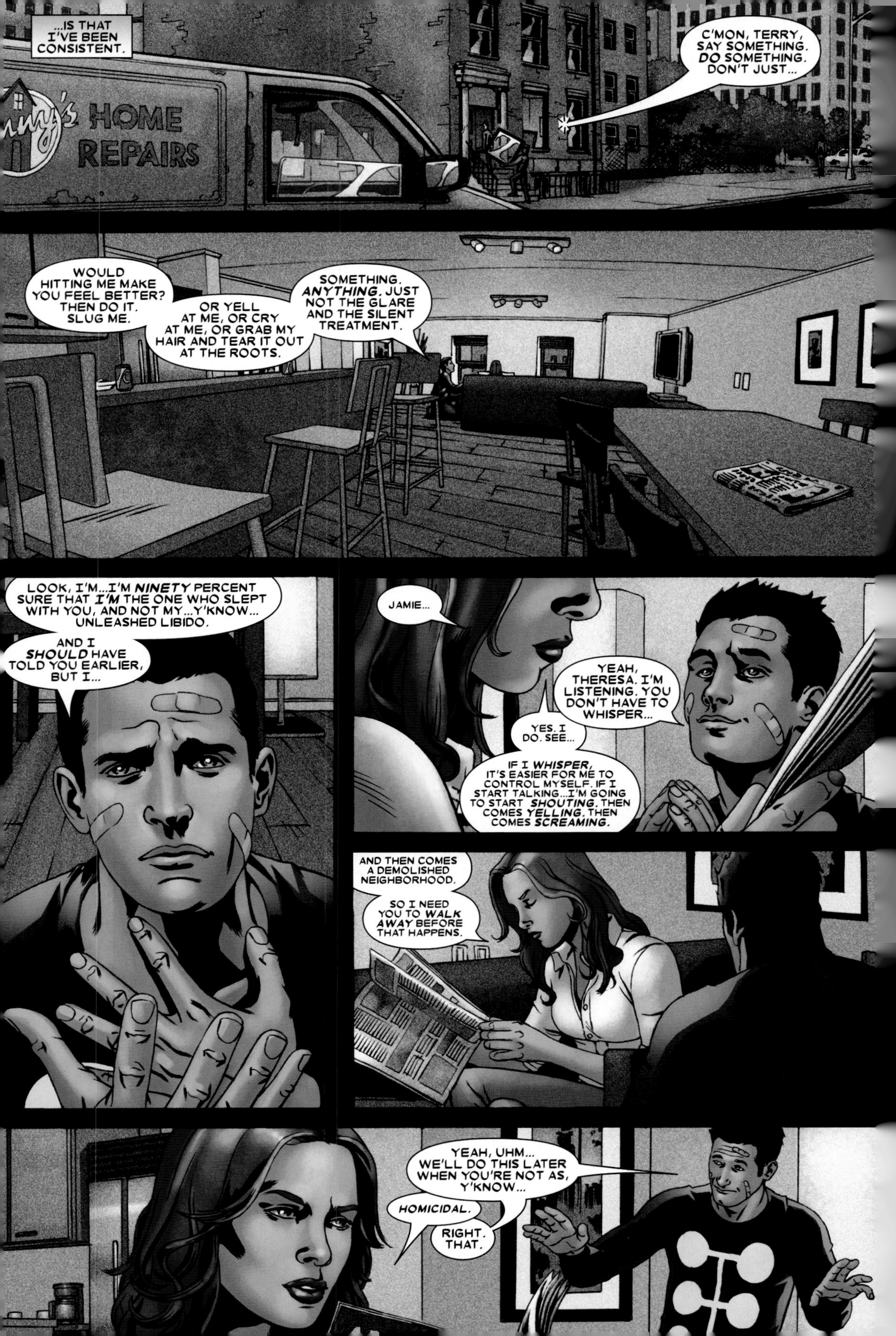

...IS THAT I'VE BEEN CONSISTENT.
C'MON, TERRY, SAY SOMETHING. DO SOMETHING. DON'T JUST...
HOME REPAIRS
WOULD HITTING ME MAKE YOU FEEL BETTER? THEN DO IT. SLUG ME.
OR YELL AT ME, OR CRY AT ME, OR GRAB MY HAIR AND TEAR IT OUT AT THE ROOTS.
SOMETHING. ANYTHING. JUST NOT THE GLARE AND THE SILENT TREATMENT.
LOOK, I'M...I'M NINETY PERCENT SURE THAT I'M THE ONE WHO SLEPT WITH YOU, AND NOT MY...Y'KNOW... UNLEASHED LIBIDO.
AND I SHOULD HAVE TOLD YOU EARLIER, BUT I...
JAMIE...
YEAH, THERESA. I'M LISTENING. YOU DON'T HAVE TO WHISPER...
YES. I DO. SEE...
IF I WHISPER, IT'S EASIER FOR ME TO CONTROL MYSELF. IF I START TALKING...I'M GOING TO START SHOUTING. THEN COMES YELLING. THEN COMES SCREAMING.
AND THEN COMES A DEMOLISHED NEIGHBORHOOD.
SO I NEED YOU TO WALK AWAY BEFORE THAT HAPPENS.
YEAH, UHM... WE'LL DO THIS LATER WHEN YOU'RE NOT AS, Y'KNOW...
HOMICIDAL.
RIGHT. THAT.

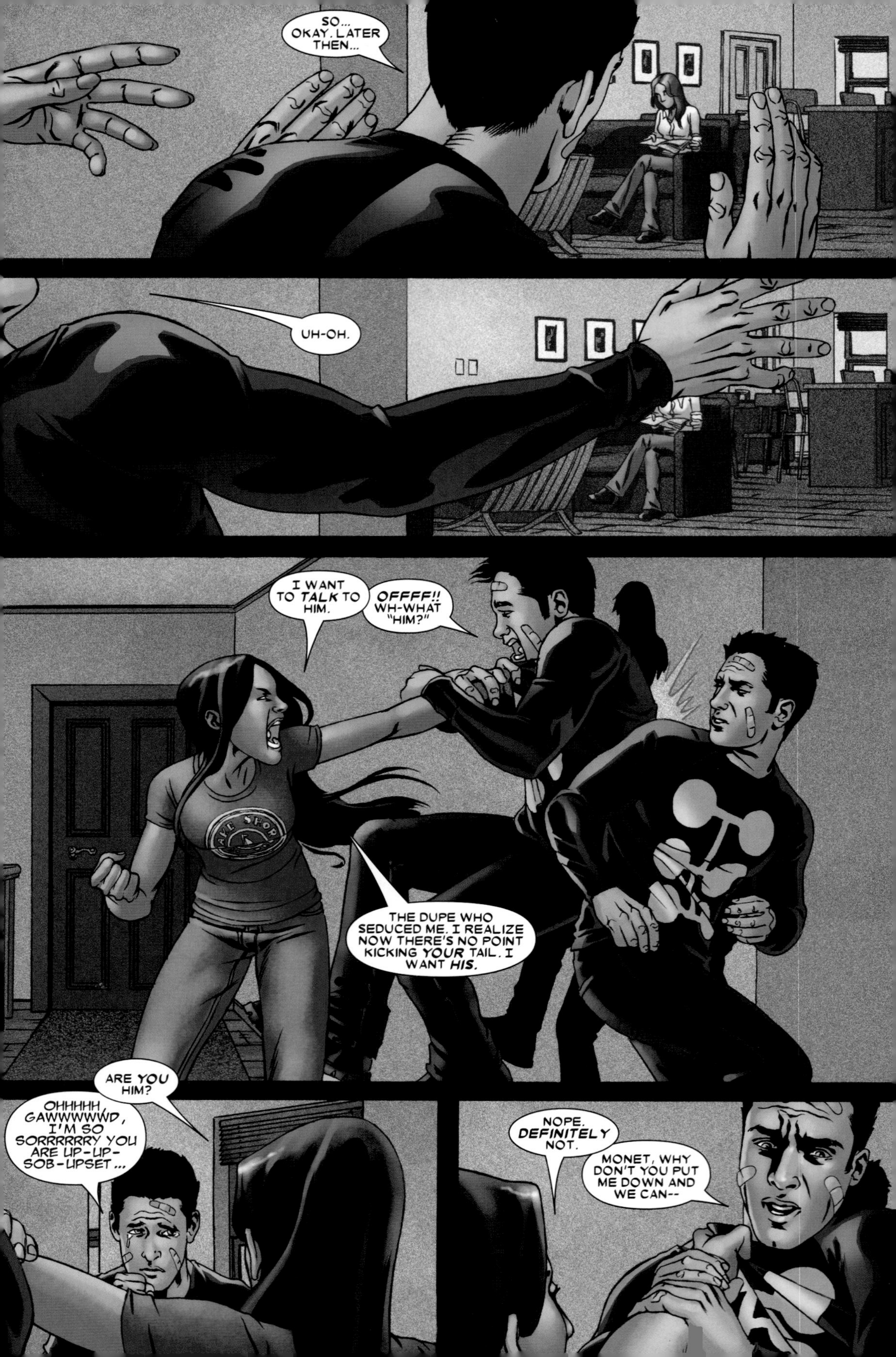
SO... OKAY. LATER THEN...
UH-OH.
I WANT TO TALK TO HIM.
OFFFF!! WH-WHAT "HIM?"
THE DUPE WHO SEDUCED ME. I REALIZE NOW THERE'S NO POINT KICKING YOUR TAIL. I WANT HIS.
ARE YOU HIM?
OHHHHH, GAWWWWWD, I'M SO SORRRRRRY YOU ARE UP-UP-SOB-UPSET...
NOPE. DEFINITELY NOT.
MONET, WHY DON'T YOU PUT ME DOWN AND WE CAN--

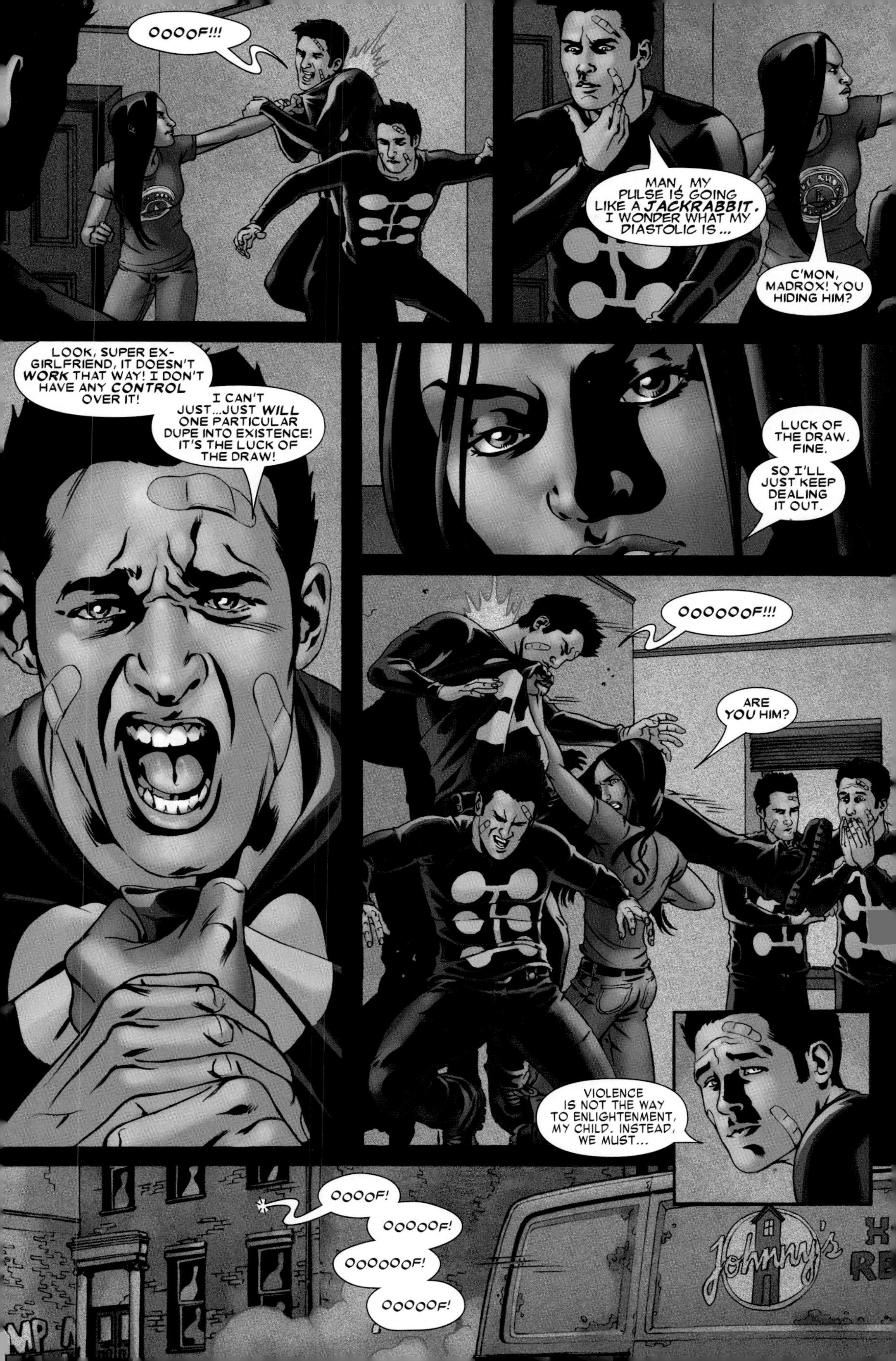
OOOOF!!!
MAN, MY PULSE IS GOING LIKE A JACKRABBIT. I WONDER WHAT MY DIASTOLIC IS...
C'MON, MADROX! YOU HIDING HIM?
LOOK, SUPER EX-GIRLFRIEND, IT DOESN'T WORK THAT WAY! I DON'T HAVE ANY CONTROL OVER IT!
I CAN'T JUST...JUST WILL ONE PARTICULAR DUPE INTO EXISTENCE! IT'S THE LUCK OF THE DRAW!
LUCK OF THE DRAW. FINE.
SO I'LL JUST KEEP DEALING IT OUT.
OOOOOOF!!!
ARE YOU HIM?
VIOLENCE IS NOT THE WAY TO ENLIGHTENMENT, MY CHILD. INSTEAD, WE MUST...
OOOOF!
OOOOOF!
OOOOOOF!
OOOOOF!
Johnny's

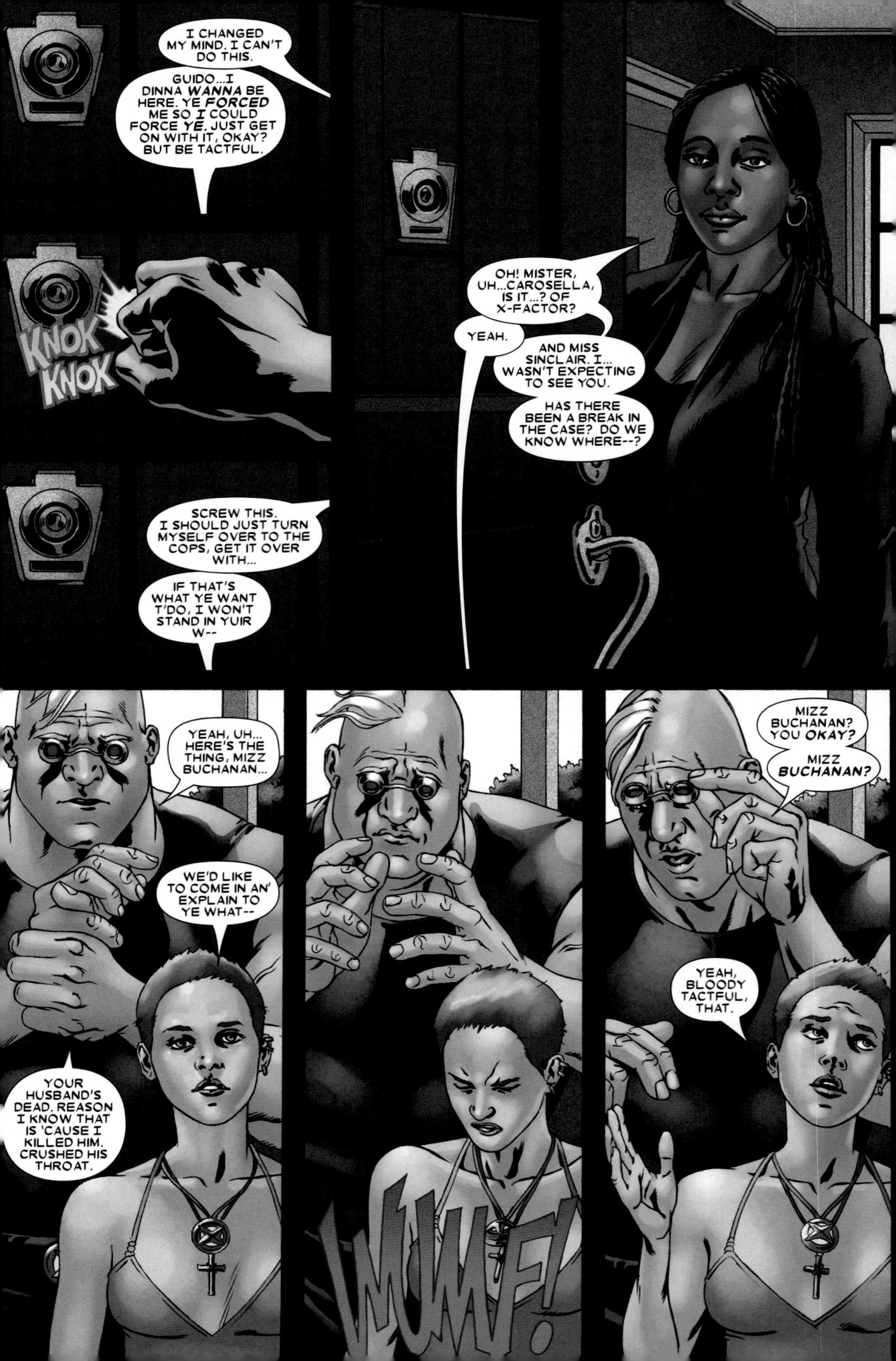
I CHANGED MY MIND. I CAN'T DO THIS.
GUIDO...I DINNA WANNA BE HERE. YE FORCED ME SO I COULD FORCE YE. JUST GET ON WITH IT, OKAY? BUT BE TACTFUL.
KNOK KNOK
SCREW THIS. I SHOULD JUST TURN MYSELF OVER TO THE COPS, GET IT OVER WITH...
IF THAT'S WHAT YE WANT T'DO, I WON'T STAND IN YUIR W--
OH! MISTER, UH...CAROSELLA, IS IT...? OF X-FACTOR?
YEAH.
AND MISS SINCLAIR. I... WASN'T EXPECTING TO SEE YOU.
HAS THERE BEEN A BREAK IN THE CASE? DO WE KNOW WHERE--?
YEAH, UH... HERE'S THE THING, MIZZ BUCHANAN...
WE'D LIKE TO COME IN AN' EXPLAIN TO YE WHAT--
YOUR HUSBAND'S DEAD. REASON I KNOW THAT IS 'CAUSE I KILLED HIM. CRUSHED HIS THROAT.
WUMF!
MIZZ BUCHANAN? YOU OKAY?
MIZZ BUCHANAN?
YEAH, BLOODY TACTFUL, THAT.

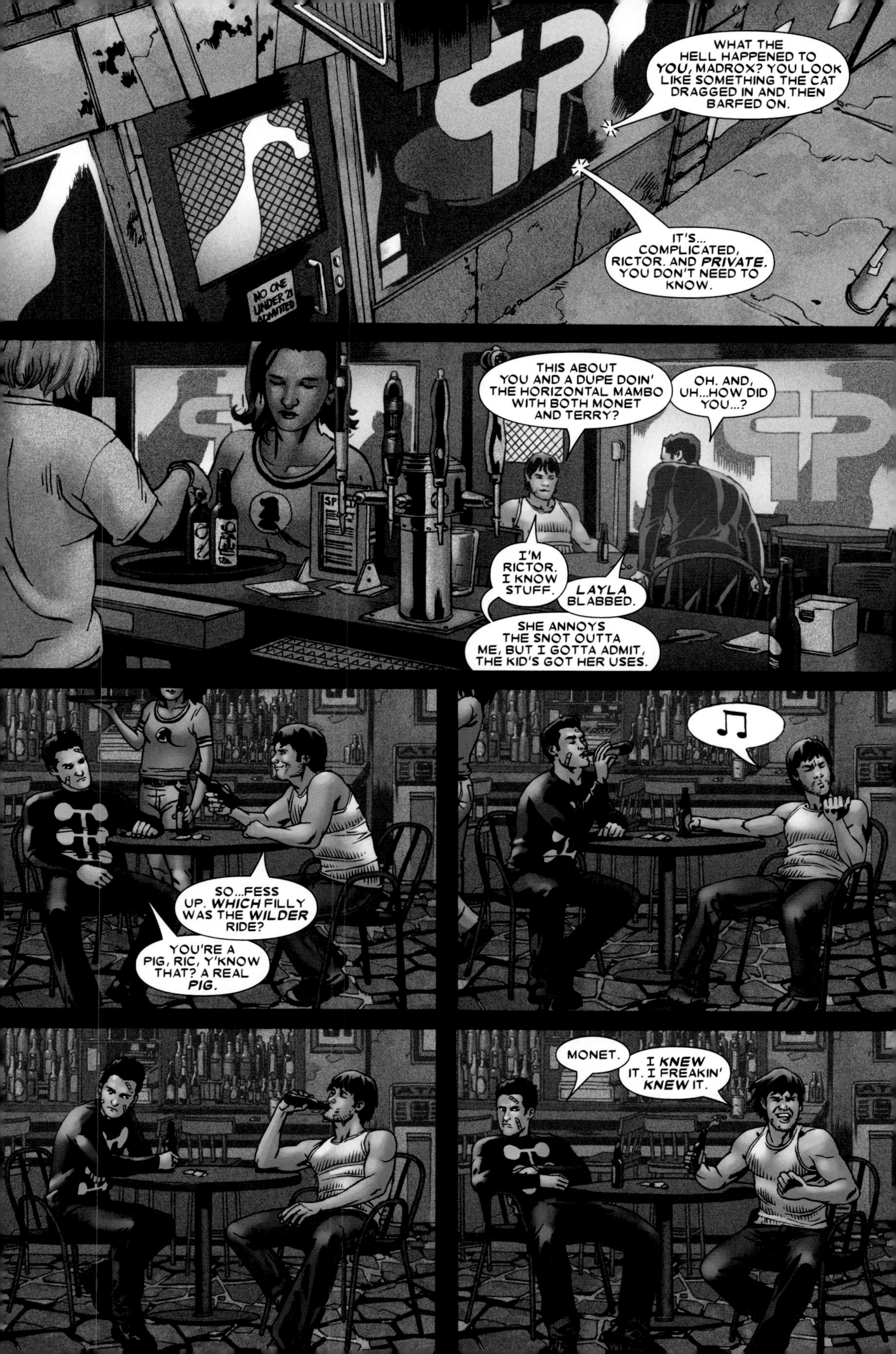
WHAT THE HELL HAPPENED TO YOU, MADROX? YOU LOOK LIKE SOMETHING THE CAT DRAGGED IN AND THEN BARFED ON.
IT'S... COMPLICATED, RICTOR. AND PRIVATE. YOU DON'T NEED TO KNOW.
NO ONE UNDER 21 ADMITTED
THIS ABOUT YOU AND A DUPE DOIN' THE HORIZONTAL MAMBO WITH BOTH MONET AND TERRY?
OH. AND, UH...HOW DID YOU...?
I'M RICTOR. I KNOW STUFF.
LAYLA BLABBED.
SHE ANNOYS THE SNOT OUTTA ME, BUT I GOTTA ADMIT, THE KID'S GOT HER USES.
SO...FESS UP. WHICH FILLY WAS THE WILDER RIDE?
YOU'RE A PIG, RIC, Y'KNOW THAT? A REAL PIG.
♫
MONET.
I KNEW IT. I FREAKIN' KNEW IT.

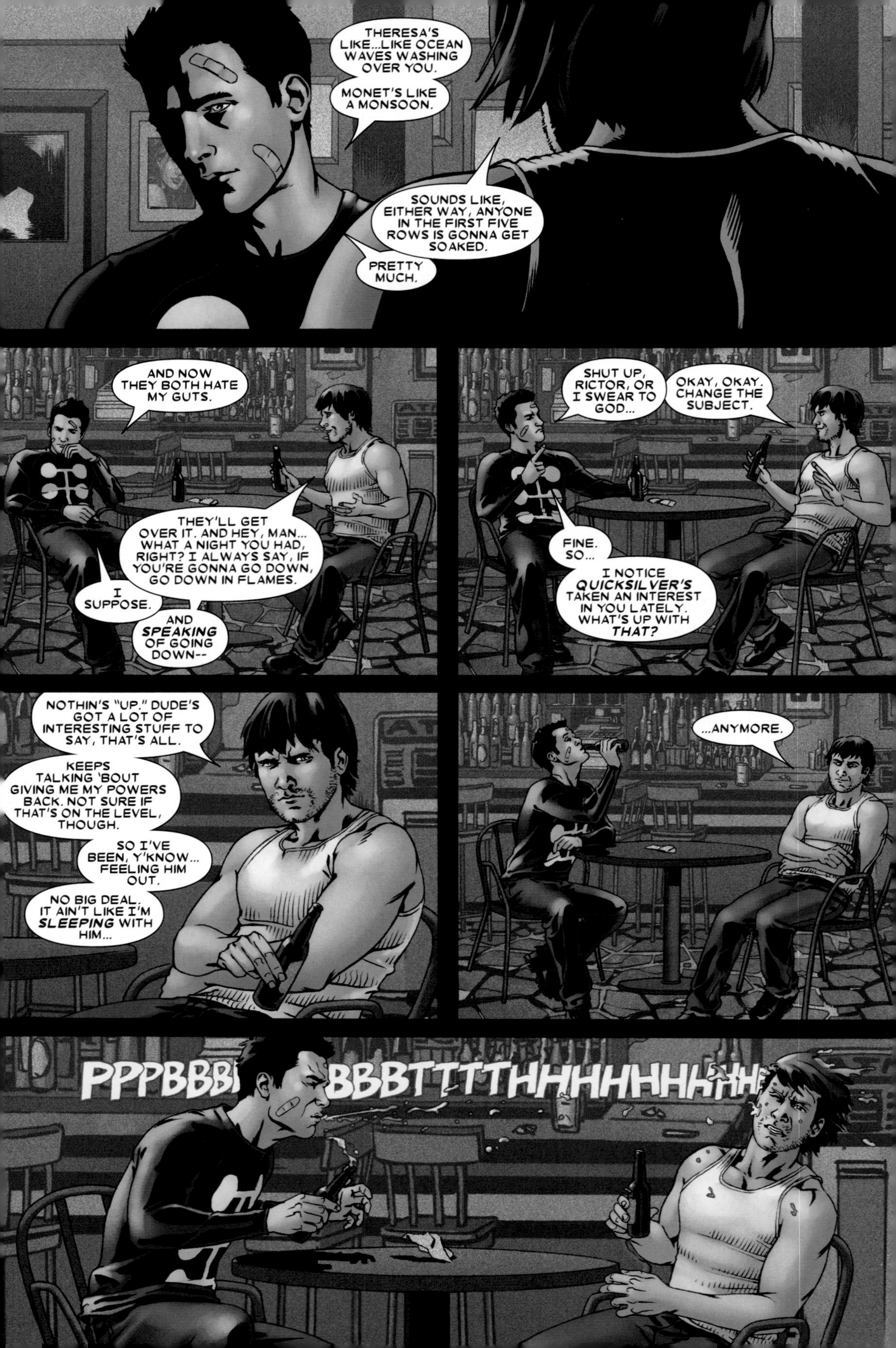

THERESA'S LIKE...LIKE OCEAN WAVES WASHING OVER YOU.
MONET'S LIKE A MONSOON.
SOUNDS LIKE, EITHER WAY, ANYONE IN THE FIRST FIVE ROWS IS GONNA GET SOAKED.
PRETTY MUCH.
AND NOW THEY BOTH HATE MY GUTS.
THEY'LL GET OVER IT. AND HEY, MAN... WHAT A NIGHT YOU HAD, RIGHT? I ALWAYS SAY, IF YOU'RE GONNA GO DOWN, GO DOWN IN FLAMES.
I SUPPOSE.
AND *SPEAKING* OF GOING DOWN--
SHUT UP, RICTOR, OR I SWEAR TO GOD...
OKAY, OKAY. CHANGE THE SUBJECT.
FINE. SO...
I NOTICE *QUICKSILVER'S* TAKEN AN INTEREST IN YOU LATELY. WHAT'S UP WITH *THAT?*
NOTHIN'S "UP." DUDE'S GOT A LOT OF INTERESTING STUFF TO SAY, THAT'S ALL.
KEEPS TALKING 'BOUT GIVING ME MY POWERS BACK. NOT SURE IF THAT'S ON THE LEVEL, THOUGH.
SO I'VE BEEN, Y'KNOW... FEELING HIM OUT.
NO BIG DEAL. IT AIN'T LIKE I'M *SLEEPING* WITH HIM...
...ANYMORE.
PPPBBB BBBTTTTHHHHHHHH

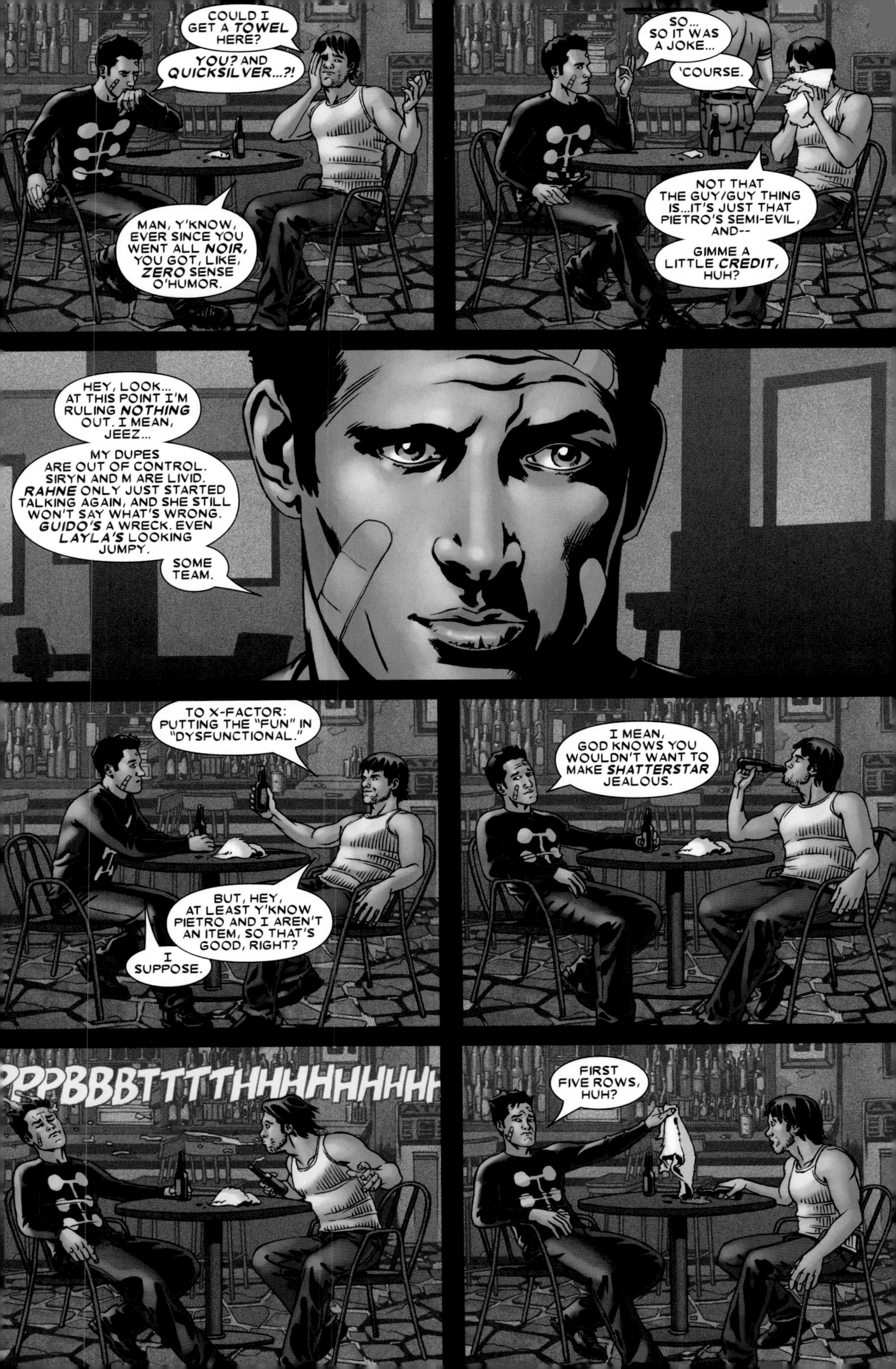
COULD I GET A TOWEL HERE?
YOU? AND QUICKSILVER...?!
MAN, Y'KNOW, EVER SINCE YOU WENT ALL NOIR, YOU GOT, LIKE, ZERO SENSE O'HUMOR.
SO... SO IT WAS A JOKE...
'COURSE.
NOT THAT THE GUY/GUY THING IS...IT'S JUST THAT PIETRO'S SEMI-EVIL, AND--
GIMME A LITTLE CREDIT, HUH?
HEY, LOOK... AT THIS POINT I'M RULING NOTHING OUT. I MEAN, JEEZ...
MY DUPES ARE OUT OF CONTROL. SIRYN AND M ARE LIVID. RAHNE ONLY JUST STARTED TALKING AGAIN, AND SHE STILL WON'T SAY WHAT'S WRONG. GUIDO'S A WRECK. EVEN LAYLA'S LOOKING JUMPY.
SOME TEAM.
TO X-FACTOR: PUTTING THE "FUN" IN "DYSFUNCTIONAL."
BUT, HEY, AT LEAST Y'KNOW PIETRO AND I AREN'T AN ITEM, SO THAT'S GOOD, RIGHT?
I SUPPOSE.
I MEAN, GOD KNOWS YOU WOULDN'T WANT TO MAKE SHATTERSTAR JEALOUS.
PPPBBBTTTTHHHHHHHH
FIRST FIVE ROWS, HUH?

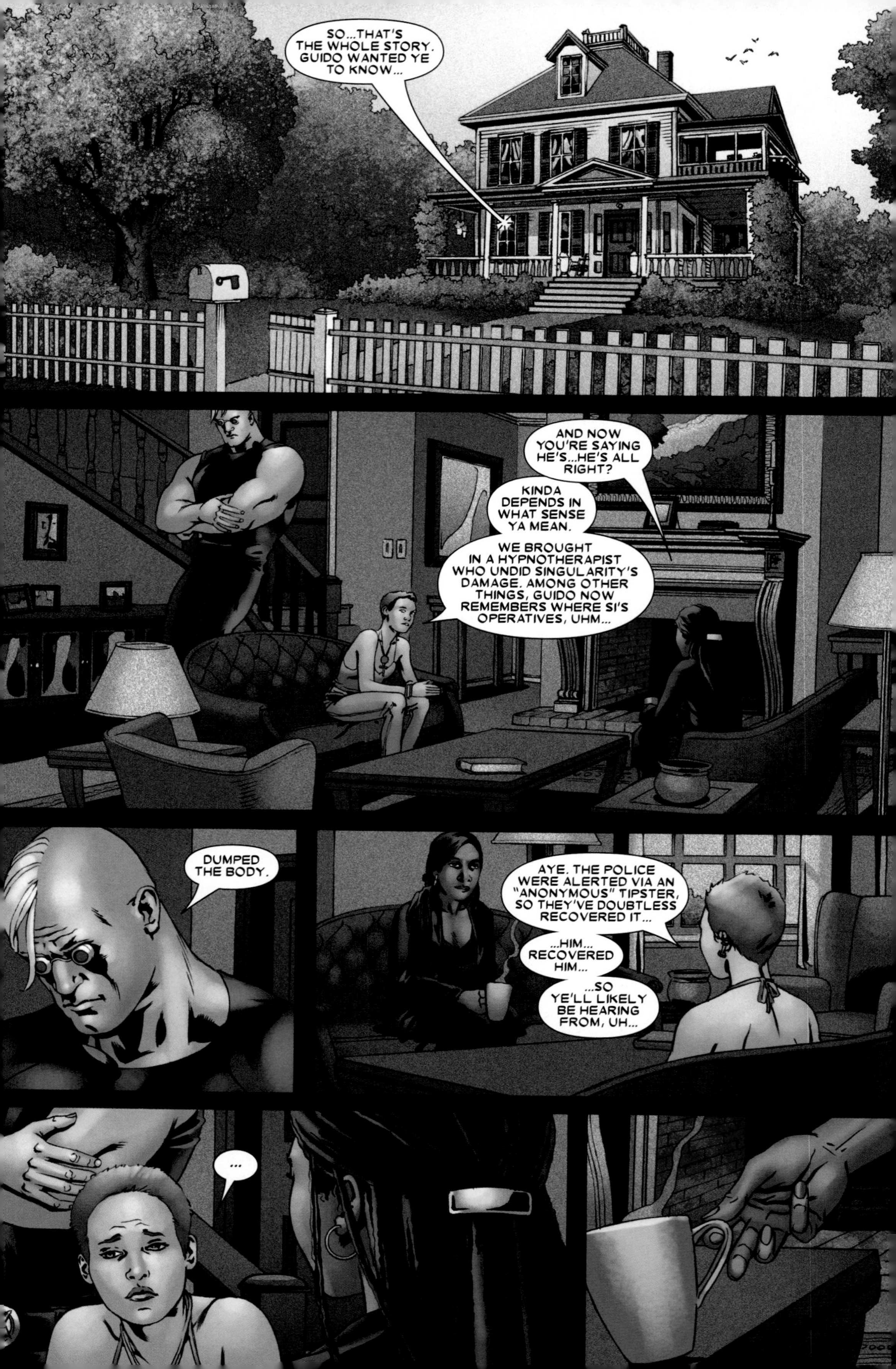

SO...THAT'S THE WHOLE STORY. GUIDO WANTED YE TO KNOW...
AND NOW YOU'RE SAYING HE'S...HE'S ALL RIGHT?
KINDA DEPENDS IN WHAT SENSE YA MEAN.
WE BROUGHT IN A HYPNOTHERAPIST WHO UNDID SINGULARITY'S DAMAGE. AMONG OTHER THINGS, GUIDO NOW REMEMBERS WHERE SI'S OPERATIVES, UHM...
DUMPED THE BODY.
AYE. THE POLICE WERE ALERTED VIA AN "ANONYMOUS" TIPSTER, SO THEY'VE DOUBTLESS RECOVERED IT...
...HIM... RECOVERED HIM...
...SO YE'LL LIKELY BE HEARING FROM, UH...
...

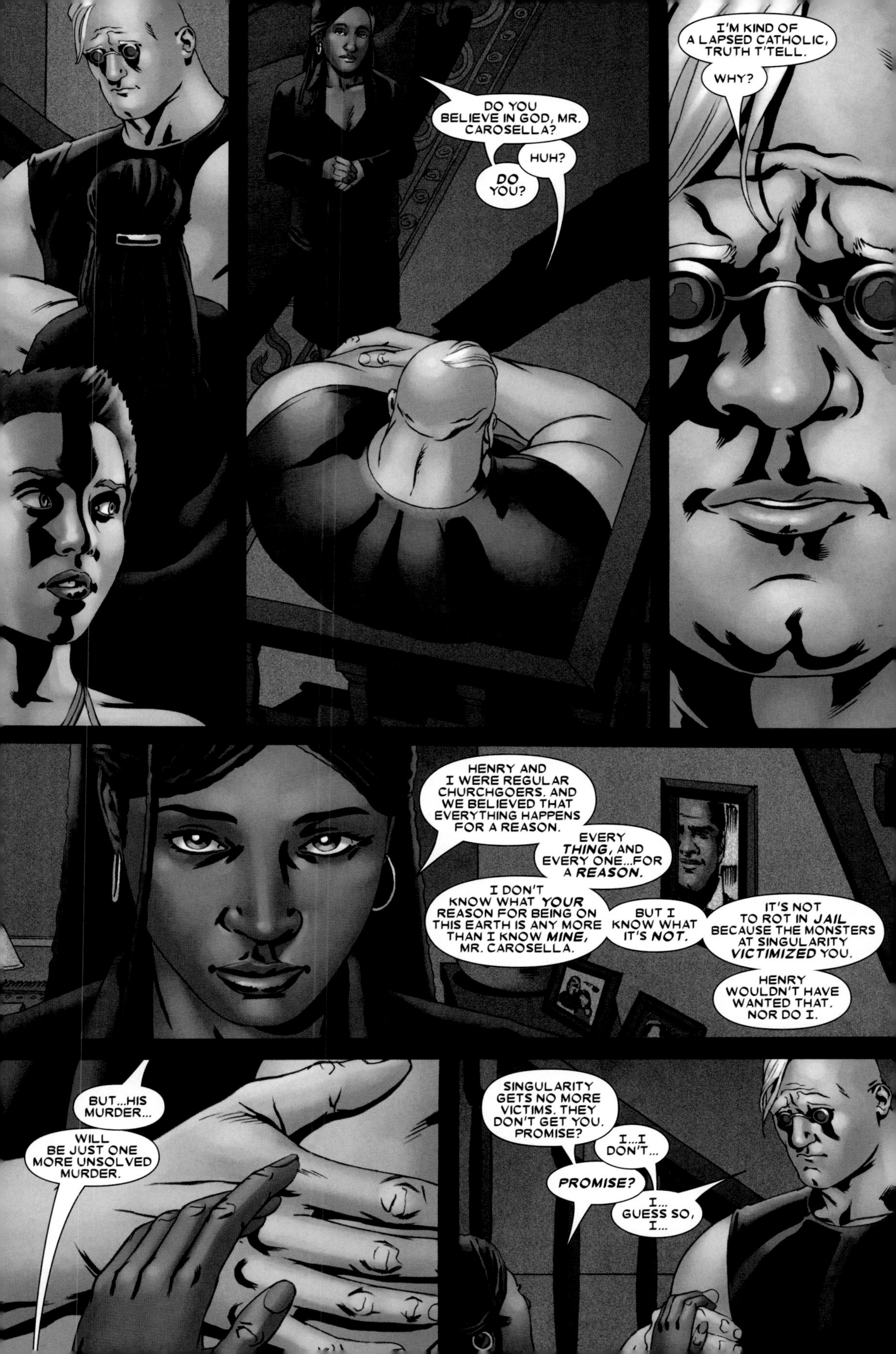
DO YOU BELIEVE IN GOD, MR. CAROSELLA?
HUH?
DO YOU?
I'M KIND OF A LAPSED CATHOLIC, TRUTH T'TELL.
WHY?
HENRY AND I WERE REGULAR CHURCHGOERS. AND WE BELIEVED THAT EVERYTHING HAPPENS FOR A REASON.
EVERY *THING*, AND EVERY ONE...FOR A *REASON*.
I DON'T KNOW WHAT *YOUR* REASON FOR BEING ON THIS EARTH IS ANY MORE THAN I KNOW *MINE*, MR. CAROSELLA.
BUT I KNOW WHAT IT'S *NOT*.
IT'S NOT TO ROT IN *JAIL* BECAUSE THE MONSTERS AT SINGULARITY *VICTIMIZED* YOU.
HENRY WOULDN'T HAVE WANTED THAT. NOR DO I.
BUT...HIS MURDER...
WILL BE JUST ONE MORE UNSOLVED MURDER.
SINGULARITY GETS NO MORE VICTIMS. THEY DON'T GET YOU. PROMISE?
I...I DON'T...
PROMISE?
I... GUESS SO, I...

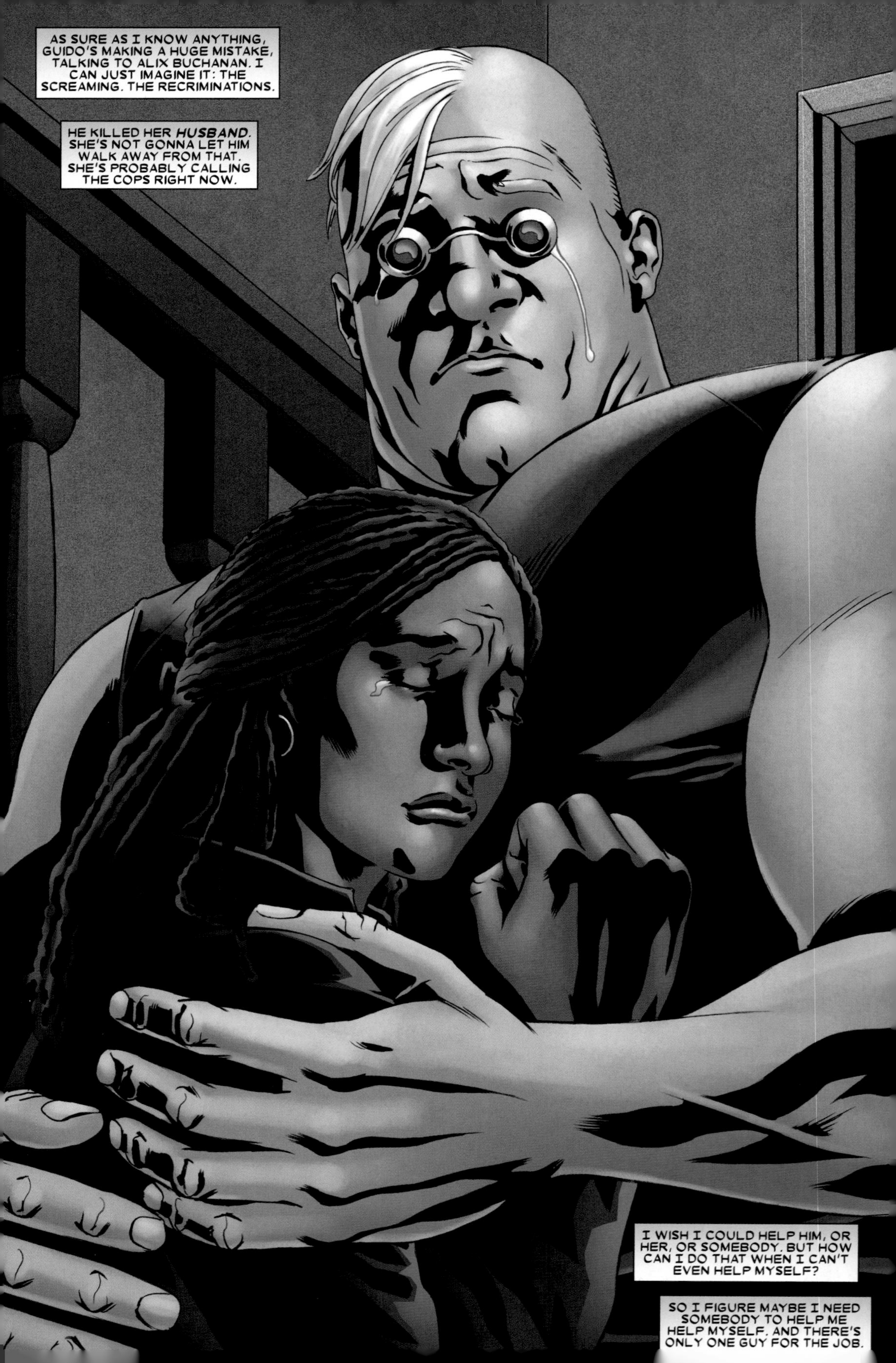
AS SURE AS I KNOW ANYTHING, GUIDO'S MAKING A HUGE MISTAKE, TALKING TO ALIX BUCHANAN. I CAN JUST IMAGINE IT: THE SCREAMING. THE RECRIMINATIONS.
HE KILLED HER *HUSBAND*. SHE'S NOT GONNA LET HIM WALK AWAY FROM THAT. SHE'S PROBABLY CALLING THE COPS RIGHT NOW.
I WISH I COULD HELP HIM, OR HER, OR SOMEBODY. BUT HOW CAN I DO THAT WHEN I CAN'T EVEN HELP MYSELF?
SO I FIGURE MAYBE I NEED SOMEBODY TO HELP ME HELP MYSELF. AND THERE'S ONLY ONE GUY FOR THE JOB.

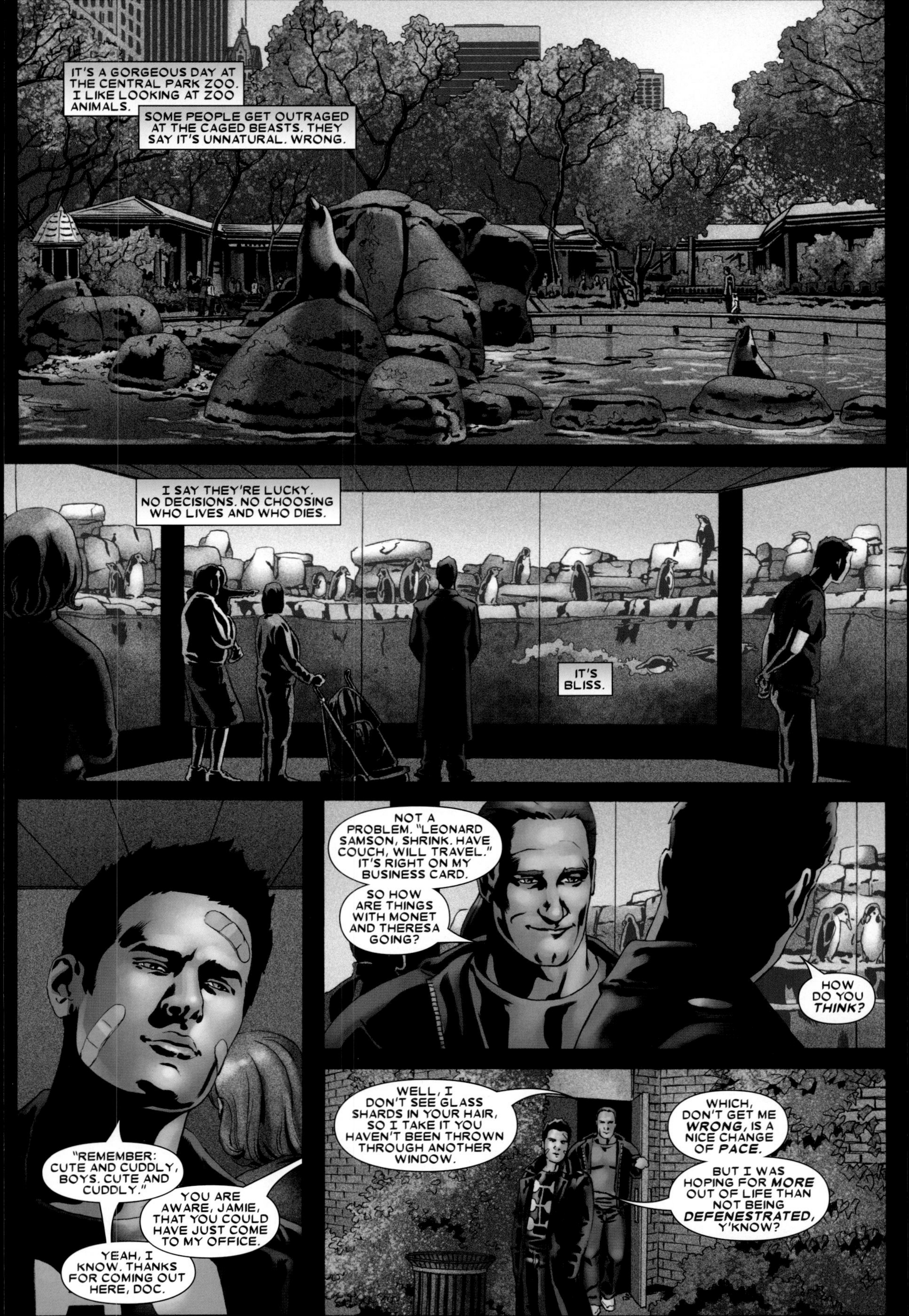
IT'S A GORGEOUS DAY AT THE CENTRAL PARK ZOO. I LIKE LOOKING AT ZOO ANIMALS.
SOME PEOPLE GET OUTRAGED AT THE CAGED BEASTS. THEY SAY IT'S UNNATURAL. WRONG.
I SAY THEY'RE LUCKY. NO DECISIONS. NO CHOOSING WHO LIVES AND WHO DIES.
IT'S BLISS.
"REMEMBER: CUTE AND CUDDLY, BOYS. CUTE AND CUDDLY."
YOU ARE AWARE, JAMIE, THAT YOU COULD HAVE JUST COME TO MY OFFICE.
YEAH, I KNOW. THANKS FOR COMING OUT HERE, DOC.
NOT A PROBLEM. "LEONARD SAMSON, SHRINK. HAVE COUCH, WILL TRAVEL." IT'S RIGHT ON MY BUSINESS CARD.
SO HOW ARE THINGS WITH MONET AND THERESA GOING?
HOW DO YOU *THINK?*
WELL, I DON'T SEE GLASS SHARDS IN YOUR HAIR, SO I TAKE IT YOU HAVEN'T BEEN THROWN THROUGH ANOTHER WINDOW.
WHICH, DON'T GET ME *WRONG,* IS A NICE CHANGE OF *PACE.*
BUT I WAS HOPING FOR *MORE* OUT OF LIFE THAN NOT BEING *DEFENESTRATED,* Y'KNOW?

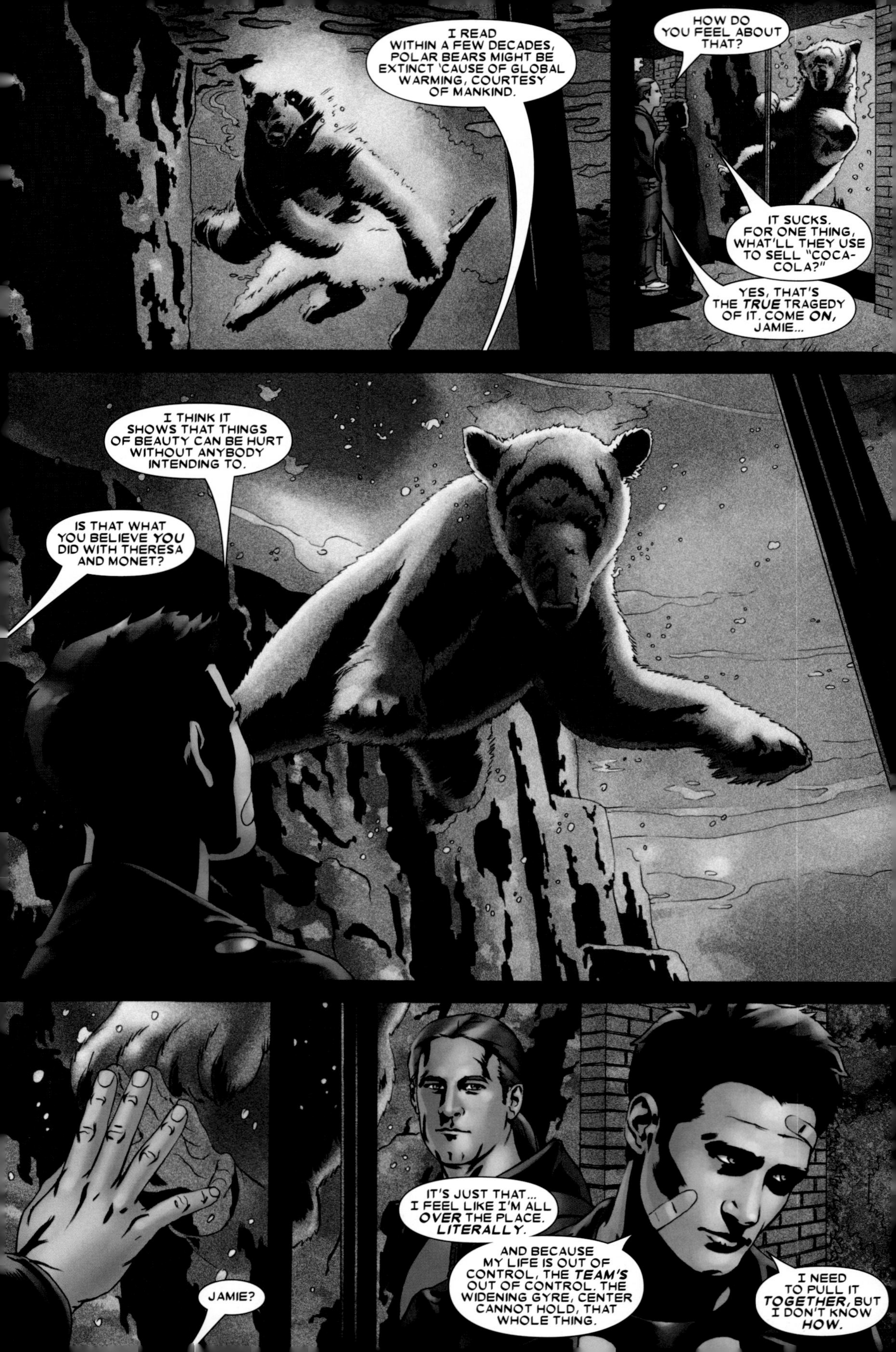
I READ WITHIN A FEW DECADES, POLAR BEARS MIGHT BE EXTINCT 'CAUSE OF GLOBAL WARMING, COURTESY OF MANKIND.
HOW DO YOU FEEL ABOUT THAT?
IT SUCKS. FOR ONE THING, WHAT'LL THEY USE TO SELL "COCA-COLA?"
YES, THAT'S THE *TRUE* TRAGEDY OF IT. COME *ON*, JAMIE...
I THINK IT SHOWS THAT THINGS OF BEAUTY CAN BE HURT WITHOUT ANYBODY INTENDING TO.
IS THAT WHAT YOU BELIEVE *YOU* DID WITH THERESA AND MONET?
JAMIE?
IT'S JUST THAT... I FEEL LIKE I'M ALL *OVER* THE PLACE. *LITERALLY*.
AND BECAUSE MY LIFE IS OUT OF CONTROL, THE *TEAM'S* OUT OF CONTROL. THE WIDENING GYRE, CENTER CANNOT HOLD, THAT WHOLE THING.
I NEED TO PULL IT *TOGETHER*, BUT I DON'T KNOW *HOW*.

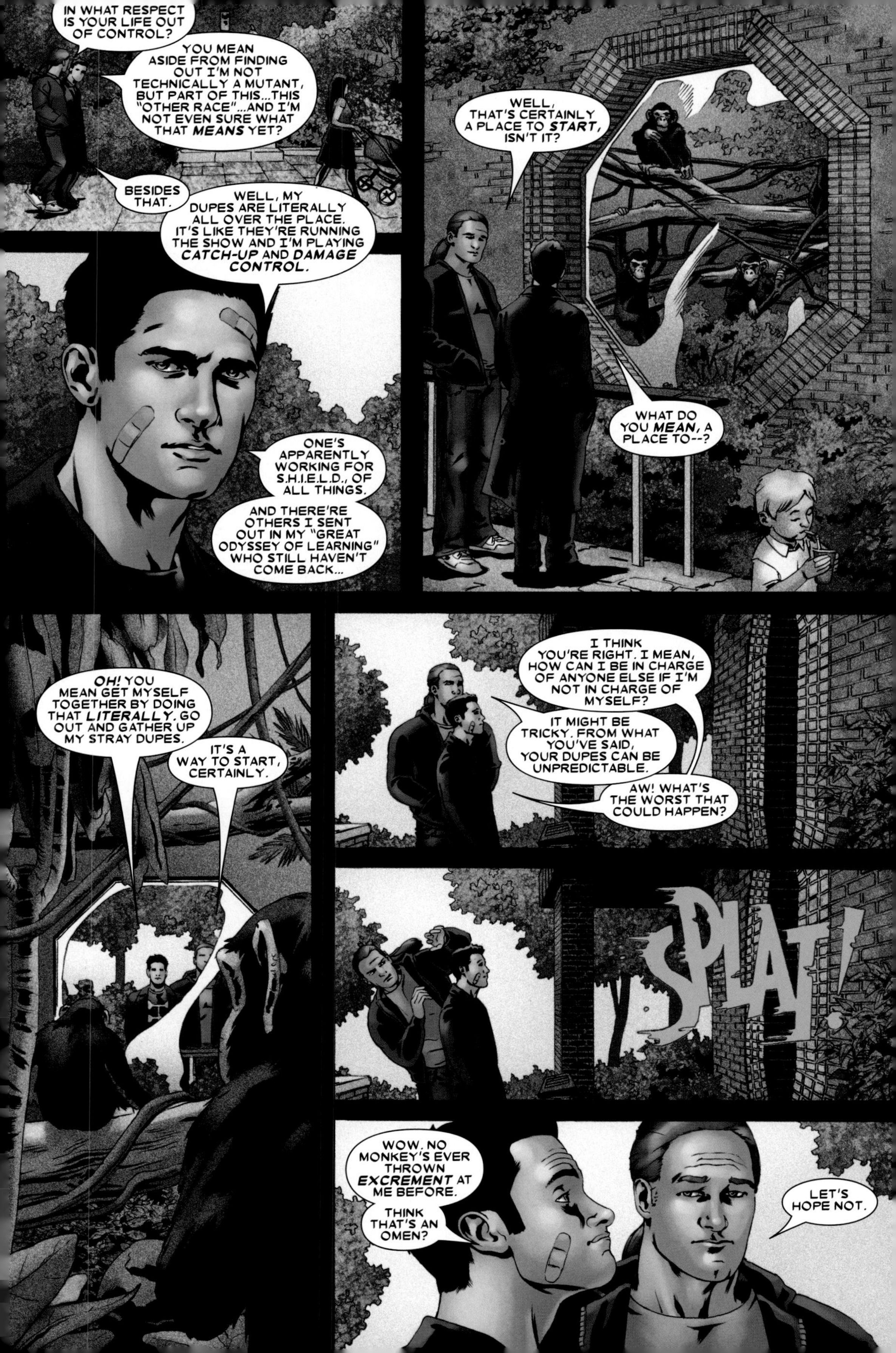
IN WHAT RESPECT IS YOUR LIFE OUT OF CONTROL?
YOU MEAN ASIDE FROM FINDING OUT I'M NOT TECHNICALLY A MUTANT, BUT PART OF THIS...THIS "OTHER RACE"...AND I'M NOT EVEN SURE WHAT THAT MEANS YET?
BESIDES THAT.
WELL, MY DUPES ARE LITERALLY ALL OVER THE PLACE. IT'S LIKE THEY'RE RUNNING THE SHOW AND I'M PLAYING CATCH-UP AND DAMAGE CONTROL.
ONE'S APPARENTLY WORKING FOR S.H.I.E.L.D., OF ALL THINGS.
AND THERE'RE OTHERS I SENT OUT IN MY "GREAT ODYSSEY OF LEARNING" WHO STILL HAVEN'T COME BACK...
WELL, THAT'S CERTAINLY A PLACE TO START, ISN'T IT?
WHAT DO YOU MEAN, A PLACE TO--?
OH! YOU MEAN GET MYSELF TOGETHER BY DOING THAT LITERALLY. GO OUT AND GATHER UP MY STRAY DUPES.
IT'S A WAY TO START, CERTAINLY.
I THINK YOU'RE RIGHT. I MEAN, HOW CAN I BE IN CHARGE OF ANYONE ELSE IF I'M NOT IN CHARGE OF MYSELF?
IT MIGHT BE TRICKY. FROM WHAT YOU'VE SAID, YOUR DUPES CAN BE UNPREDICTABLE.
AW! WHAT'S THE WORST THAT COULD HAPPEN?
SPLAT!
WOW. NO MONKEY'S EVER THROWN EXCREMENT AT ME BEFORE.
THINK THAT'S AN OMEN?
LET'S HOPE NOT.

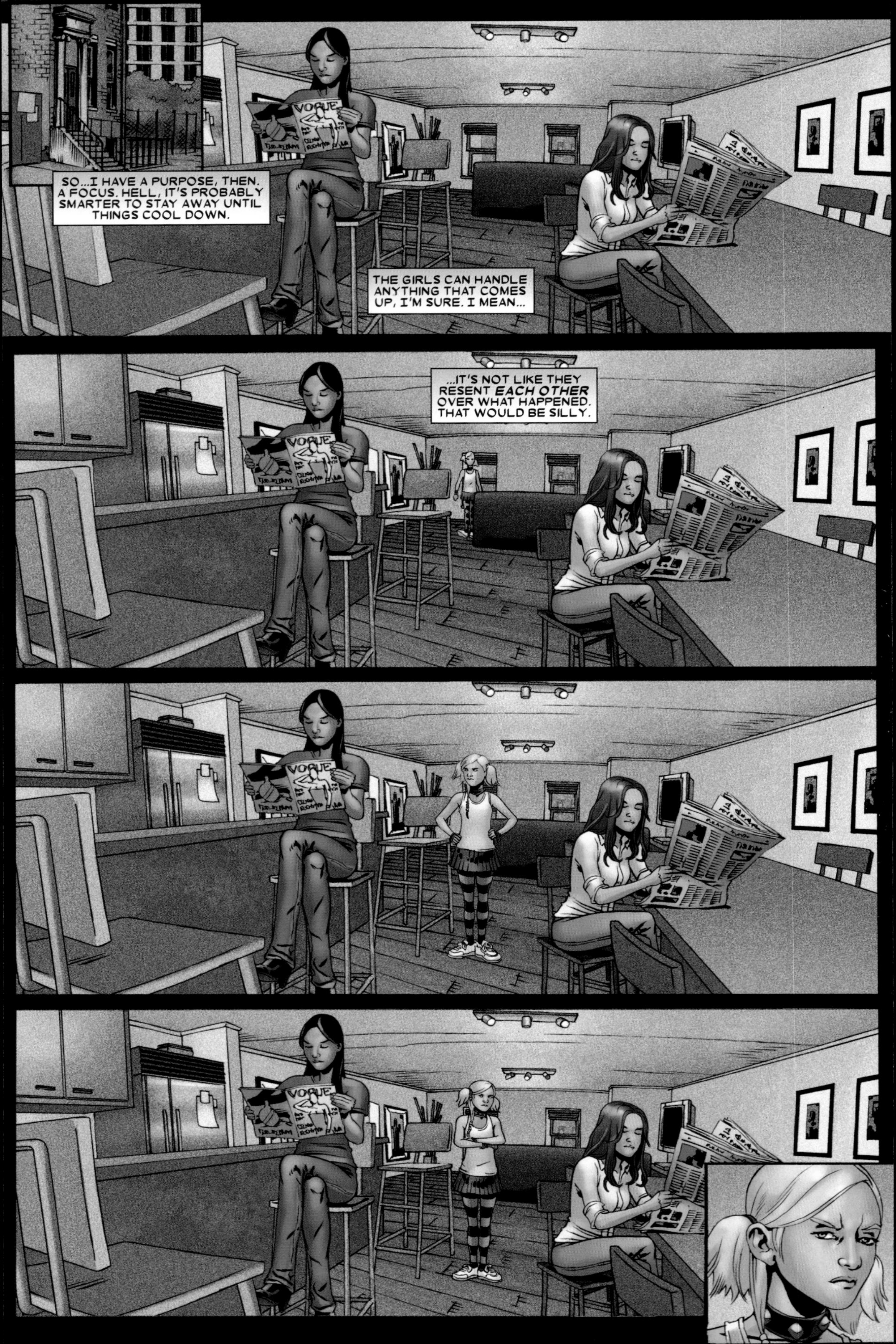

SO...I HAVE A PURPOSE, THEN. A FOCUS. HELL, IT'S PROBABLY SMARTER TO STAY AWAY UNTIL THINGS COOL DOWN.
THE GIRLS CAN HANDLE ANYTHING THAT COMES UP, I'M SURE. I MEAN...
...IT'S NOT LIKE THEY RESENT *EACH OTHER* OVER WHAT HAPPENED. THAT WOULD BE SILLY.

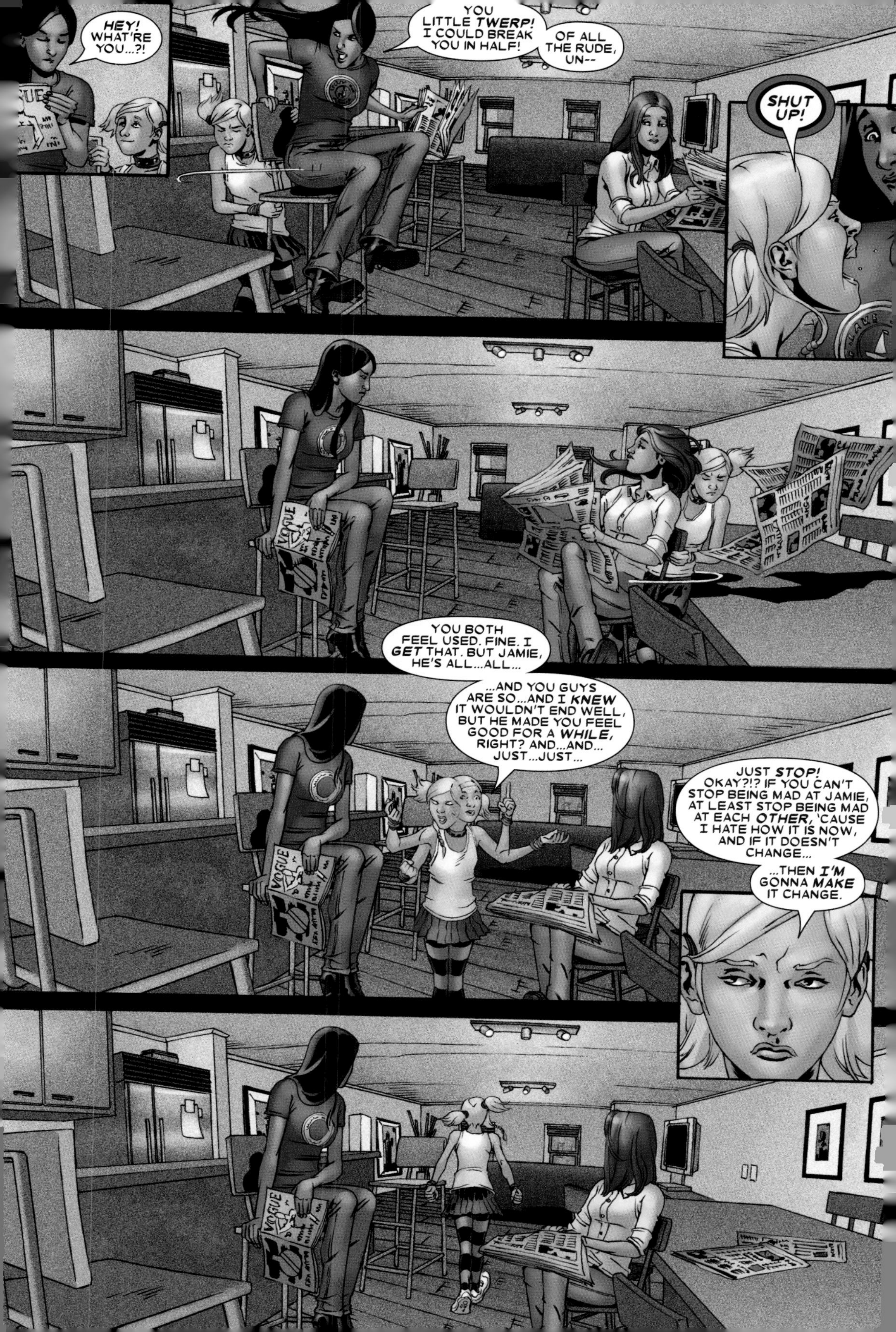
HEY! WHAT'RE YOU...?!
YOU LITTLE TWERP! I COULD BREAK YOU IN HALF!
OF ALL THE RUDE, UN--
SHUT UP!
YOU BOTH FEEL USED. FINE. I GET THAT. BUT JAMIE, HE'S ALL...ALL...
...AND YOU GUYS ARE SO...AND I KNEW IT WOULDN'T END WELL, BUT HE MADE YOU FEEL GOOD FOR A WHILE, RIGHT? AND...AND... JUST...JUST...
JUST STOP! OKAY?!? IF YOU CAN'T STOP BEING MAD AT JAMIE, AT LEAST STOP BEING MAD AT EACH OTHER, 'CAUSE I HATE HOW IT IS NOW, AND IF IT DOESN'T CHANGE...
...THEN I'M GONNA MAKE IT CHANGE.

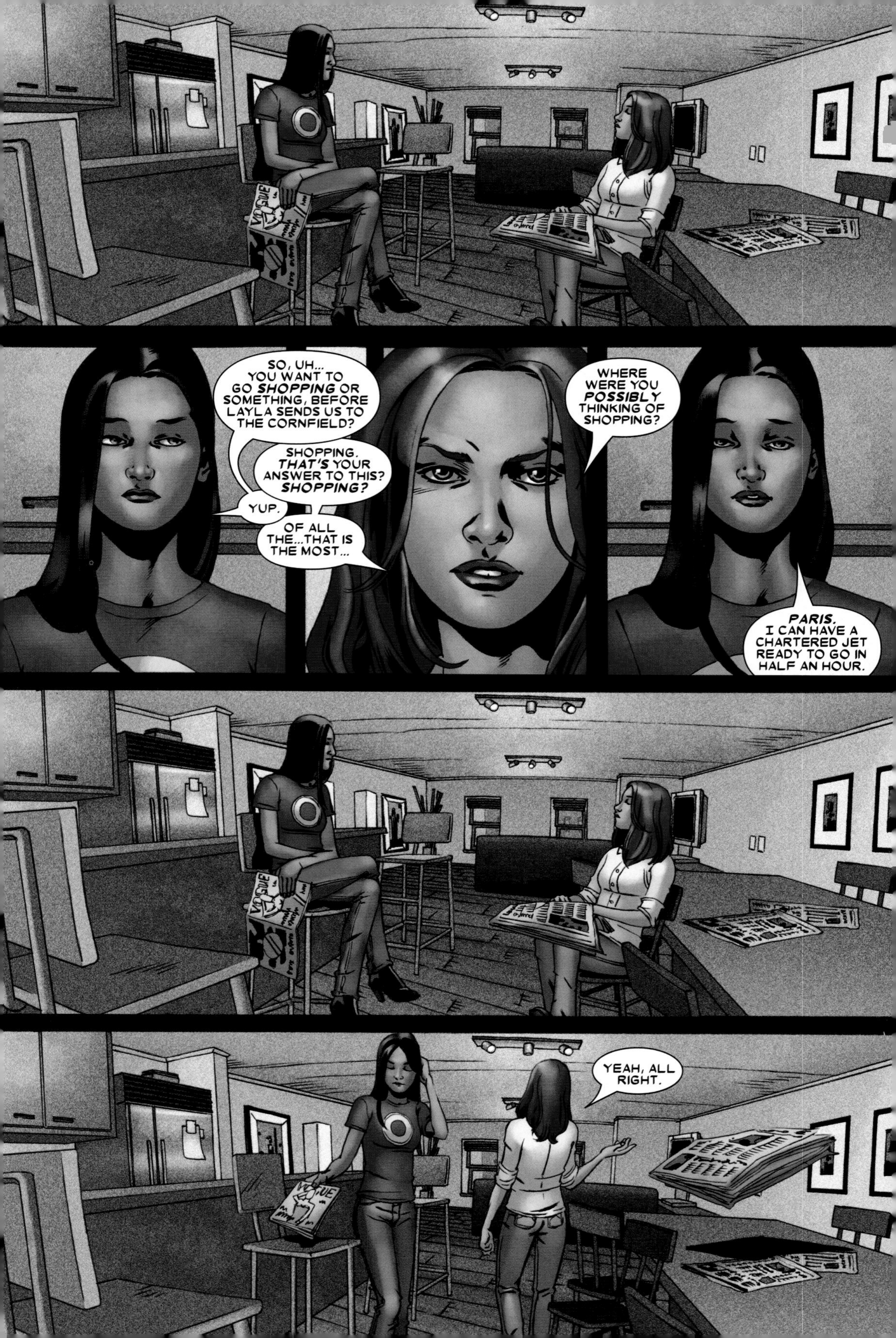
SO, UH... YOU WANT TO GO SHOPPING OR SOMETHING, BEFORE LAYLA SENDS US TO THE CORNFIELD?
SHOPPING. THAT'S YOUR ANSWER TO THIS? SHOPPING?
YUP.
OF ALL THE...THAT IS THE MOST...
WHERE WERE YOU POSSIBLY THINKING OF SHOPPING?
PARIS. I CAN HAVE A CHARTERED JET READY TO GO IN HALF AN HOUR.
YEAH, ALL RIGHT.

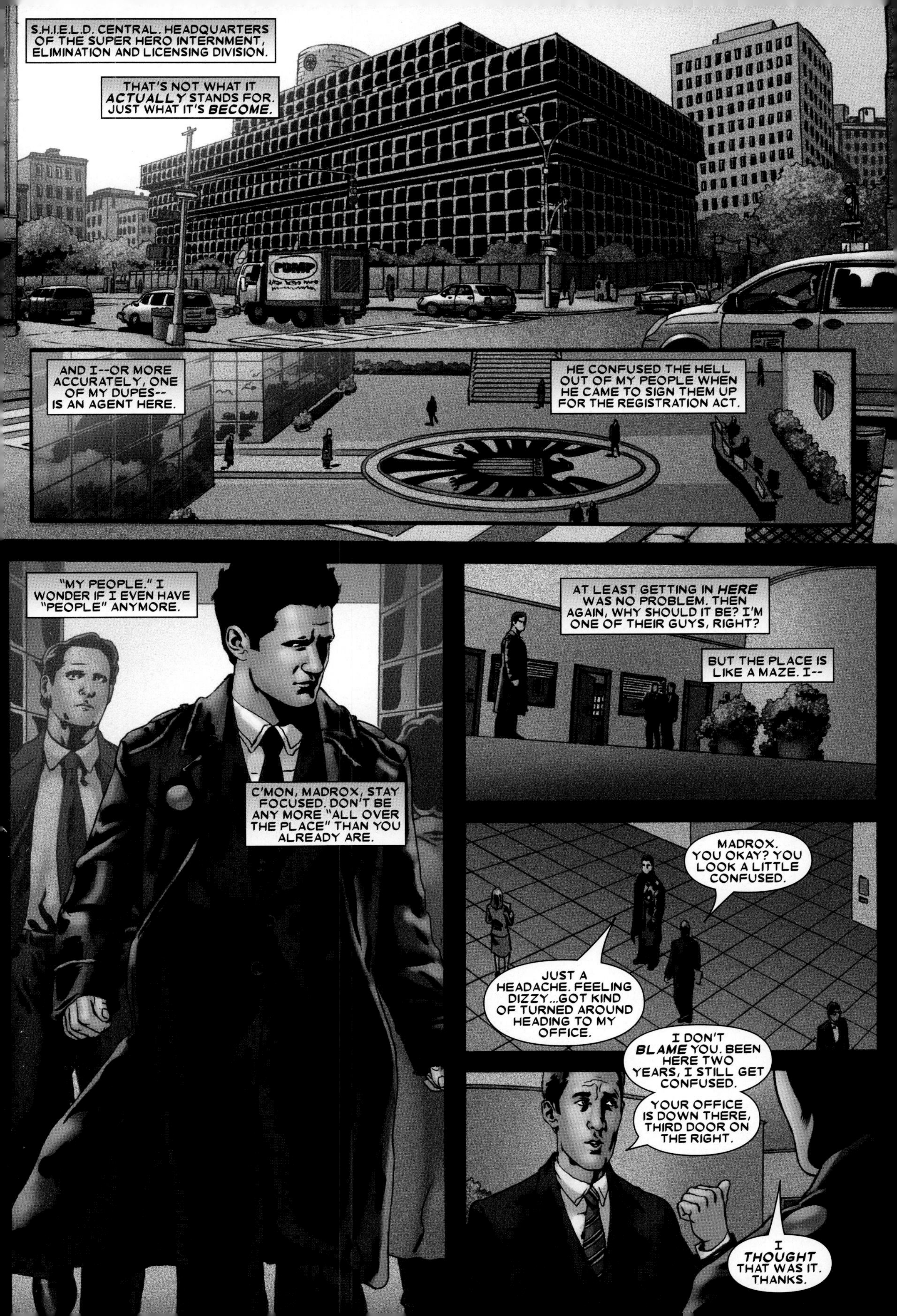
S.H.I.E.L.D. CENTRAL. HEADQUARTERS OF THE SUPER HERO INTERNMENT, ELIMINATION AND LICENSING DIVISION.
THAT'S NOT WHAT IT *ACTUALLY* STANDS FOR. JUST WHAT IT'S *BECOME.*
AND I--OR MORE ACCURATELY, ONE OF MY DUPES--IS AN AGENT HERE.
HE CONFUSED THE HELL OUT OF MY PEOPLE WHEN HE CAME TO SIGN THEM UP FOR THE REGISTRATION ACT.
"MY PEOPLE." I WONDER IF I EVEN HAVE "PEOPLE" ANYMORE.
C'MON, MADROX, STAY FOCUSED. DON'T BE ANY MORE "ALL OVER THE PLACE" THAN YOU ALREADY ARE.
AT LEAST GETTING IN *HERE* WAS NO PROBLEM. THEN AGAIN, WHY SHOULD IT BE? I'M ONE OF THEIR GUYS, RIGHT?
BUT THE PLACE IS LIKE A MAZE. I--
MADROX. YOU OKAY? YOU LOOK A LITTLE CONFUSED.
JUST A HEADACHE. FEELING DIZZY...GOT KIND OF TURNED AROUND HEADING TO MY OFFICE.
I DON'T *BLAME* YOU. BEEN HERE TWO YEARS, I STILL GET CONFUSED.
YOUR OFFICE IS DOWN THERE, THIRD DOOR ON THE RIGHT.
I *THOUGHT* THAT WAS IT. THANKS.

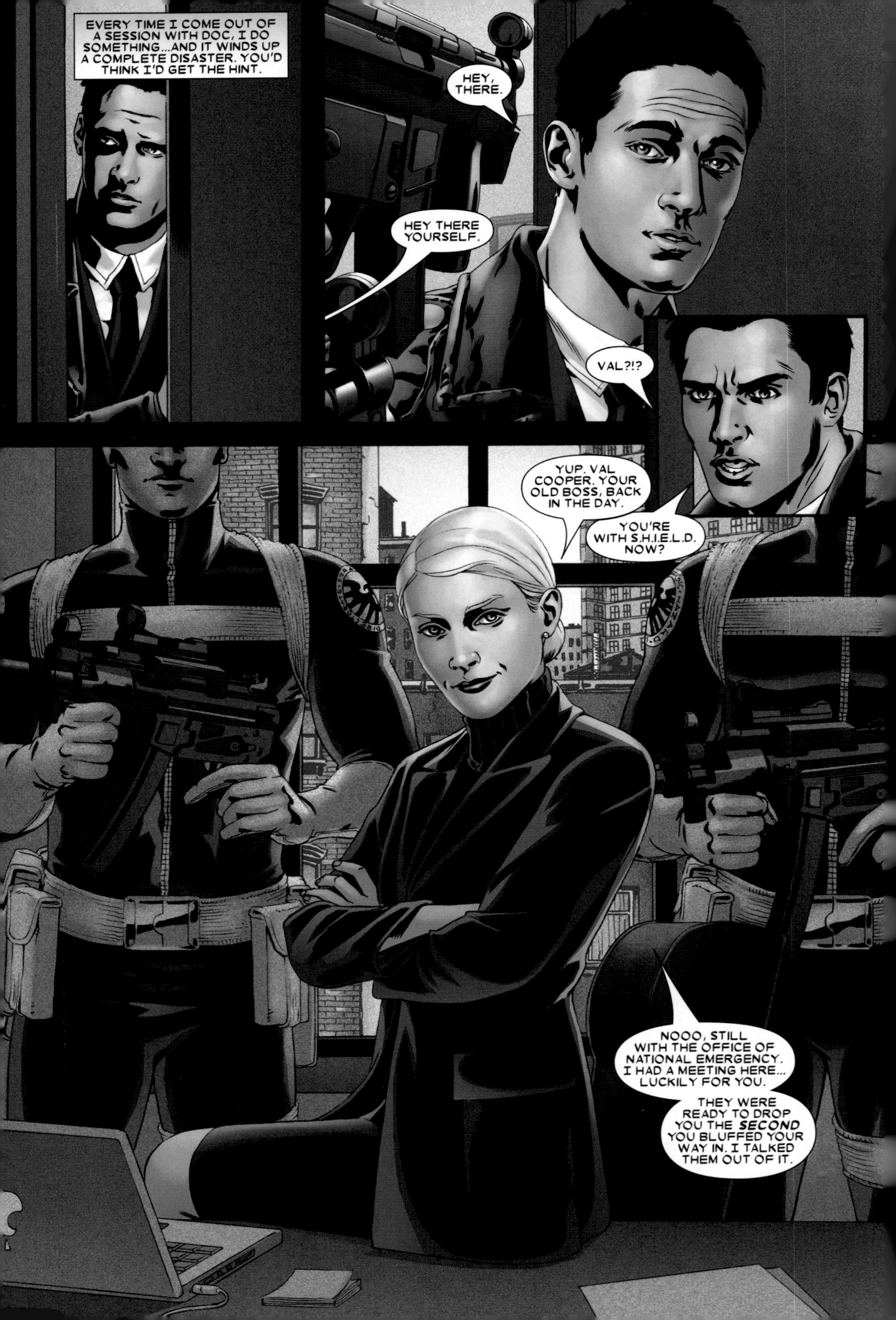
EVERY TIME I COME OUT OF A SESSION WITH DOC, I DO SOMETHING...AND IT WINDS UP A COMPLETE DISASTER. YOU'D THINK I'D GET THE HINT.
HEY, THERE.
HEY THERE YOURSELF.
VAL?!?
YUP. VAL COOPER. YOUR OLD BOSS, BACK IN THE DAY.
YOU'RE WITH S.H.I.E.L.D. NOW?
NOOO, STILL WITH THE OFFICE OF NATIONAL EMERGENCY. I HAD A MEETING HERE... LUCKILY FOR YOU.
THEY WERE READY TO DROP YOU THE *SECOND* YOU BLUFFED YOUR WAY IN. I TALKED THEM OUT OF IT.

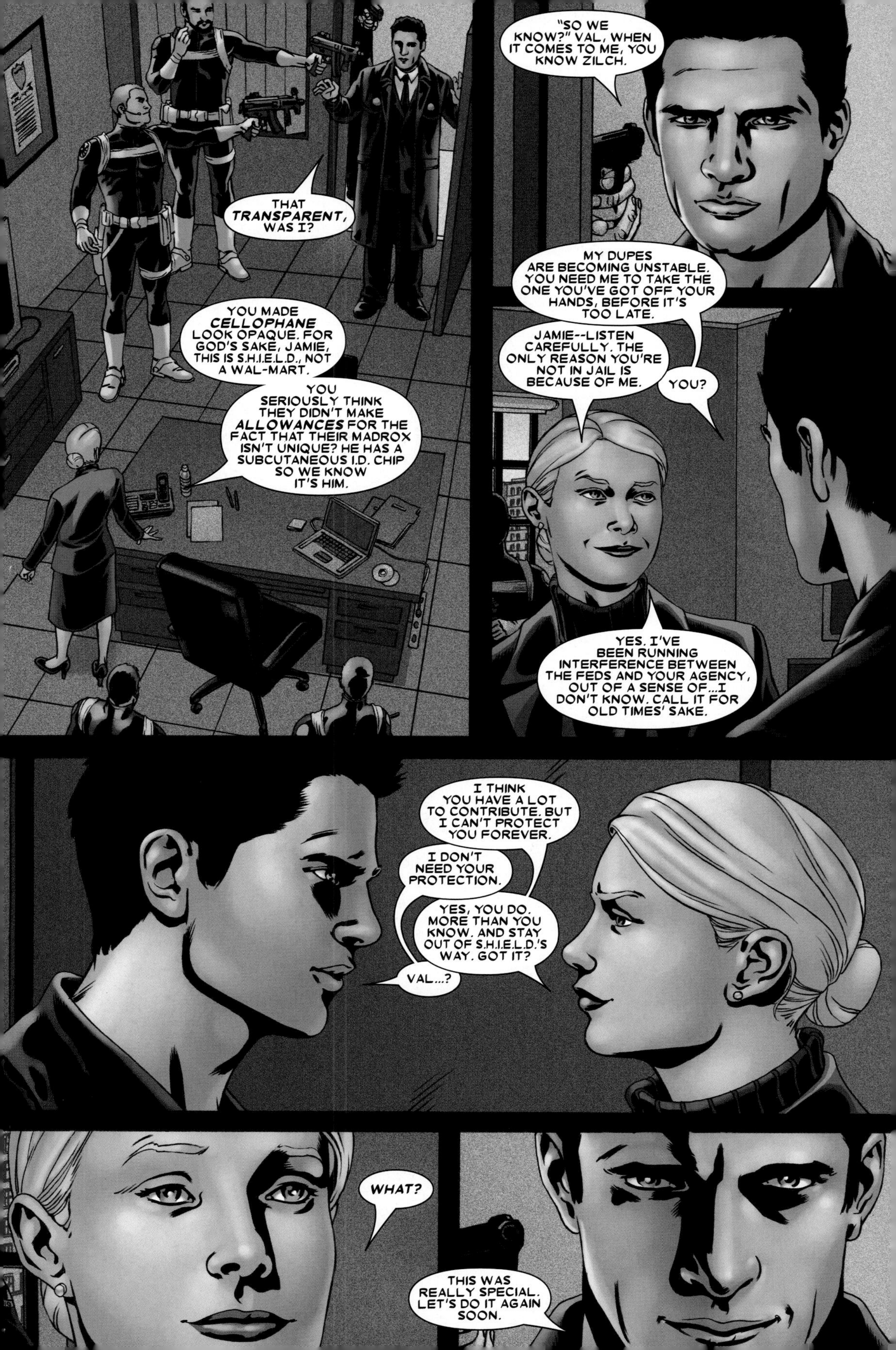
THAT TRANSPARENT, WAS I?
YOU MADE CELLOPHANE LOOK OPAQUE. FOR GOD'S SAKE, JAMIE, THIS IS S.H.I.E.L.D., NOT A WAL-MART.
YOU SERIOUSLY THINK THEY DIDN'T MAKE ALLOWANCES FOR THE FACT THAT THEIR MADROX ISN'T UNIQUE? HE HAS A SUBCUTANEOUS I.D. CHIP SO WE KNOW IT'S HIM.
"SO WE KNOW?" VAL, WHEN IT COMES TO ME, YOU KNOW ZILCH.
MY DUPES ARE BECOMING UNSTABLE. YOU NEED ME TO TAKE THE ONE YOU'VE GOT OFF YOUR HANDS, BEFORE IT'S TOO LATE.
JAMIE--LISTEN CAREFULLY. THE ONLY REASON YOU'RE NOT IN JAIL IS BECAUSE OF ME.
YOU?
YES. I'VE BEEN RUNNING INTERFERENCE BETWEEN THE FEDS AND YOUR AGENCY, OUT OF A SENSE OF...I DON'T KNOW. CALL IT FOR OLD TIMES' SAKE.
I THINK YOU HAVE A LOT TO CONTRIBUTE. BUT I CAN'T PROTECT YOU FOREVER.
I DON'T NEED YOUR PROTECTION.
YES, YOU DO. MORE THAN YOU KNOW. AND STAY OUT OF S.H.I.E.L.D.'S WAY. GOT IT?
VAL...?
WHAT?
THIS WAS REALLY SPECIAL. LET'S DO IT AGAIN SOON.

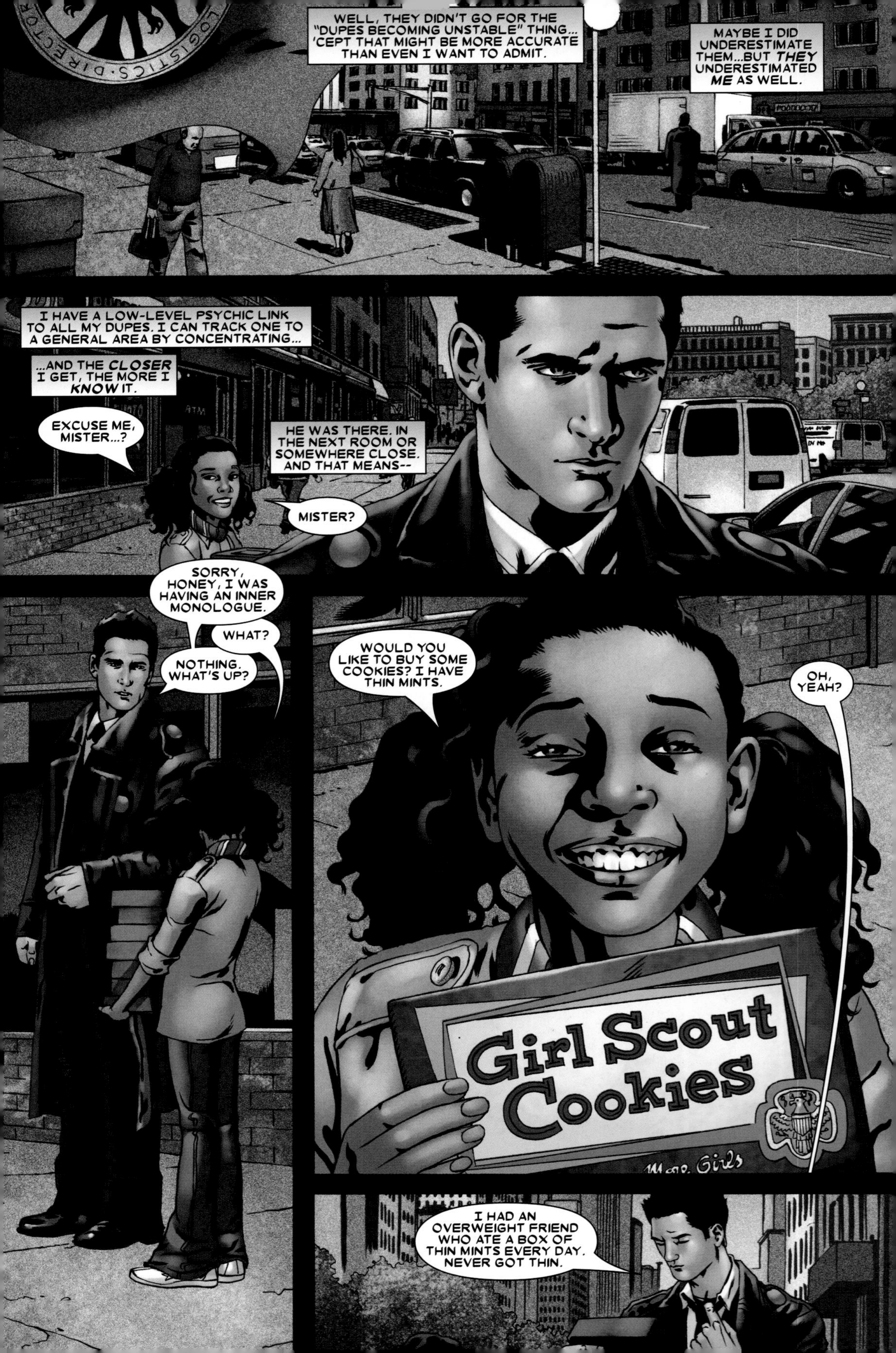

LOGISTICS · DIRECTOR
WELL, THEY DIDN'T GO FOR THE "DUPES BECOMING UNSTABLE" THING... 'CEPT THAT MIGHT BE MORE ACCURATE THAN EVEN I WANT TO ADMIT.
MAYBE I DID UNDERESTIMATE THEM...BUT THEY UNDERESTIMATED ME AS WELL.
I HAVE A LOW-LEVEL PSYCHIC LINK TO ALL MY DUPES. I CAN TRACK ONE TO A GENERAL AREA BY CONCENTRATING...
...AND THE CLOSER I GET, THE MORE I KNOW IT.
EXCUSE ME, MISTER...?
HE WAS THERE. IN THE NEXT ROOM OR SOMEWHERE CLOSE. AND THAT MEANS--
MISTER?
SORRY, HONEY, I WAS HAVING AN INNER MONOLOGUE.
WHAT?
NOTHING. WHAT'S UP?
WOULD YOU LIKE TO BUY SOME COOKIES? I HAVE THIN MINTS.
OH, YEAH?
Girl Scout Cookies
I HAD AN OVERWEIGHT FRIEND WHO ATE A BOX OF THIN MINTS EVERY DAY. NEVER GOT THIN.

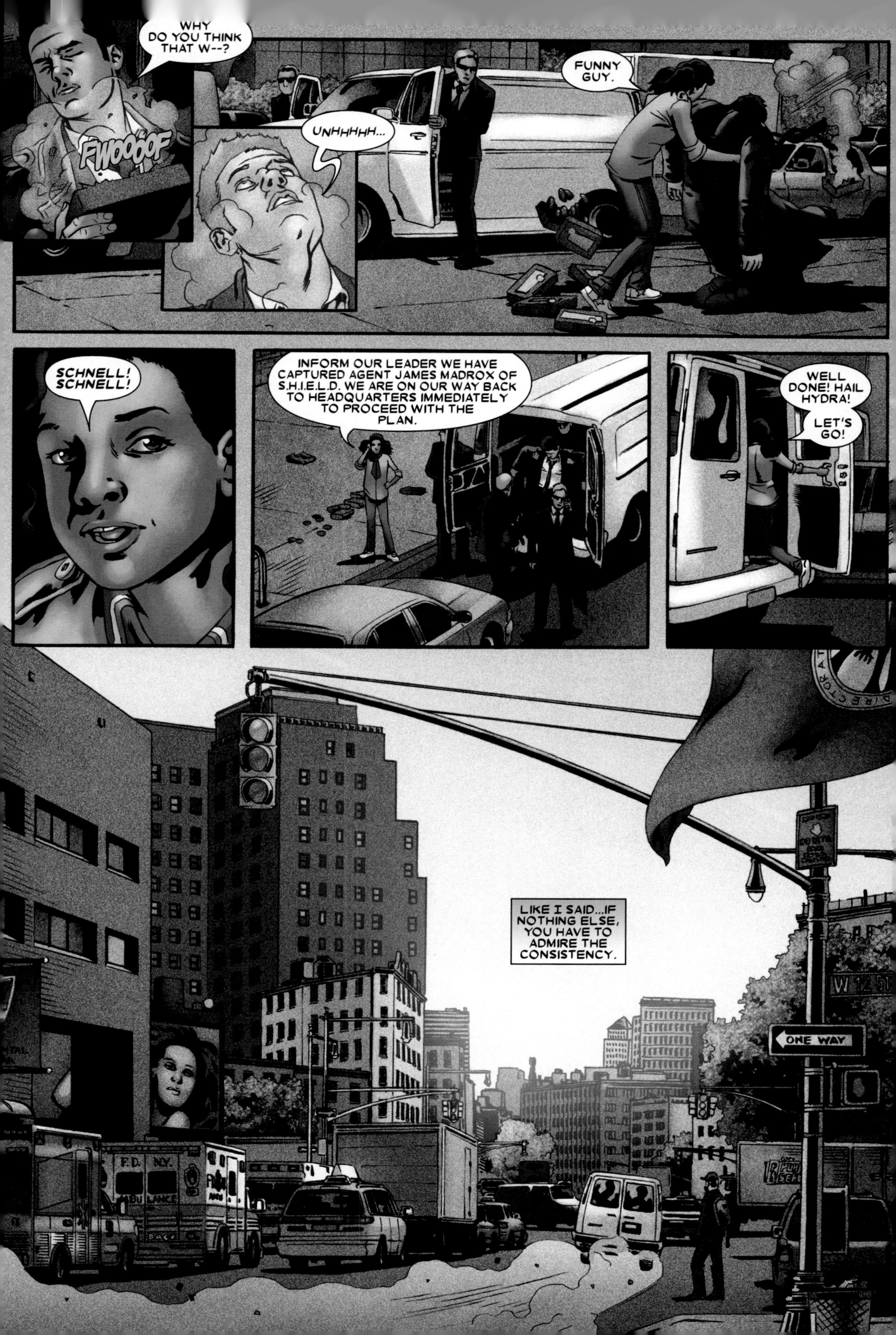
WHY DO YOU THINK THAT W--?
FWOOOOF
UNHHHHH...
FUNNY GUY.
SCHNELL! SCHNELL!
INFORM OUR LEADER WE HAVE CAPTURED AGENT JAMES MADROX OF S.H.I.E.L.D. WE ARE ON OUR WAY BACK TO HEADQUARTERS IMMEDIATELY TO PROCEED WITH THE PLAN.
WELL DONE! HAIL HYDRA!
LET'S GO!
LIKE I SAID...IF NOTHING ELSE, YOU HAVE TO ADMIRE THE CONSISTENCY.
ONE WAY
W 12 ST
F.D. N.Y.

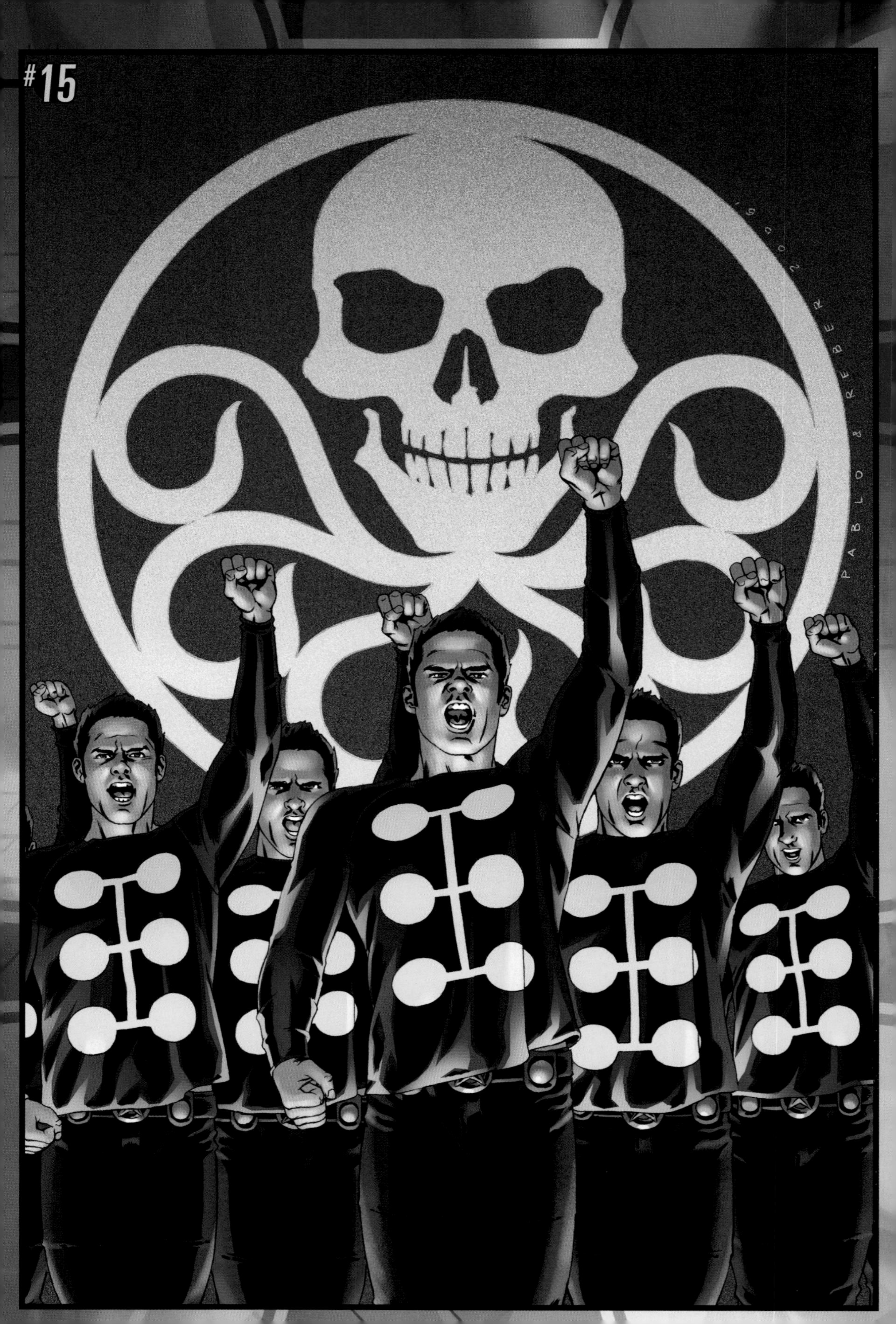
#15

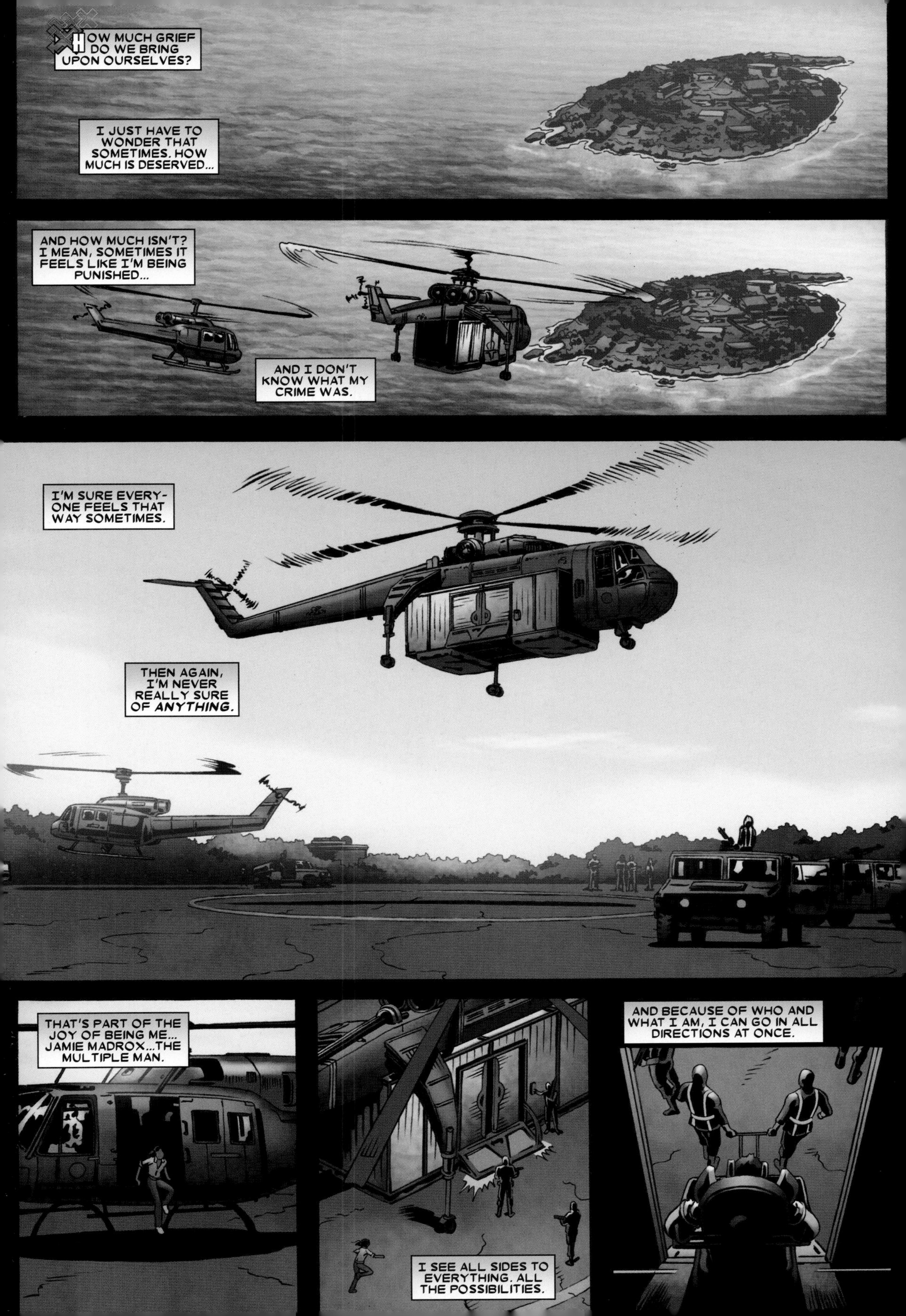
HOW MUCH GRIEF DO WE BRING UPON OURSELVES?
I JUST HAVE TO WONDER THAT SOMETIMES. HOW MUCH IS DESERVED...
AND HOW MUCH ISN'T? I MEAN, SOMETIMES IT FEELS LIKE I'M BEING PUNISHED...
AND I DON'T KNOW WHAT MY CRIME WAS.
I'M SURE EVERYONE FEELS THAT WAY SOMETIMES.
THEN AGAIN, I'M NEVER REALLY SURE OF *ANYTHING*.
THAT'S PART OF THE JOY OF BEING ME... JAMIE MADROX...THE MULTIPLE MAN.
I SEE ALL SIDES TO EVERYTHING. ALL THE POSSIBILITIES.
AND BECAUSE OF WHO AND WHAT I AM, I CAN GO IN ALL DIRECTIONS AT ONCE.

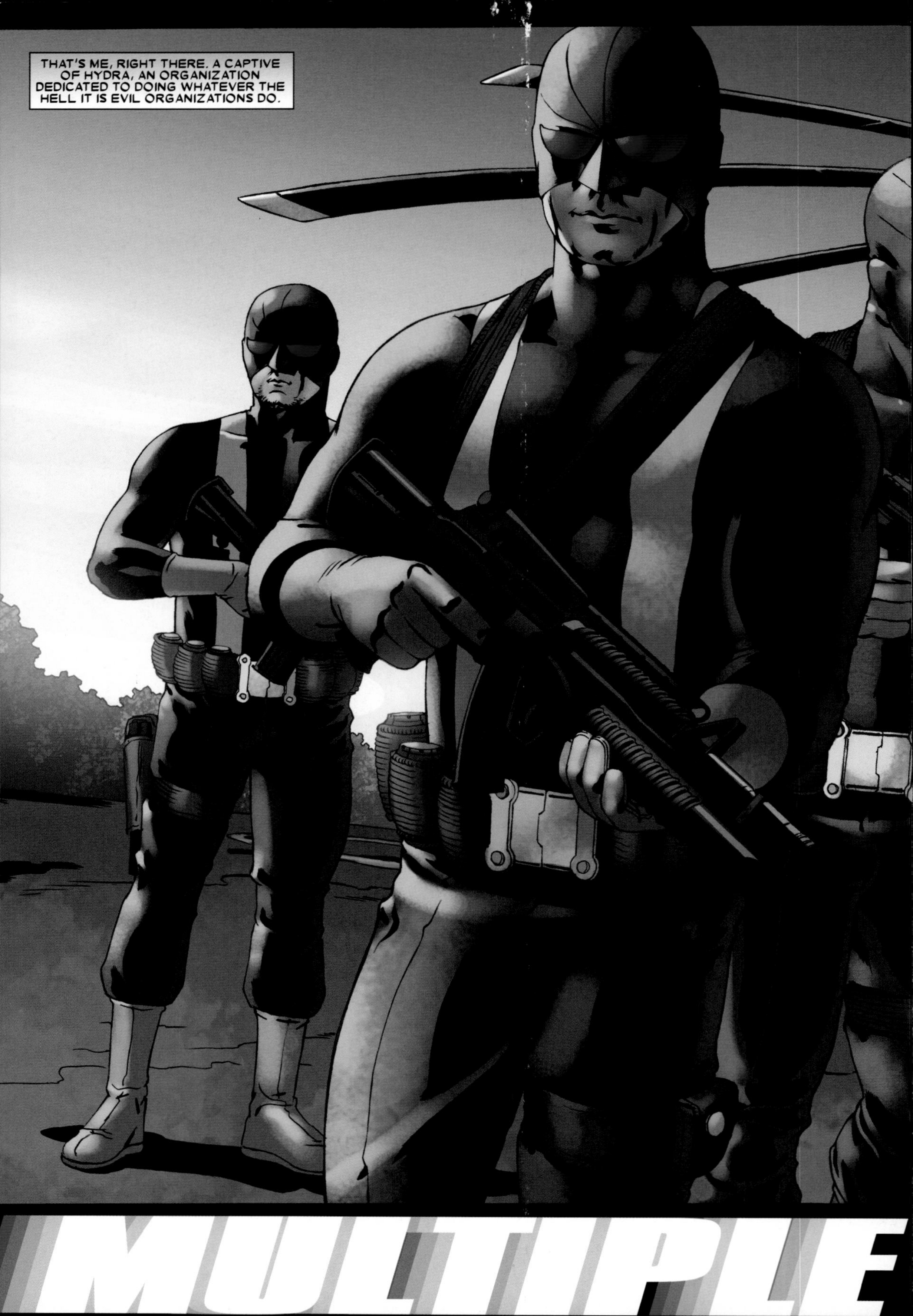
THAT'S ME, RIGHT THERE. A CAPTIVE OF HYDRA, AN ORGANIZATION DEDICATED TO DOING WHATEVER THE HELL IT IS EVIL ORGANIZATIONS DO.
MULTIPLE

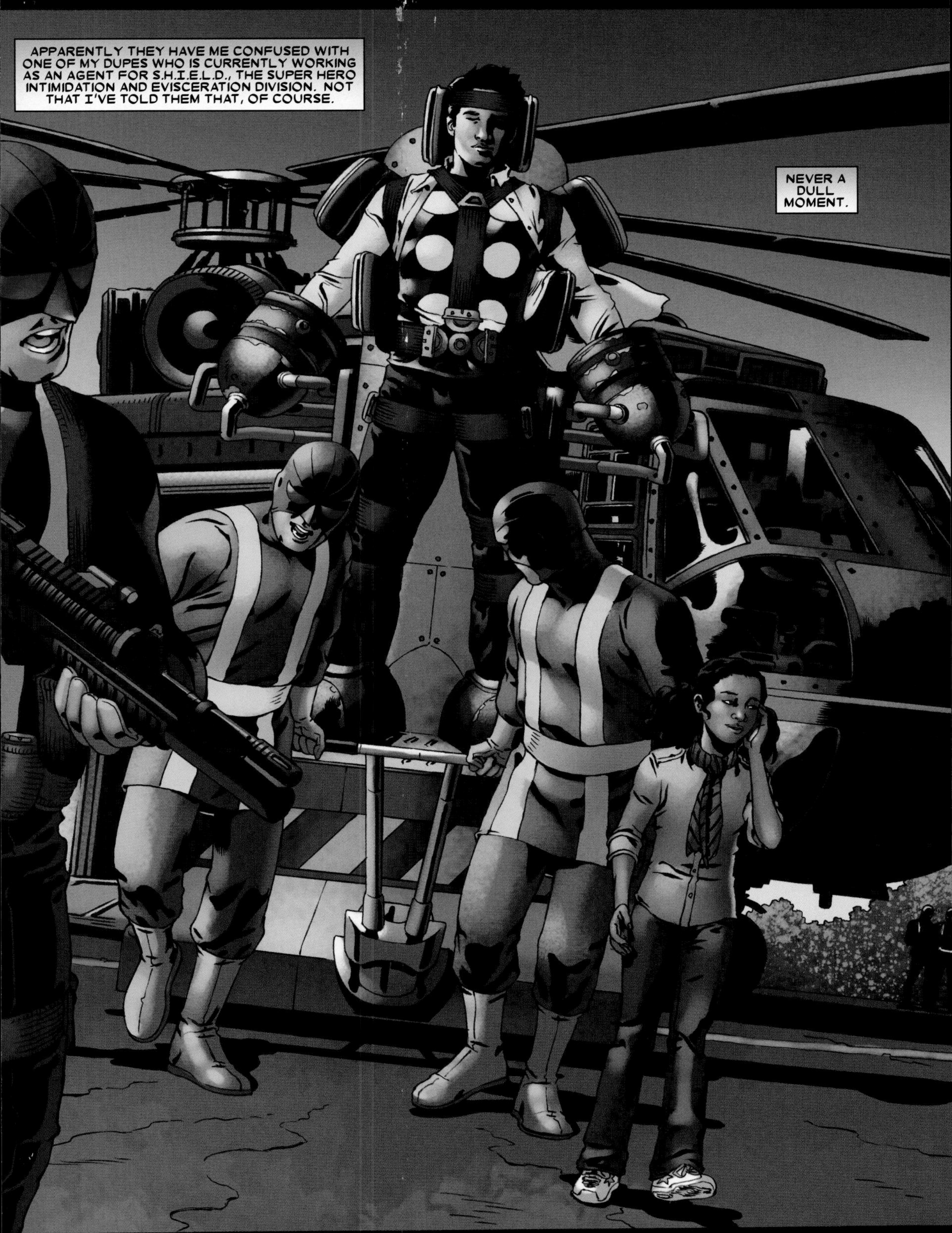

APPARENTLY THEY HAVE ME CONFUSED WITH ONE OF MY DUPES WHO IS CURRENTLY WORKING AS AN AGENT FOR S.H.I.E.L.D., THE SUPER HERO INTIMIDATION AND EVISCERATION DIVISION. NOT THAT I'VE TOLD THEM THAT, OF COURSE.
NEVER A DULL MOMENT.

ISSUES PART 2

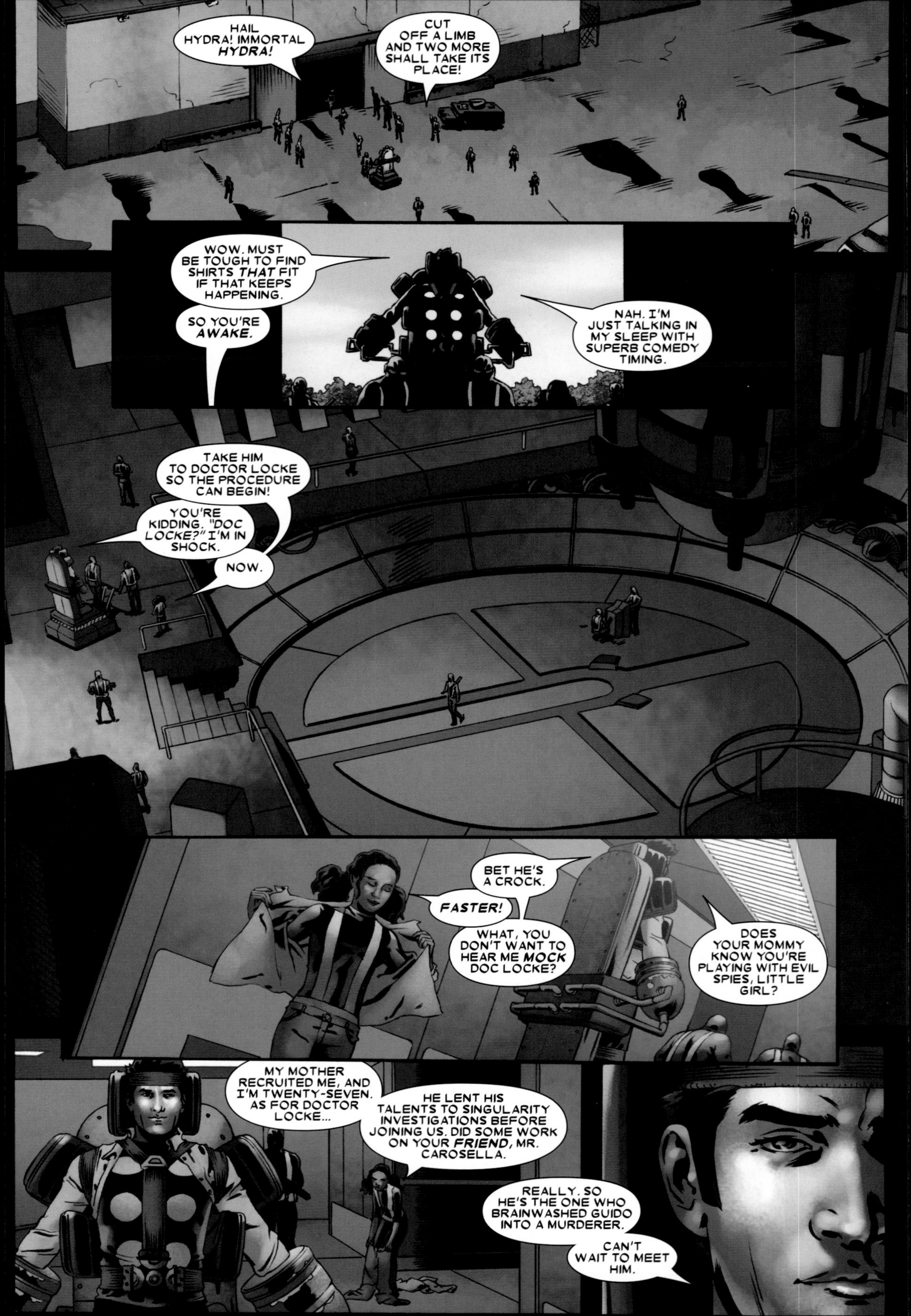
HAIL HYDRA! IMMORTAL *HYDRA!*
CUT OFF A LIMB AND TWO MORE SHALL TAKE ITS PLACE!
WOW. MUST BE TOUGH TO FIND SHIRTS *THAT* FIT IF THAT KEEPS HAPPENING.
SO YOU'RE *AWAKE.*
NAH. I'M JUST TALKING IN MY SLEEP WITH SUPERB COMEDY TIMING.
TAKE HIM TO DOCTOR LOCKE SO THE PROCEDURE CAN BEGIN!
YOU'RE KIDDING. *"DOC LOCKE?"* I'M IN SHOCK.
NOW.
BET HE'S A CROCK.
FASTER!
WHAT, YOU DON'T WANT TO HEAR ME *MOCK* DOC LOCKE?
DOES YOUR MOMMY KNOW YOU'RE PLAYING WITH EVIL SPIES, LITTLE GIRL?
MY MOTHER RECRUITED ME, AND I'M TWENTY-SEVEN. AS FOR DOCTOR LOCKE...
HE LENT HIS TALENTS TO SINGULARITY INVESTIGATIONS BEFORE JOINING US. DID SOME WORK ON YOUR *FRIEND*, MR. CAROSELLA.
REALLY. SO HE'S THE ONE WHO BRAINWASHED GUIDO INTO A MURDERER.
CAN'T WAIT TO MEET HIM.

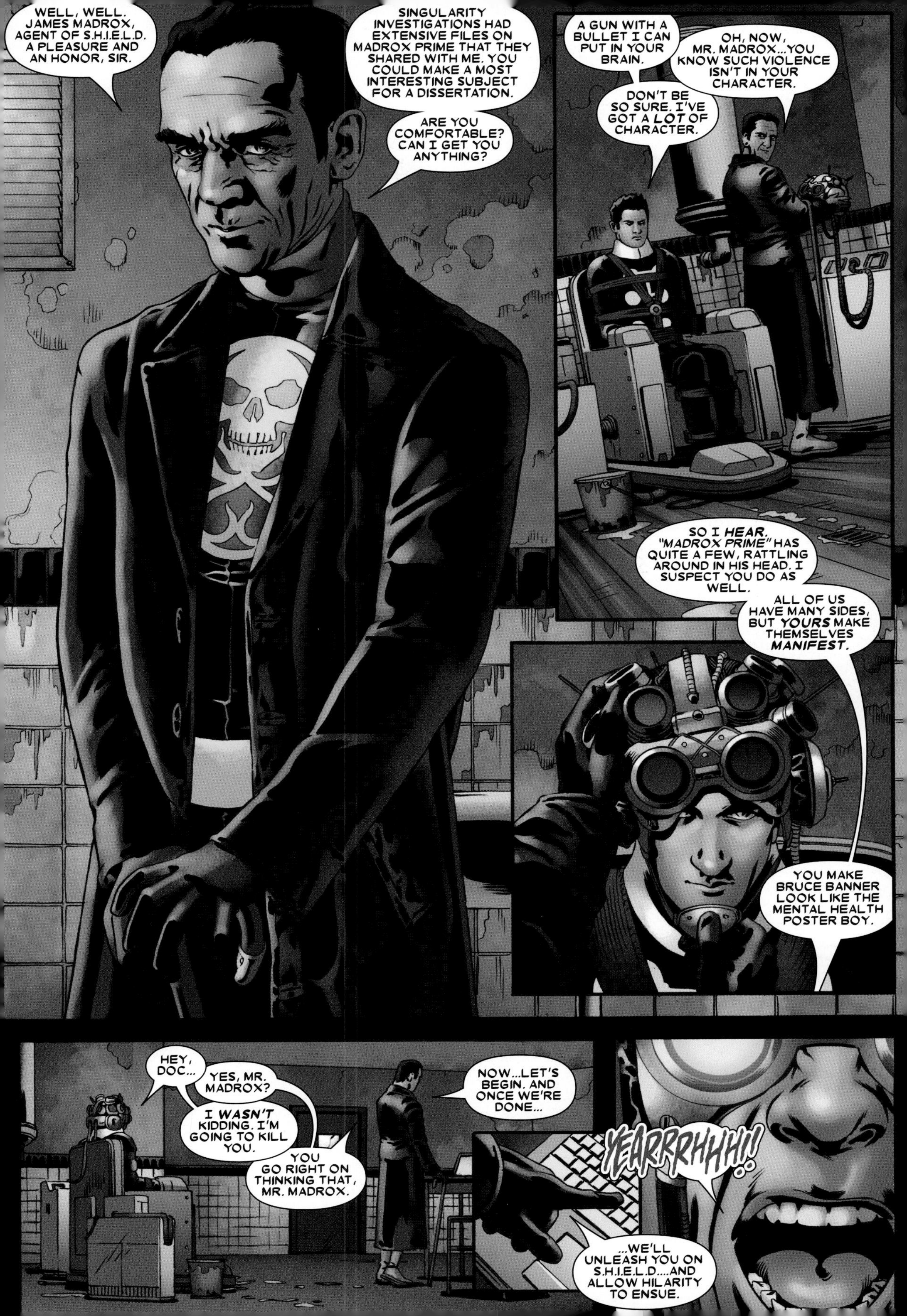
WELL, WELL. JAMES MADROX, AGENT OF S.H.I.E.L.D. A PLEASURE AND AN HONOR, SIR.
SINGULARITY INVESTIGATIONS HAD EXTENSIVE FILES ON MADROX PRIME THAT THEY SHARED WITH ME. YOU COULD MAKE A MOST INTERESTING SUBJECT FOR A DISSERTATION.
ARE YOU COMFORTABLE? CAN I GET YOU ANYTHING?
A GUN WITH A BULLET I CAN PUT IN YOUR BRAIN.
OH, NOW, MR. MADROX...YOU KNOW SUCH VIOLENCE ISN'T IN YOUR CHARACTER.
DON'T BE SO SURE. I'VE GOT A *LOT* OF CHARACTER.
SO I *HEAR*. "*MADROX PRIME*" HAS QUITE A FEW, RATTLING AROUND IN HIS HEAD. I SUSPECT YOU DO AS WELL.
ALL OF US HAVE MANY SIDES, BUT *YOURS* MAKE THEMSELVES *MANIFEST*.
YOU MAKE BRUCE BANNER LOOK LIKE THE MENTAL HEALTH POSTER BOY.
HEY, DOC...
YES, MR. MADROX?
I *WASN'T* KIDDING. I'M GOING TO KILL YOU.
YOU GO RIGHT ON THINKING THAT, MR. MADROX.
NOW...LET'S BEGIN. AND ONCE WE'RE DONE...
YEARRRHHH!!
...WE'LL UNLEASH YOU ON S.H.I.E.L.D....AND ALLOW HILARITY TO ENSUE.

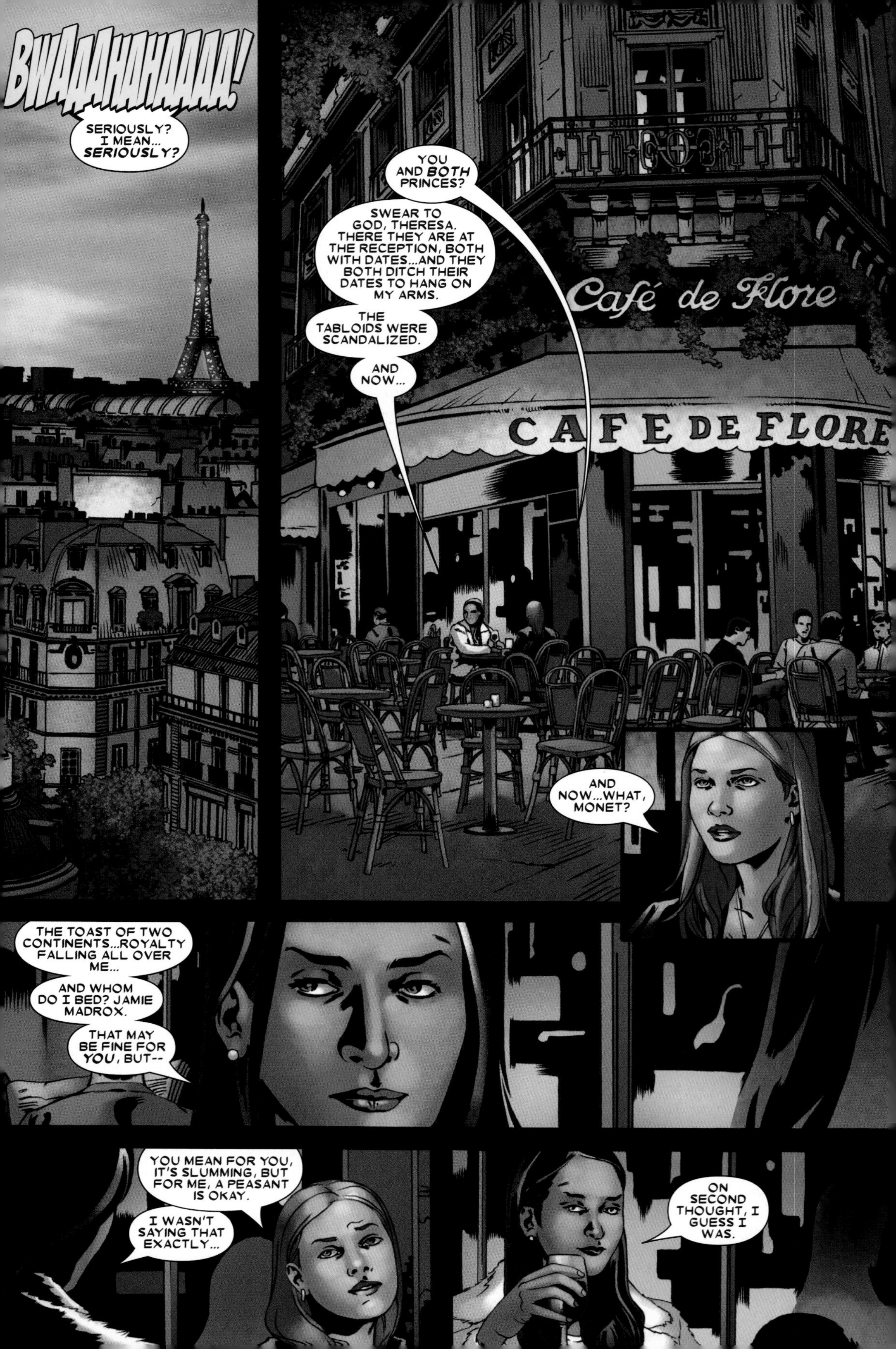
BWAAAHAHAAAA!
SERIOUSLY? I MEAN... SERIOUSLY?
YOU AND BOTH PRINCES?
SWEAR TO GOD, THERESA. THERE THEY ARE AT THE RECEPTION, BOTH WITH DATES...AND THEY BOTH DITCH THEIR DATES TO HANG ON MY ARMS.
THE TABLOIDS WERE SCANDALIZED.
AND NOW...
Café de Flore
CAFE DE FLORE
AND NOW...WHAT, MONET?
THE TOAST OF TWO CONTINENTS...ROYALTY FALLING ALL OVER ME...
AND WHOM DO I BED? JAMIE MADROX.
THAT MAY BE FINE FOR YOU, BUT--
YOU MEAN FOR YOU, IT'S SLUMMING, BUT FOR ME, A PEASANT IS OKAY.
I WASN'T SAYING THAT EXACTLY...
ON SECOND THOUGHT, I GUESS I WAS.

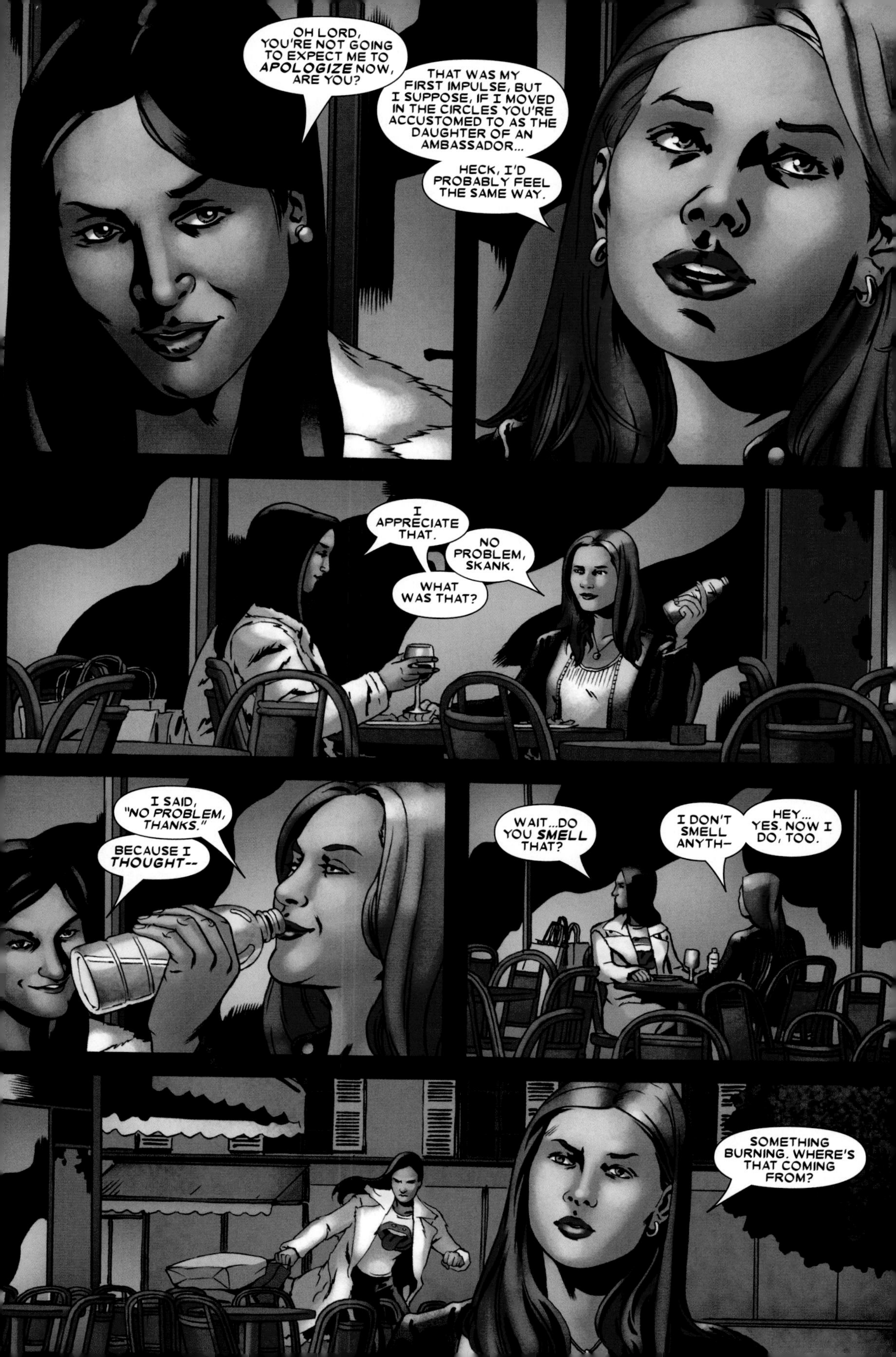
OH LORD, YOU'RE NOT GOING TO EXPECT ME TO APOLOGIZE NOW, ARE YOU?
THAT WAS MY FIRST IMPULSE, BUT I SUPPOSE, IF I MOVED IN THE CIRCLES YOU'RE ACCUSTOMED TO AS THE DAUGHTER OF AN AMBASSADOR...
HECK, I'D PROBABLY FEEL THE SAME WAY.
I APPRECIATE THAT.
NO PROBLEM, SKANK.
WHAT WAS THAT?
I SAID, "NO PROBLEM, THANKS."
BECAUSE I THOUGHT--
WAIT...DO YOU SMELL THAT?
I DON'T SMELL ANYTH—
HEY... YES. NOW I DO, TOO.
SOMETHING BURNING. WHERE'S THAT COMING FROM?

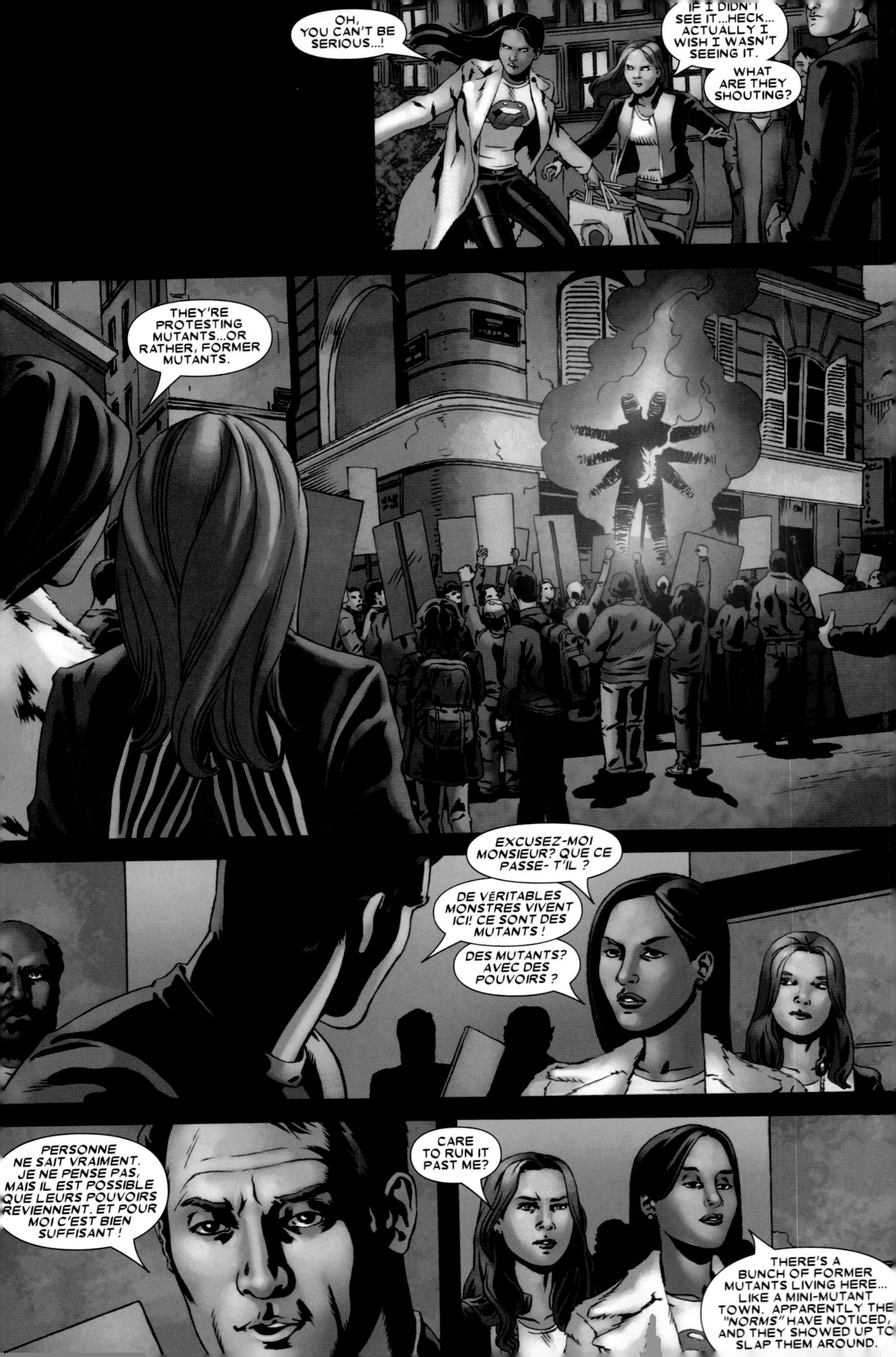
OH, YOU CAN'T BE SERIOUS...!
IF I DIDN'T SEE IT...HECK... ACTUALLY I WISH I WASN'T SEEING IT.
WHAT ARE THEY SHOUTING?
THEY'RE PROTESTING MUTANTS...OR RATHER, FORMER MUTANTS.
EXCUSEZ-MOI MONSIEUR? QUE CE PASSE- T'IL ?
DE VÉRITABLES MONSTRES VIVENT ICI! CE SONT DES MUTANTS !
DES MUTANTS? AVEC DES POUVOIRS ?
PERSONNE NE SAIT VRAIMENT. JE NE PENSE PAS, MAIS IL EST POSSIBLE QUE LEURS POUVOIRS REVIENNENT. ET POUR MOI C'EST BIEN SUFFISANT !
CARE TO RUN IT PAST ME?
THERE'S A BUNCH OF FORMER MUTANTS LIVING HERE... LIKE A MINI-MUTANT TOWN. APPARENTLY THE "NORMS" HAVE NOTICED, AND THEY SHOWED UP TO SLAP THEM AROUND.

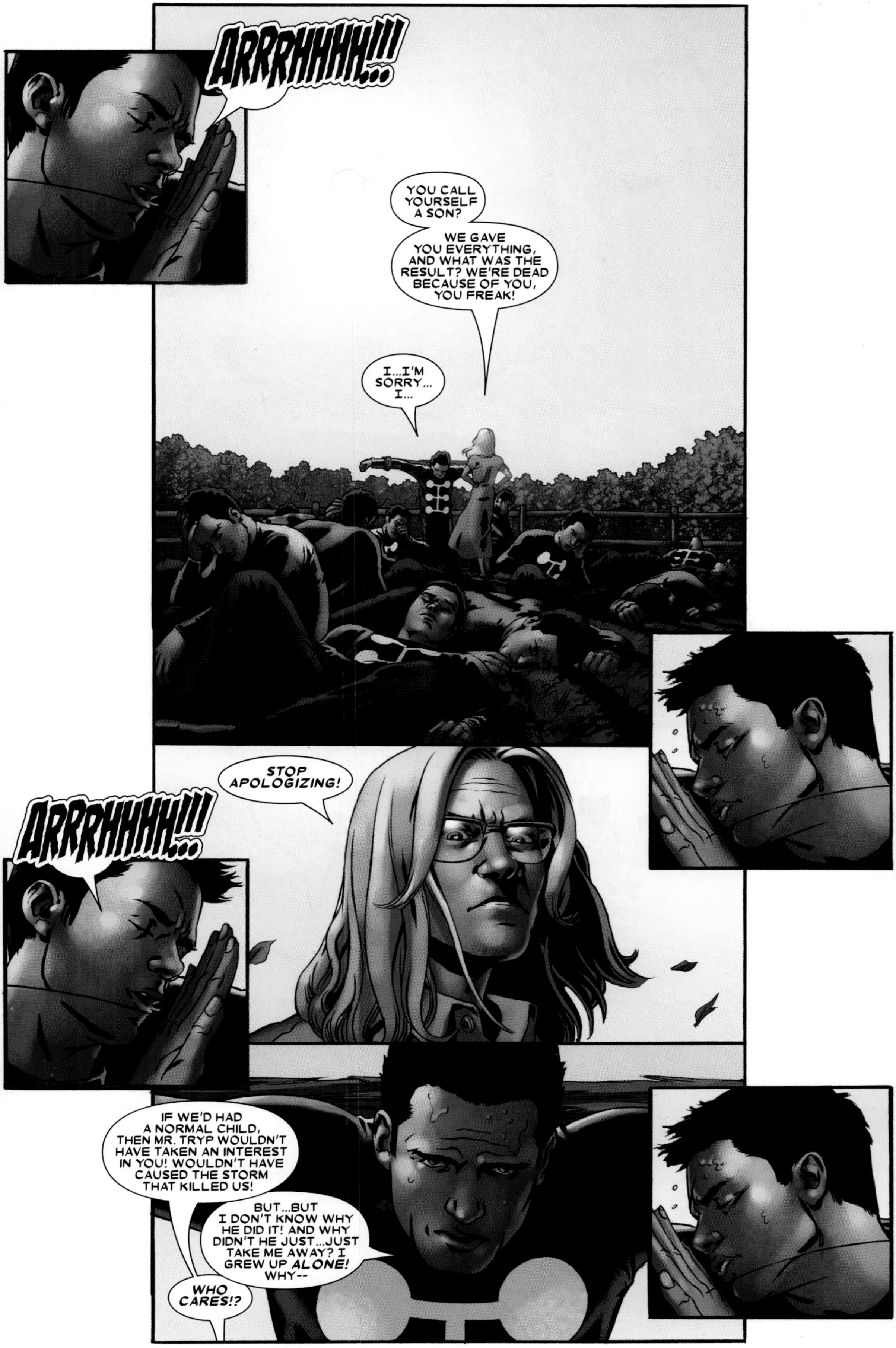
ARRRHHHH!!!...
YOU CALL YOURSELF A SON?
WE GAVE YOU EVERYTHING, AND WHAT WAS THE RESULT? WE'RE DEAD BECAUSE OF YOU, YOU FREAK!
I...I'M SORRY... I...
STOP APOLOGIZING!
ARRRHHHH!!!...
IF WE'D HAD A NORMAL CHILD, THEN MR. TRYP WOULDN'T HAVE TAKEN AN INTEREST IN YOU! WOULDN'T HAVE CAUSED THE STORM THAT KILLED US!
BUT...BUT I DON'T KNOW WHY HE DID IT! AND WHY DIDN'T HE JUST...JUST TAKE ME AWAY? I GREW UP ALONE! WHY--
WHO CARES!?

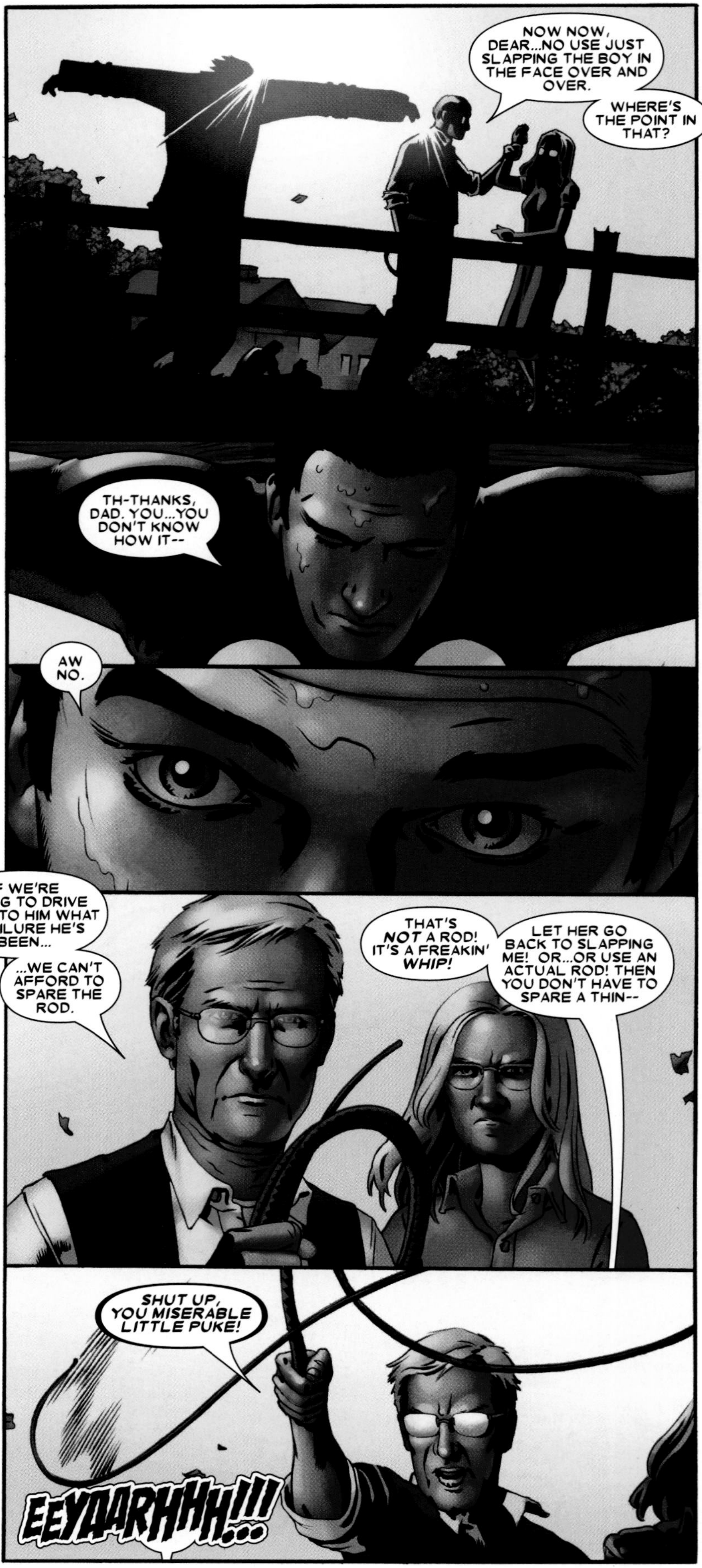
NOW NOW, DEAR...NO USE JUST SLAPPING THE BOY IN THE FACE OVER AND OVER.
WHERE'S THE POINT IN THAT?
TH-THANKS, DAD. YOU...YOU DON'T KNOW HOW IT--
AW NO.
IF WE'RE GOING TO DRIVE HOME TO HIM WHAT A FAILURE HE'S BEEN...
...WE CAN'T AFFORD TO SPARE THE ROD.
THAT'S NOT A ROD! IT'S A FREAKIN' WHIP!
LET HER GO BACK TO SLAPPING ME! OR...OR USE AN ACTUAL ROD! THEN YOU DON'T HAVE TO SPARE A THIN--
SHUT UP, YOU MISERABLE LITTLE PUKE!
EEYAARHHH!!!...

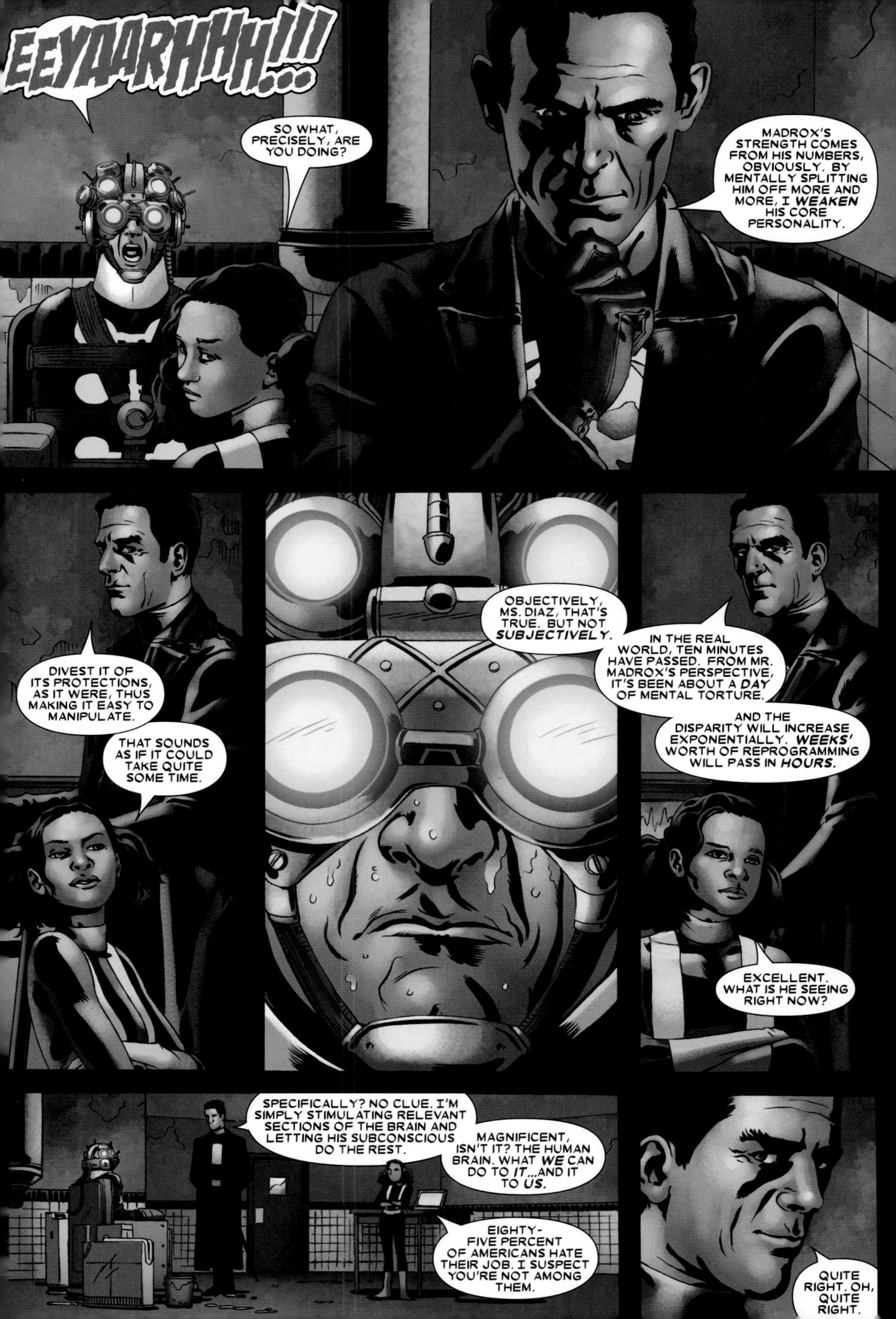
EEYAARHHH!!!...
SO WHAT, PRECISELY, ARE YOU DOING?
MADROX'S STRENGTH COMES FROM HIS NUMBERS, OBVIOUSLY. BY MENTALLY SPLITTING HIM OFF MORE AND MORE, I WEAKEN HIS CORE PERSONALITY.
DIVEST IT OF ITS PROTECTIONS, AS IT WERE, THUS MAKING IT EASY TO MANIPULATE.
THAT SOUNDS AS IF IT COULD TAKE QUITE SOME TIME.
OBJECTIVELY, MS. DIAZ, THAT'S TRUE. BUT NOT SUBJECTIVELY.
IN THE REAL WORLD, TEN MINUTES HAVE PASSED. FROM MR. MADROX'S PERSPECTIVE, IT'S BEEN ABOUT A DAY OF MENTAL TORTURE.
AND THE DISPARITY WILL INCREASE EXPONENTIALLY. WEEKS' WORTH OF REPROGRAMMING WILL PASS IN HOURS.
EXCELLENT. WHAT IS HE SEEING RIGHT NOW?
SPECIFICALLY? NO CLUE. I'M SIMPLY STIMULATING RELEVANT SECTIONS OF THE BRAIN AND LETTING HIS SUBCONSCIOUS DO THE REST.
MAGNIFICENT, ISN'T IT? THE HUMAN BRAIN. WHAT WE CAN DO TO IT...AND IT TO US.
EIGHTY-FIVE PERCENT OF AMERICANS HATE THEIR JOB. I SUSPECT YOU'RE NOT AMONG THEM.
QUITE RIGHT. OH, QUITE RIGHT.

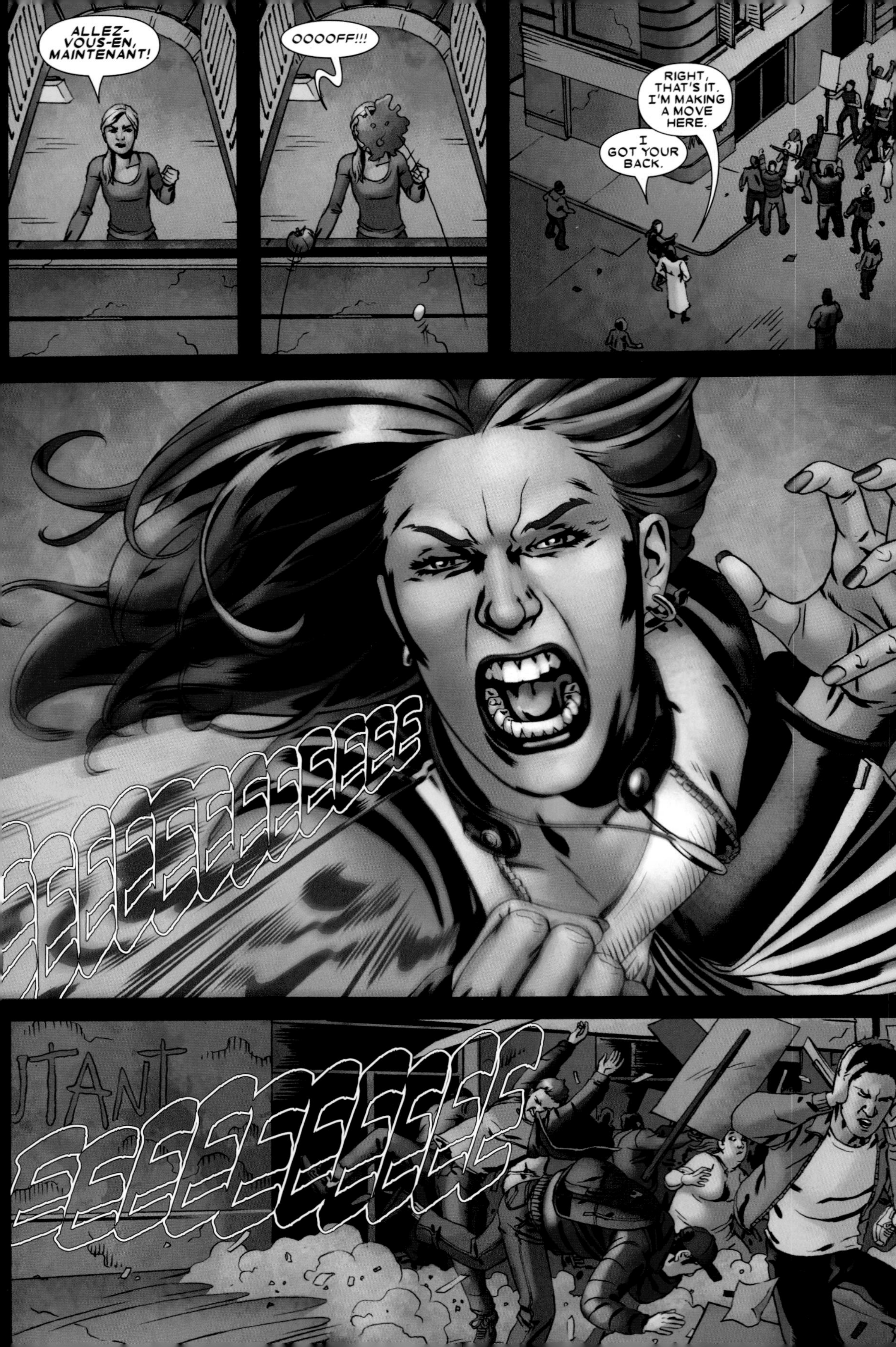
ALLEZ-VOUS-EN, MAINTENANT!
OOOOFF!!!
RIGHT, THAT'S IT. I'M MAKING A MOVE HERE.
I GOT YOUR BACK.

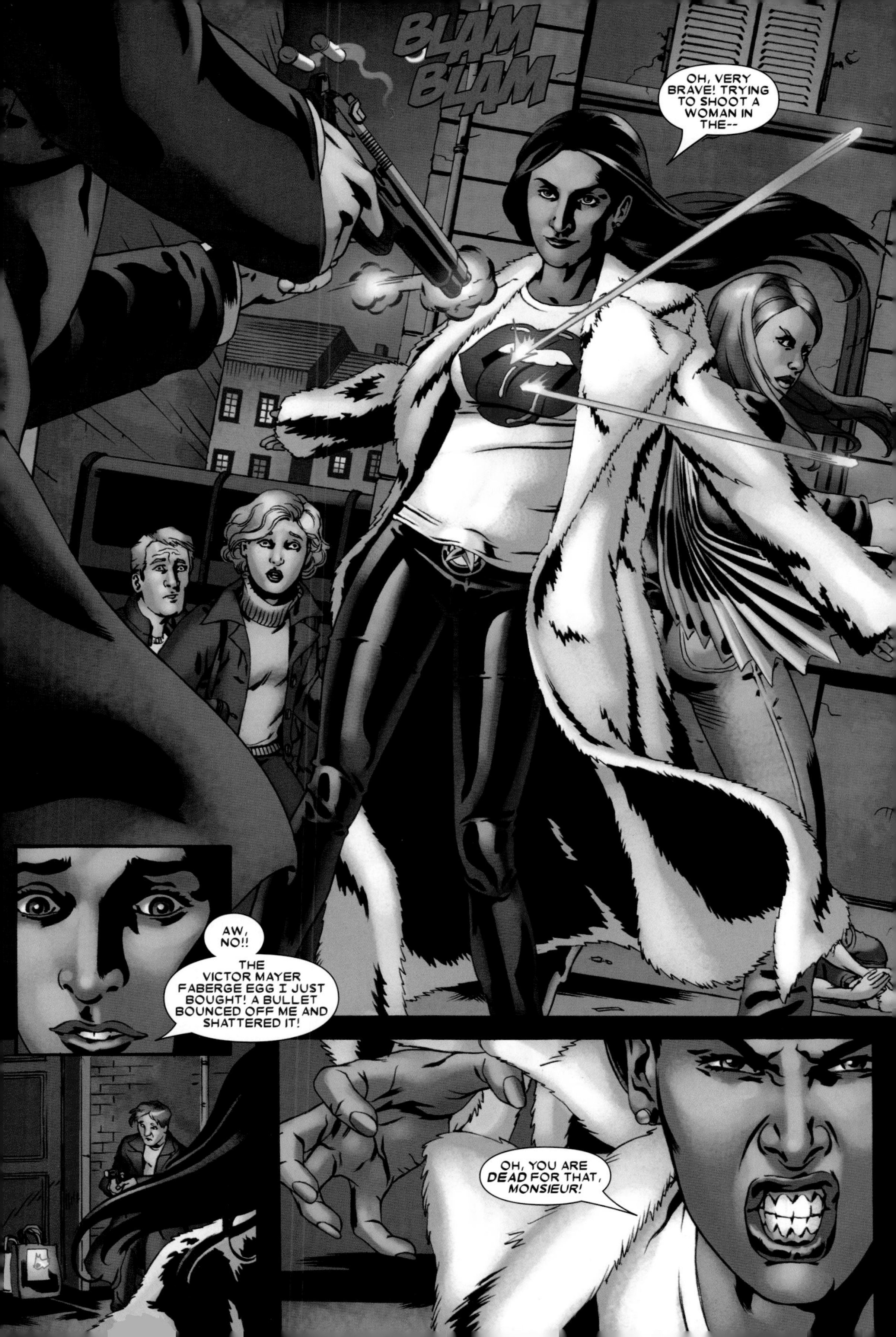
BLAM
BLAM
OH, VERY BRAVE! TRYING TO SHOOT A WOMAN IN THE--
AW, NO!!
THE VICTOR MAYER FABERGE EGG I JUST BOUGHT! A BULLET BOUNCED OFF ME AND SHATTERED IT!
OH, YOU ARE *DEAD* FOR THAT, *MONSIEUR!*

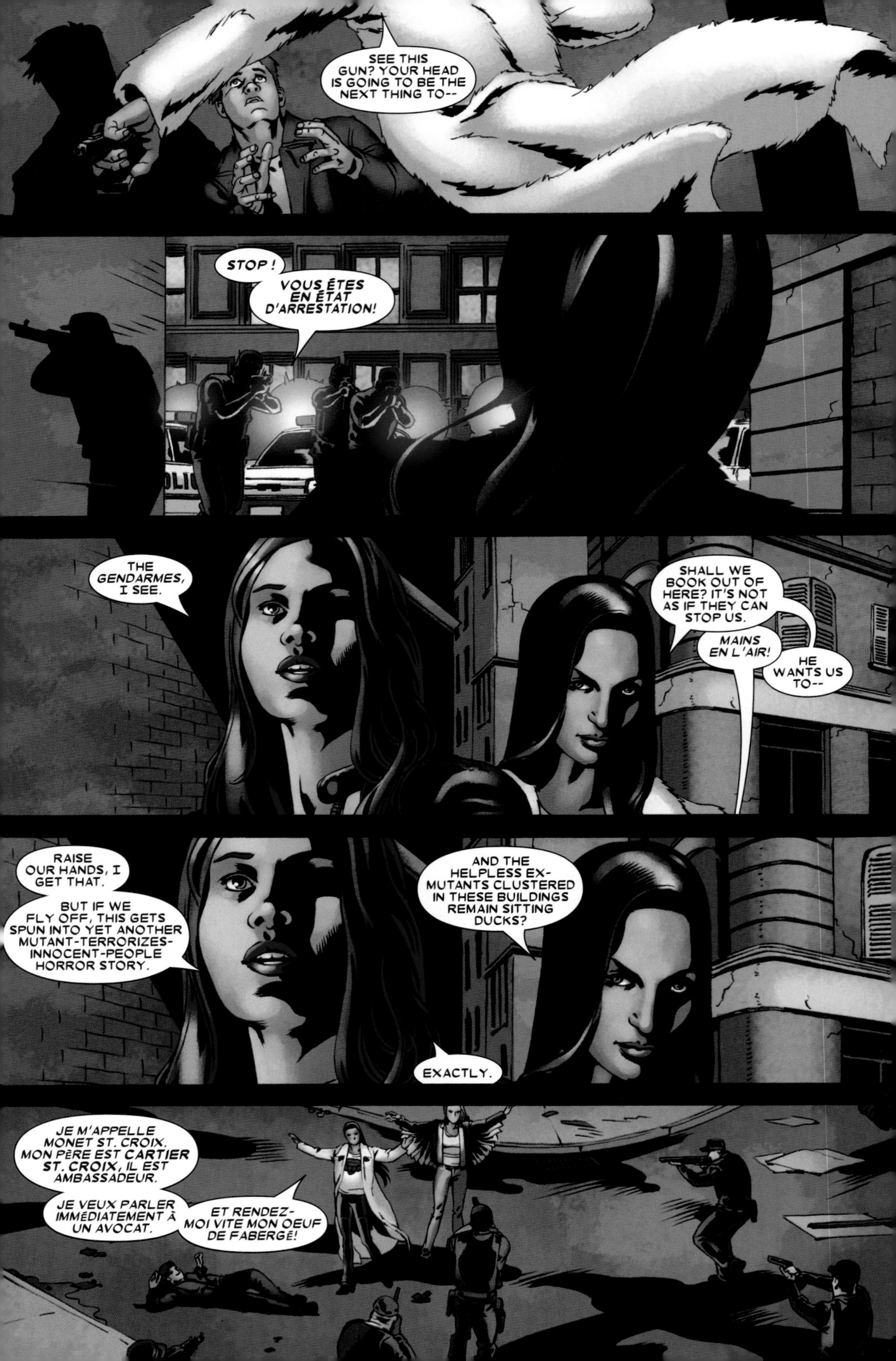
SEE THIS GUN? YOUR HEAD IS GOING TO BE THE NEXT THING TO--
STOP!
VOUS ÊTES EN ÉTAT D'ARRESTATION!
THE GENDARMES, I SEE.
SHALL WE BOOK OUT OF HERE? IT'S NOT AS IF THEY CAN STOP US.
MAINS EN L'AIR!
HE WANTS US TO--
RAISE OUR HANDS, I GET THAT.
BUT IF WE FLY OFF, THIS GETS SPUN INTO YET ANOTHER MUTANT-TERRORIZES-INNOCENT-PEOPLE HORROR STORY.
AND THE HELPLESS EX-MUTANTS CLUSTERED IN THESE BUILDINGS REMAIN SITTING DUCKS?
EXACTLY.
JE M'APPELLE MONET ST. CROIX. MON PÈRE EST CARTIER ST. CROIX, IL EST AMBASSADEUR.
JE VEUX PARLER IMMÉDIATEMENT À UN AVOCAT.
ET RENDEZ-MOI VITE MON OEUF DE FABERGÉ!
POLICE

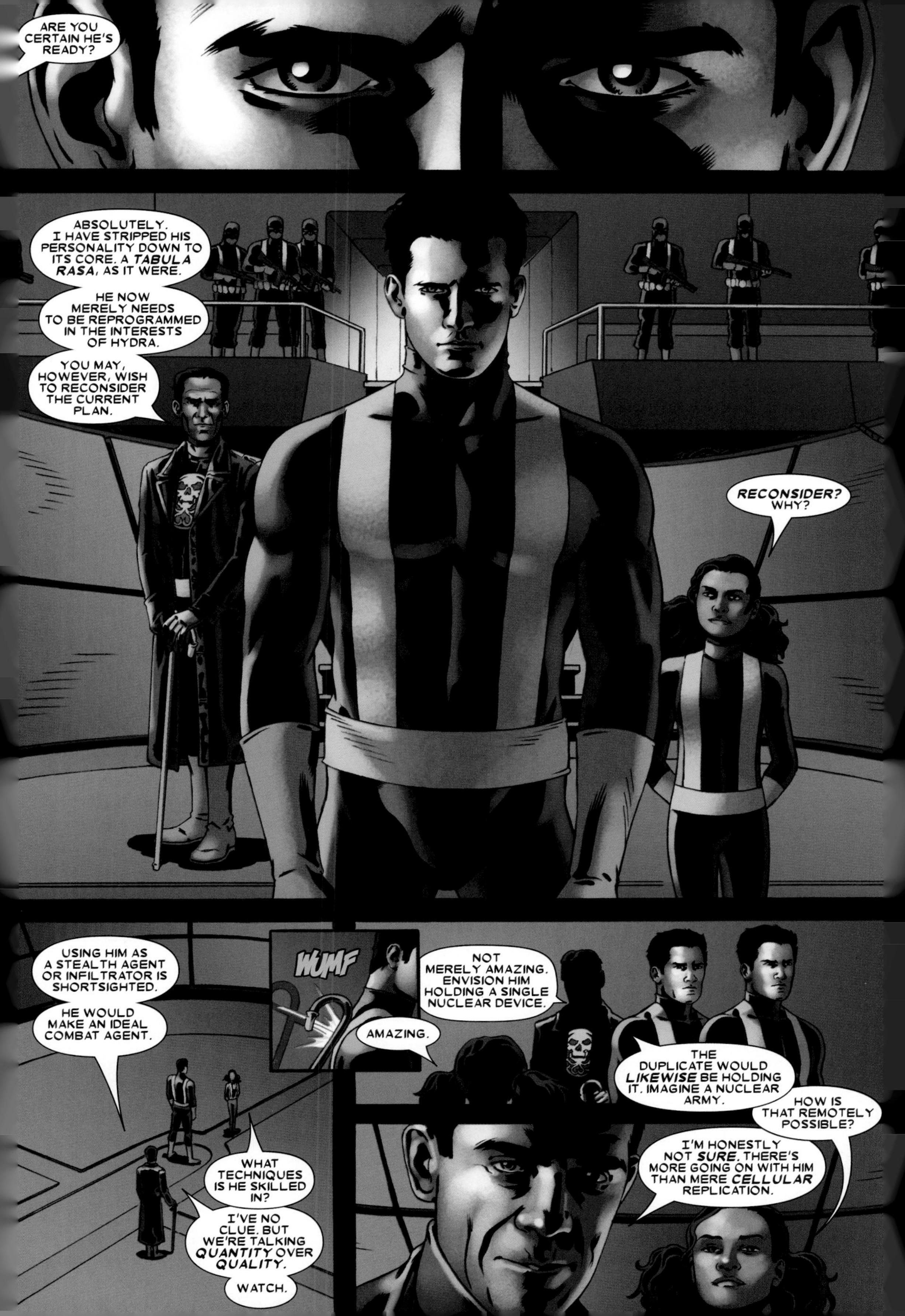
ARE YOU CERTAIN HE'S READY?
ABSOLUTELY. I HAVE STRIPPED HIS PERSONALITY DOWN TO ITS CORE. A *TABULA RASA*, AS IT WERE.
HE NOW MERELY NEEDS TO BE REPROGRAMMED IN THE INTERESTS OF HYDRA.
YOU MAY, HOWEVER, WISH TO RECONSIDER THE CURRENT PLAN.
RECONSIDER? WHY?
USING HIM AS A STEALTH AGENT OR INFILTRATOR IS SHORTSIGHTED.
HE WOULD MAKE AN IDEAL COMBAT AGENT.
WHAT TECHNIQUES IS HE SKILLED IN?
I'VE NO CLUE. BUT WE'RE TALKING *QUANTITY* OVER *QUALITY*.
WATCH.
WUMF
AMAZING.
NOT MERELY AMAZING. ENVISION HIM HOLDING A SINGLE NUCLEAR DEVICE.
THE DUPLICATE WOULD *LIKEWISE* BE HOLDING IT. IMAGINE A NUCLEAR ARMY.
HOW IS THAT REMOTELY POSSIBLE?
I'M HONESTLY NOT *SURE*. THERE'S MORE GOING ON WITH HIM THAN MERE *CELLULAR* REPLICATION.

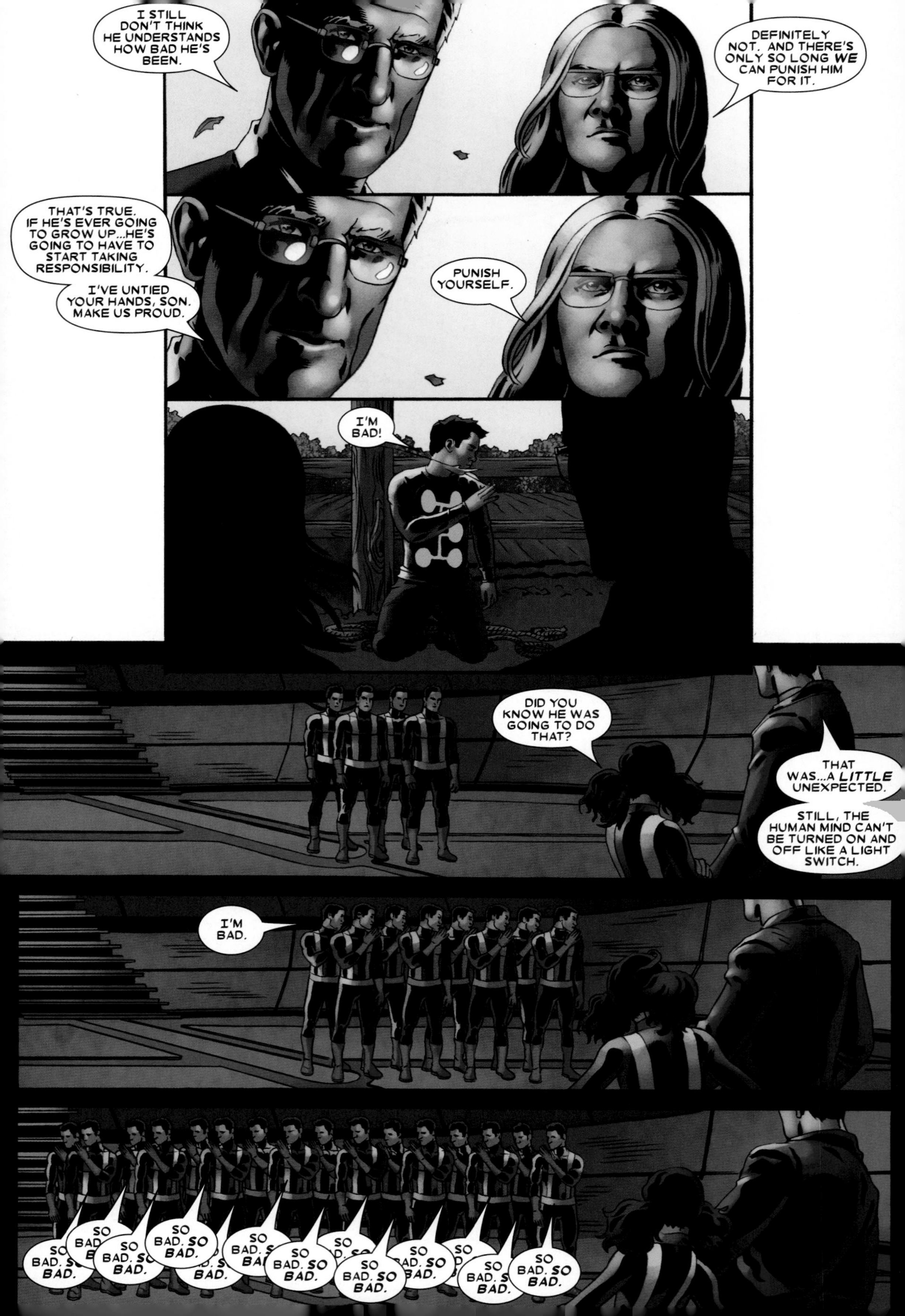
I STILL DON'T THINK HE UNDERSTANDS HOW BAD HE'S BEEN.
DEFINITELY NOT. AND THERE'S ONLY SO LONG *WE* CAN PUNISH HIM FOR IT.
THAT'S TRUE. IF HE'S EVER GOING TO GROW UP...HE'S GOING TO HAVE TO START TAKING RESPONSIBILITY.
I'VE UNTIED YOUR HANDS, SON. MAKE US PROUD.
PUNISH YOURSELF.
I'M BAD!
DID YOU KNOW HE WAS GOING TO DO THAT?
THAT WAS...A *LITTLE* UNEXPECTED.
STILL, THE HUMAN MIND CAN'T BE TURNED ON AND OFF LIKE A LIGHT SWITCH.
I'M BAD.
SO BAD. *SO BAD.*
SO BAD. *SO BAD.*
SO BAD. *SO BAD.*
SO BAD. *SO BAD.*
SO BAD. *SO BAD.*
SO BAD. *SO BAD.*
SO BAD. *SO BAD.*

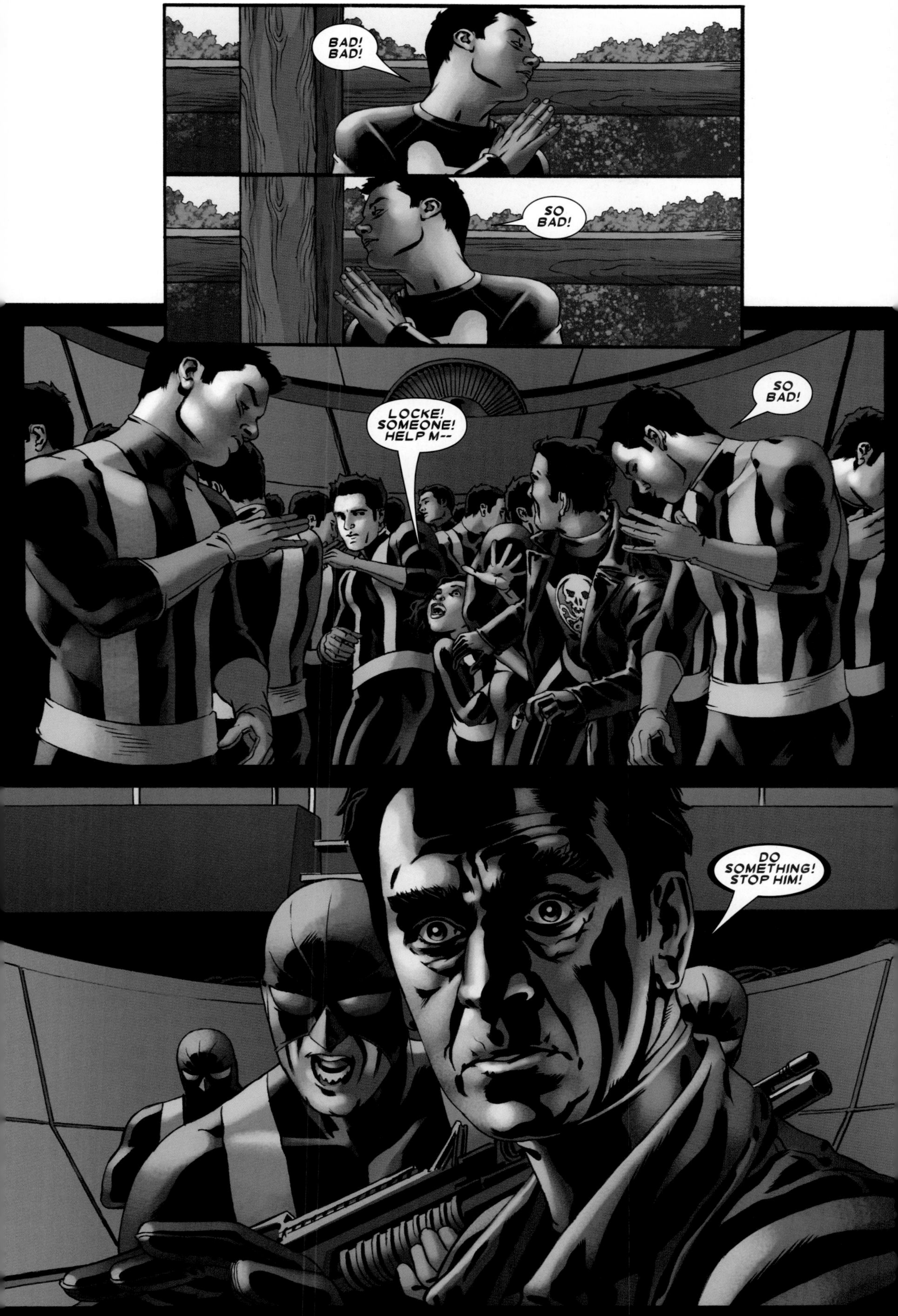
BAD! BAD!
SO BAD!
LOCKE! SOMEONE! HELP M--
SO BAD!
DO SOMETHING! STOP HIM!

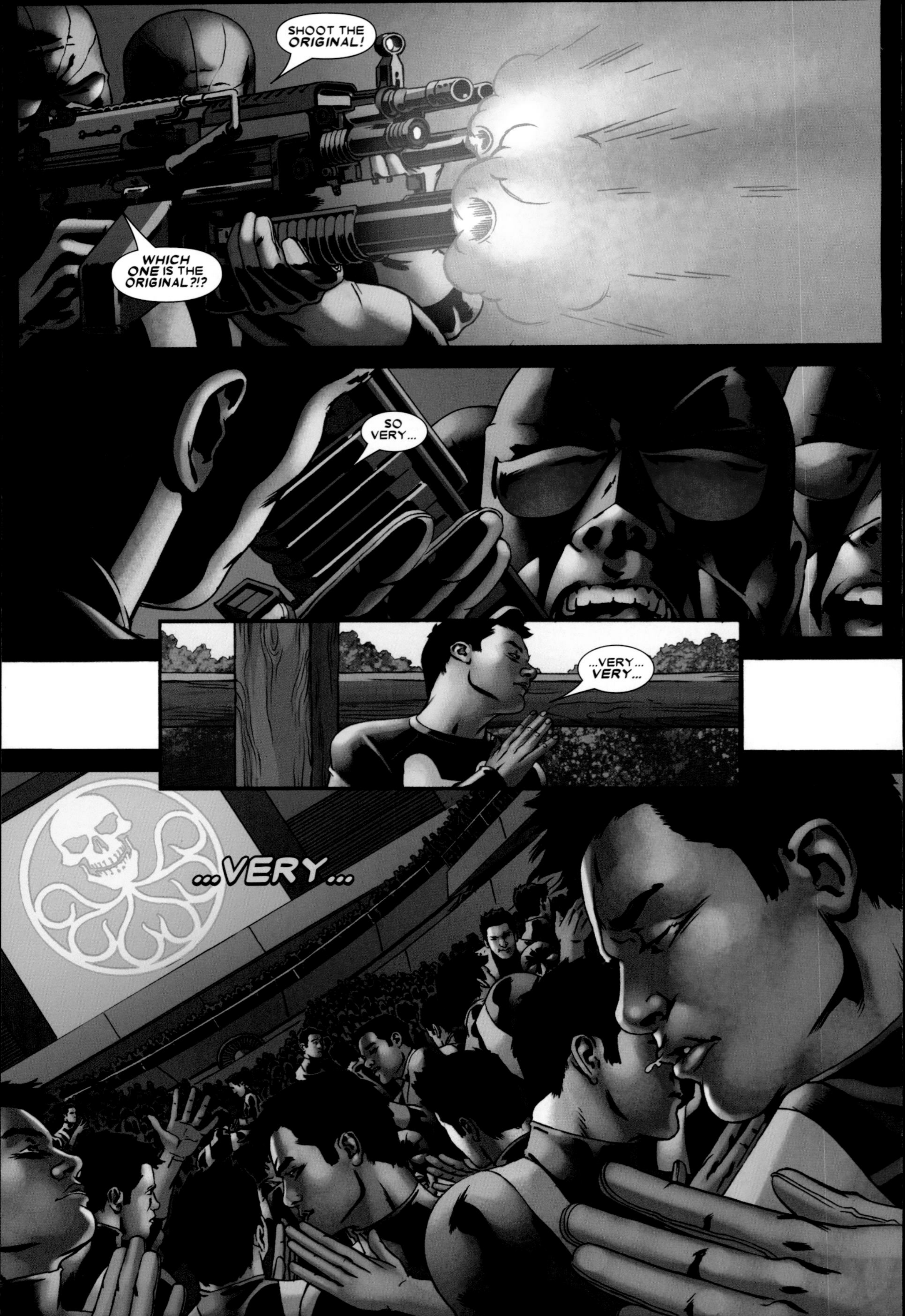

SHOOT THE ORIGINAL!
WHICH ONE IS THE ORIGINAL?!?
SO VERY...
...VERY... VERY...
...VERY...

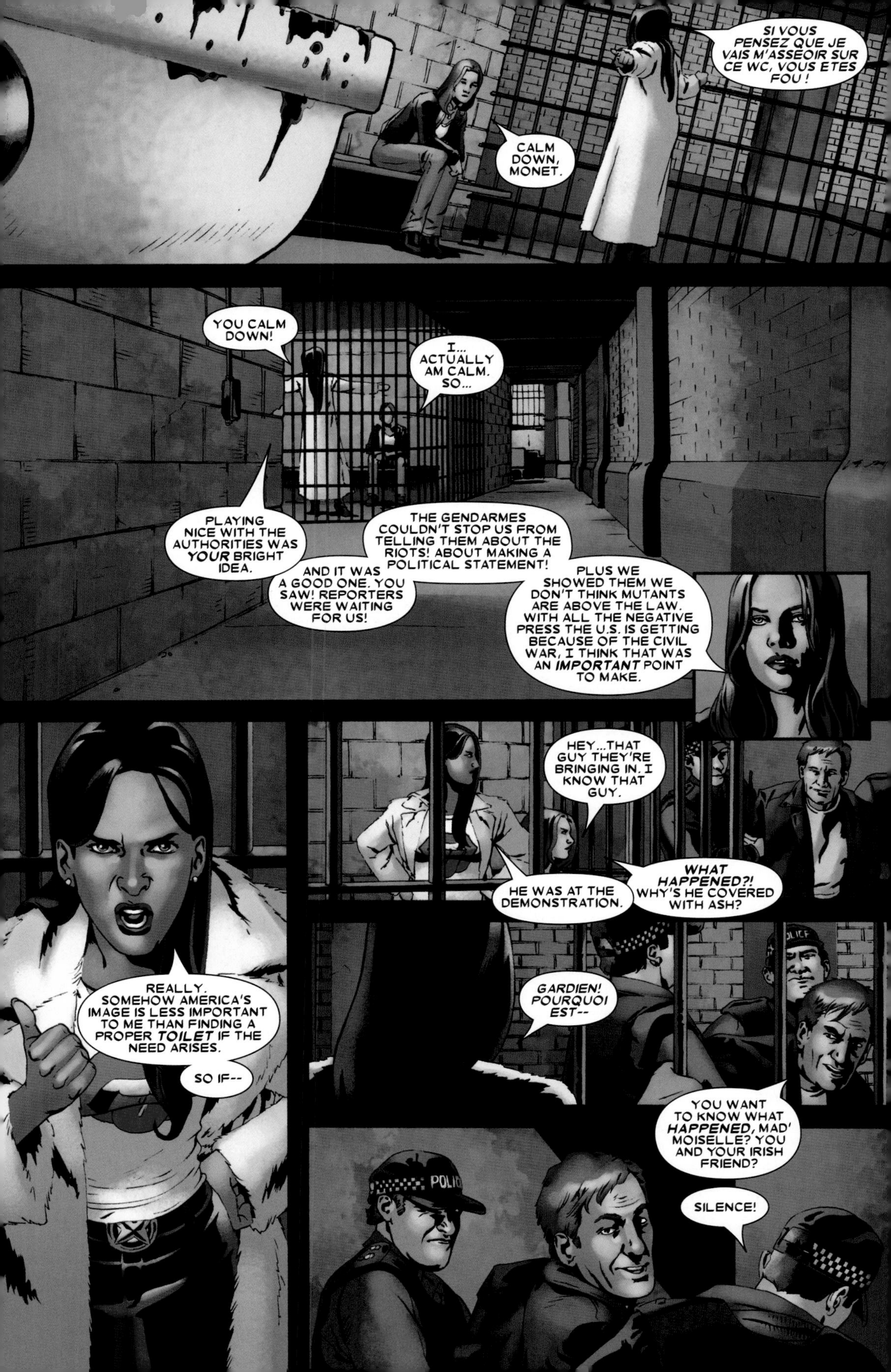
SI VOUS PENSEZ QUE JE VAIS M'ASSEOIR SUR CE WC, VOUS ETES FOU !
CALM DOWN, MONET.
YOU CALM DOWN!
I... ACTUALLY AM CALM. SO...
PLAYING NICE WITH THE AUTHORITIES WAS *YOUR* BRIGHT IDEA.
THE GENDARMES COULDN'T STOP US FROM TELLING THEM ABOUT THE RIOTS! ABOUT MAKING A POLITICAL STATEMENT!
AND IT WAS A GOOD ONE. YOU SAW! REPORTERS WERE WAITING FOR US!
PLUS WE SHOWED THEM WE DON'T THINK MUTANTS ARE ABOVE THE LAW. WITH ALL THE NEGATIVE PRESS THE U.S. IS GETTING BECAUSE OF THE CIVIL WAR, I THINK THAT WAS AN *IMPORTANT* POINT TO MAKE.
REALLY. SOMEHOW AMERICA'S IMAGE IS LESS IMPORTANT TO ME THAN FINDING A PROPER *TOILET* IF THE NEED ARISES.
SO IF--
HEY...THAT GUY THEY'RE BRINGING IN. I KNOW THAT GUY.
HE WAS AT THE DEMONSTRATION.
WHAT HAPPENED?! WHY'S HE COVERED WITH ASH?
GARDIEN! POURQUOI EST--
YOU WANT TO KNOW WHAT *HAPPENED,* MAD' MOISELLE? YOU AND YOUR IRISH FRIEND?
SILENCE!
POLICE

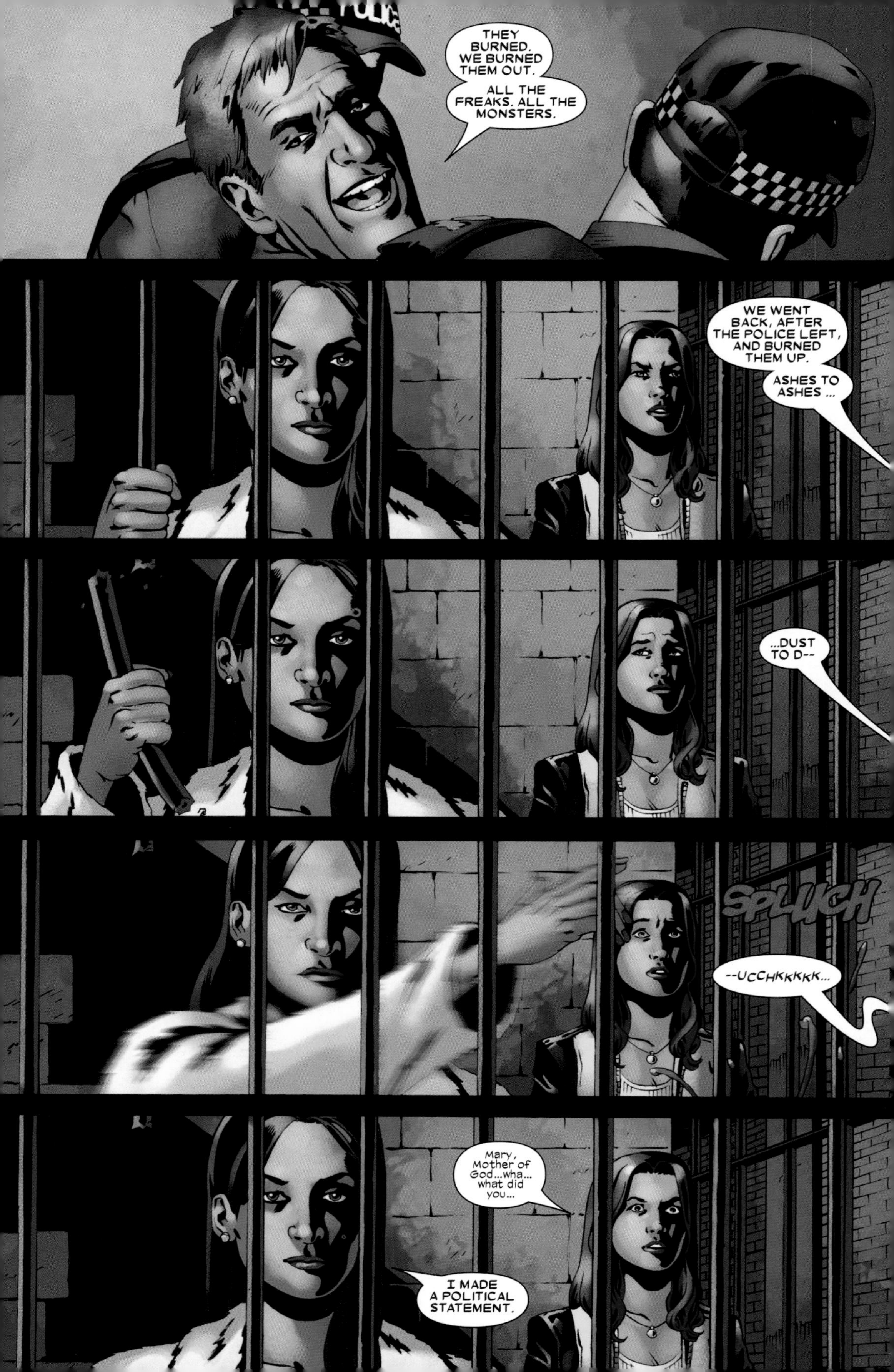
POLICE
THEY BURNED. WE BURNED THEM OUT.
ALL THE FREAKS. ALL THE MONSTERS.
WE WENT BACK, AFTER THE POLICE LEFT, AND BURNED THEM UP.
ASHES TO ASHES ...
...DUST TO D--
SPLUCH
--UCCHKKKKK...
Mary, Mother of God...wha... what did you...
I MADE A POLITICAL STATEMENT.

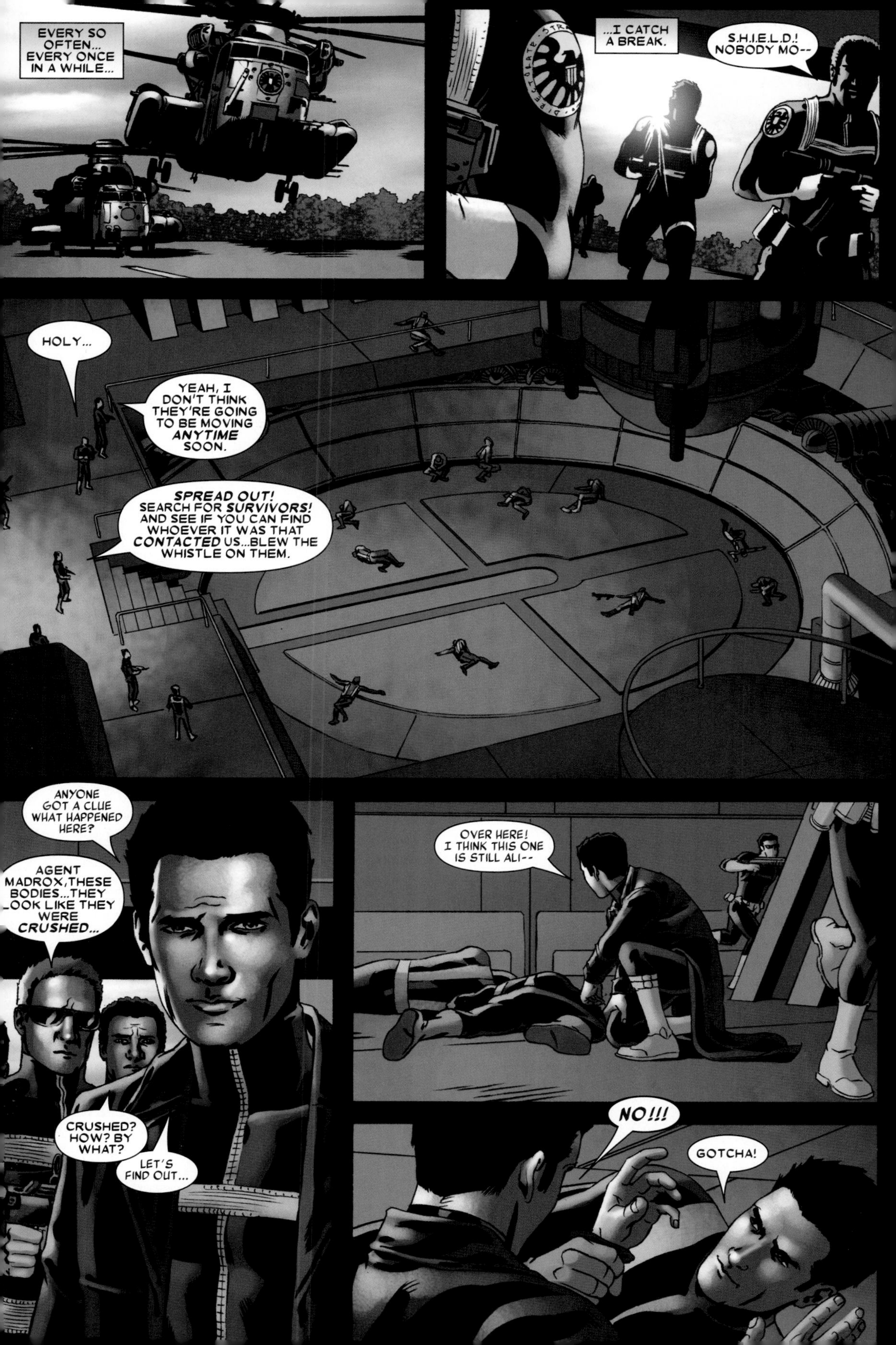
EVERY SO OFTEN... EVERY ONCE IN A WHILE...
...I CATCH A BREAK.
S.H.I.E.L.D.! NOBODY MO--
HOLY...
YEAH, I DON'T THINK THEY'RE GOING TO BE MOVING ANYTIME SOON.
SPREAD OUT! SEARCH FOR SURVIVORS! AND SEE IF YOU CAN FIND WHOEVER IT WAS THAT CONTACTED US...BLEW THE WHISTLE ON THEM.
ANYONE GOT A CLUE WHAT HAPPENED HERE?
AGENT MADROX, THESE BODIES...THEY LOOK LIKE THEY WERE CRUSHED...
CRUSHED? HOW? BY WHAT?
LET'S FIND OUT...
OVER HERE! I THINK THIS ONE IS STILL ALI--
NO!!!
GOTCHA!

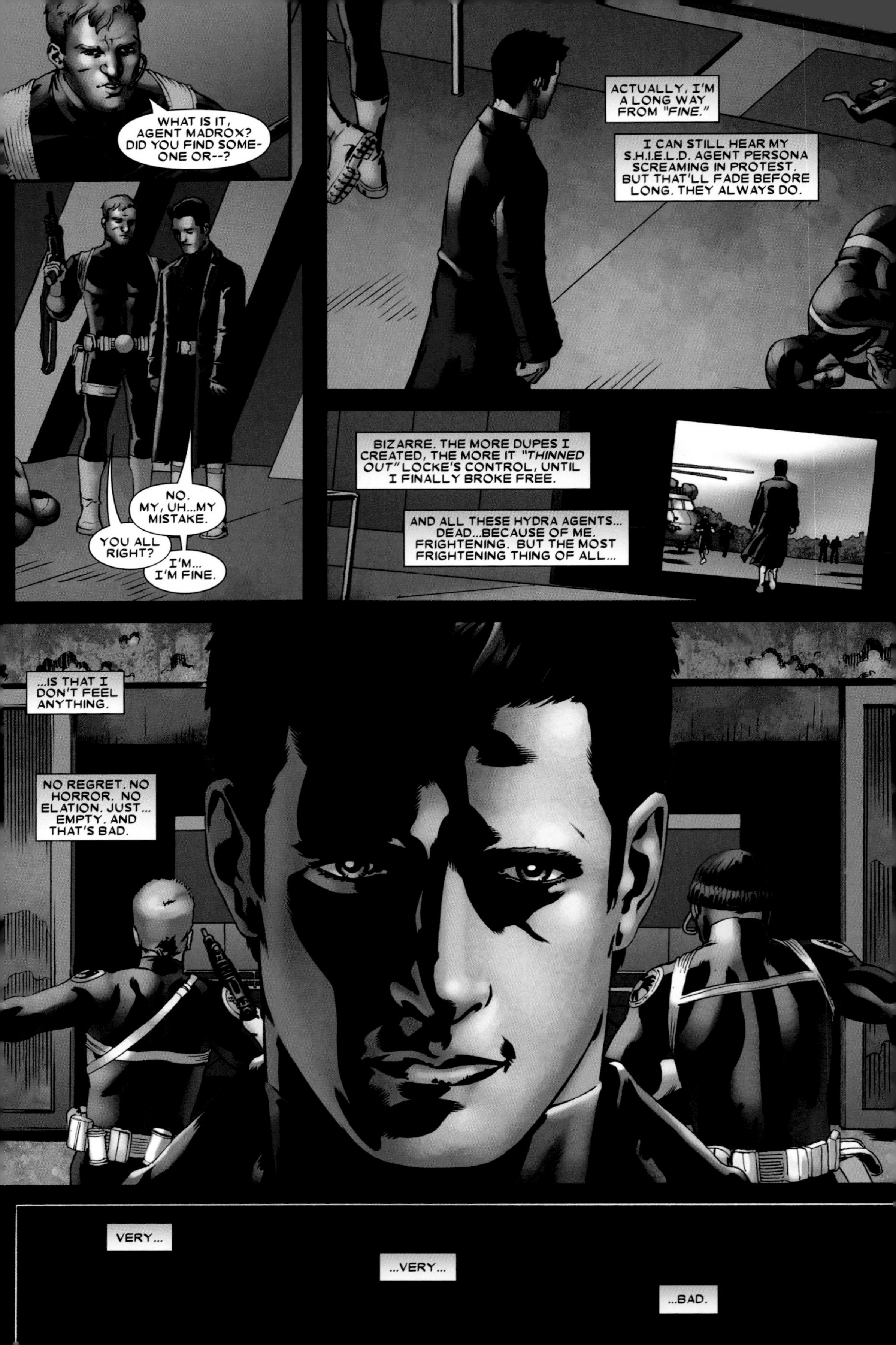
WHAT IS IT, AGENT MADROX? DID YOU FIND SOME-ONE OR--?
NO. MY, UH...MY MISTAKE.
YOU ALL RIGHT?
I'M... I'M FINE.
ACTUALLY, I'M A LONG WAY FROM "FINE."
I CAN STILL HEAR MY S.H.I.E.L.D. AGENT PERSONA SCREAMING IN PROTEST. BUT THAT'LL FADE BEFORE LONG. THEY ALWAYS DO.
BIZARRE. THE MORE DUPES I CREATED, THE MORE IT "THINNED OUT" LOCKE'S CONTROL, UNTIL I FINALLY BROKE FREE.
AND ALL THESE HYDRA AGENTS... DEAD...BECAUSE OF ME. FRIGHTENING. BUT THE MOST FRIGHTENING THING OF ALL...
...IS THAT I DON'T FEEL ANYTHING.
NO REGRET. NO HORROR. NO ELATION. JUST... EMPTY. AND THAT'S BAD.
VERY...
...VERY...
...BAD.

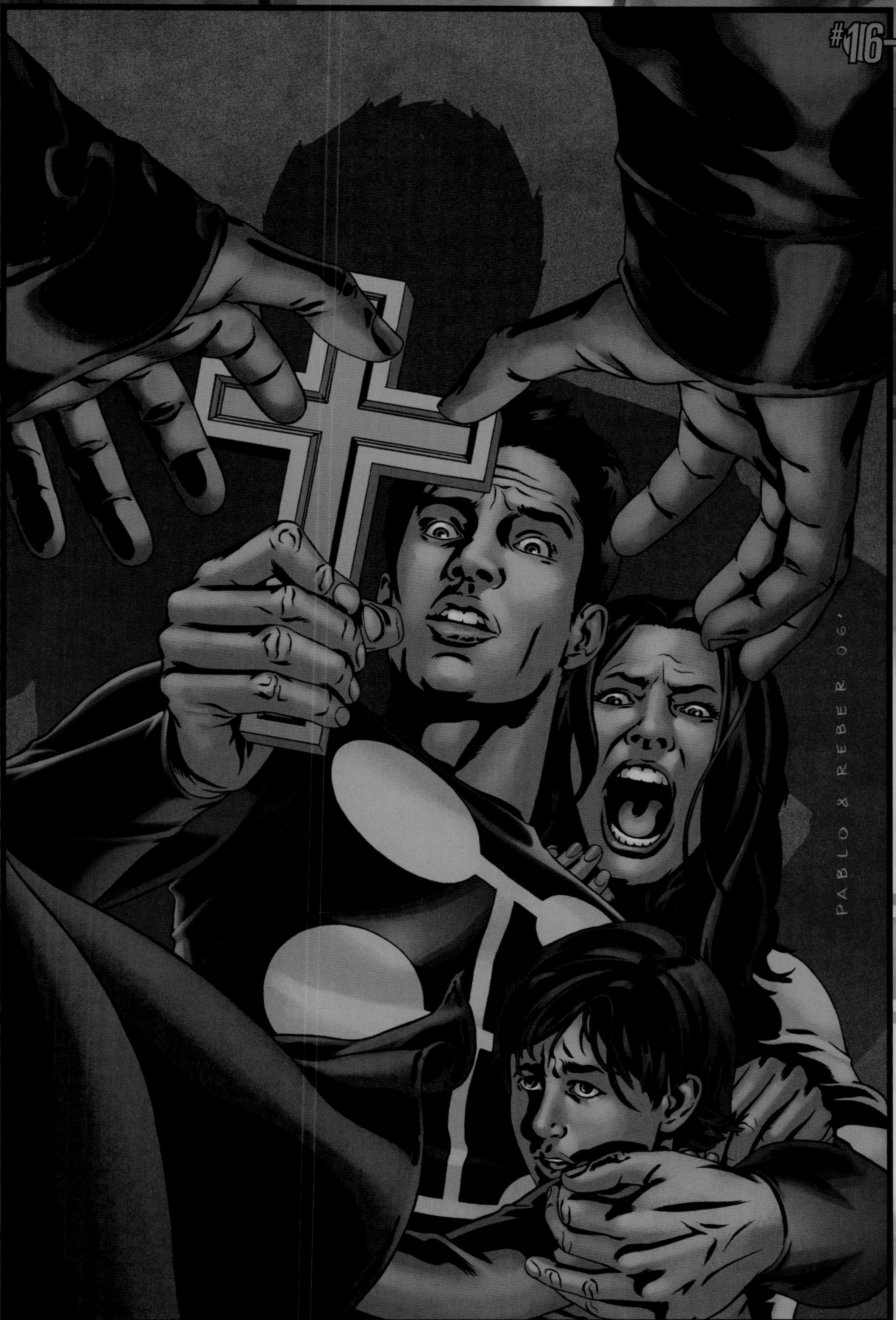
#16
PABLO & REBER 06'

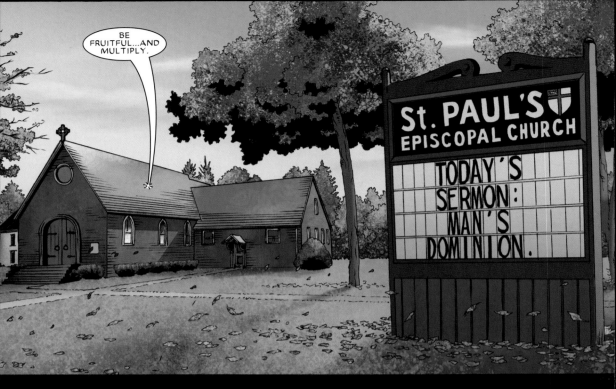

BE FRUITFUL...AND MULTIPLY.

St. PAUL'S EPISCOPAL CHURCH

TODAY'S SERMON: MAN'S DOMINION.

THAT WAS THE INSTRUCTION THE LORD GAVE ADAM AND EVE IN GENESIS 1:28. "BE FRUITFUL AND MULTIPLY, AND REPLENISH THE EARTH, AND SUBDUE IT...

"...AND HAVE DOMINION OVER THE FISH OF THE SEA, AND OVER THE FOWL OF THE AIR, AND OVER EVERY LIVING THING THAT MOVETH UPON THE EARTH."

THAT SEEMS PRETTY CLEAR IN THE READING. THE LORD IS GIVING OVER EARTH TO HIS CREATION. IT'S OURS TO DO WITH AS WE WILL.

DANIEL! STOP IT!

BUT IS IT REALLY OURS? REALLY OUR PROPERTY?

ARE WE KINGS? ABSOLUTE RULERS OF ALL THAT WE SEE?

HOW PRESUMPTUOUS WOULD THAT BE, FOR US TO CONSIDER OURSELVES IN THAT WAY?

THERE IS ONLY ONE ABSOLUTE RULER, AND WE KNOW WHO THAT IS, DON'T WE? HE PROVIDED US THIS WORLD, BUT IT REMAINS HIS. AFTER ALL, WE DO CALL STORMS, EARTHQUAKES AND SUCH "ACTS OF GOD," DON'T WE?

WE ARE NOT MASTERS OF THIS WORLD. THAT'S BEEN PROVEN OVER AND OVER AGAIN.

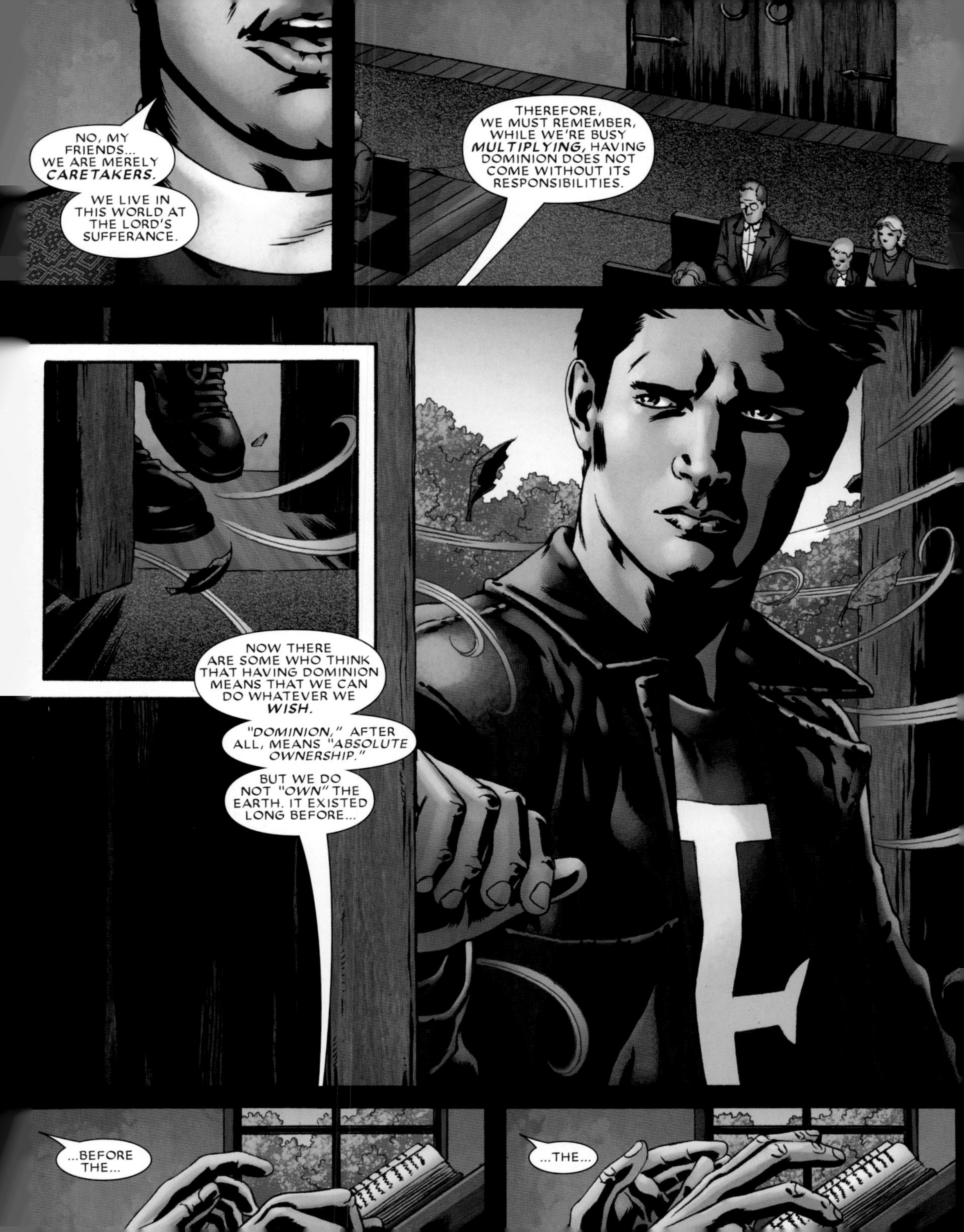
NO, MY FRIENDS... WE ARE MERELY *CARETAKERS.*
WE LIVE IN THIS WORLD AT THE LORD'S SUFFERANCE.
THEREFORE, WE MUST REMEMBER, WHILE WE'RE BUSY *MULTIPLYING,* HAVING DOMINION DOES NOT COME WITHOUT ITS RESPONSIBILITIES.
NOW THERE ARE SOME WHO THINK THAT HAVING DOMINION MEANS THAT WE CAN DO WHATEVER WE *WISH.*
"DOMINION," AFTER ALL, MEANS *"ABSOLUTE OWNERSHIP."*
BUT WE DO NOT *"OWN"* THE EARTH. IT EXISTED LONG BEFORE...
...BEFORE THE...
...THE...

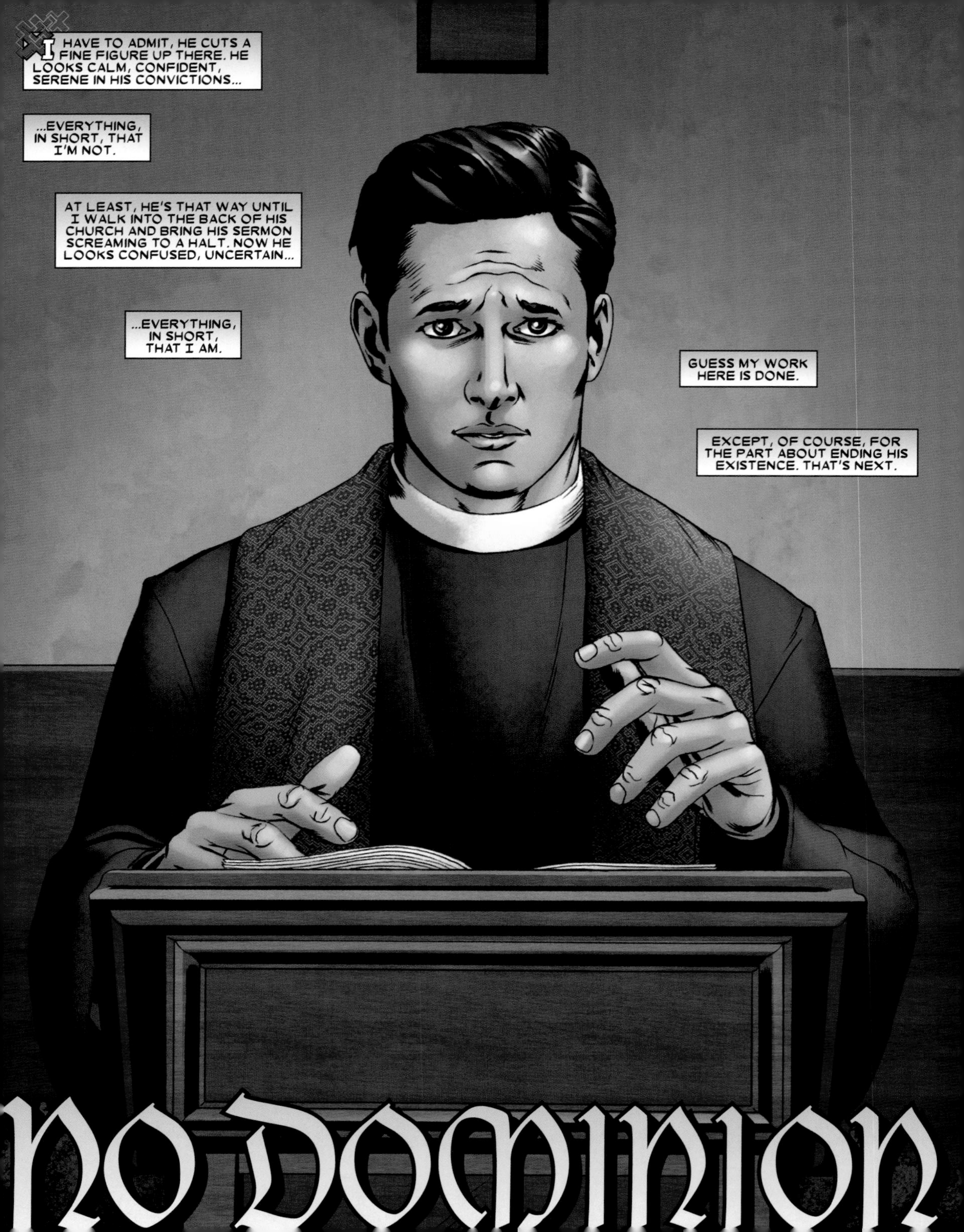
I HAVE TO ADMIT, HE CUTS A FINE FIGURE UP THERE. HE LOOKS CALM, CONFIDENT, SERENE IN HIS CONVICTIONS...
...EVERYTHING, IN SHORT, THAT I'M NOT.
AT LEAST, HE'S THAT WAY UNTIL I WALK INTO THE BACK OF HIS CHURCH AND BRING HIS SERMON SCREAMING TO A HALT. NOW HE LOOKS CONFUSED, UNCERTAIN...
...EVERYTHING, IN SHORT, THAT I AM.
GUESS MY WORK HERE IS DONE.
EXCEPT, OF COURSE, FOR THE PART ABOUT ENDING HIS EXISTENCE. THAT'S NEXT.
NO DOMINION

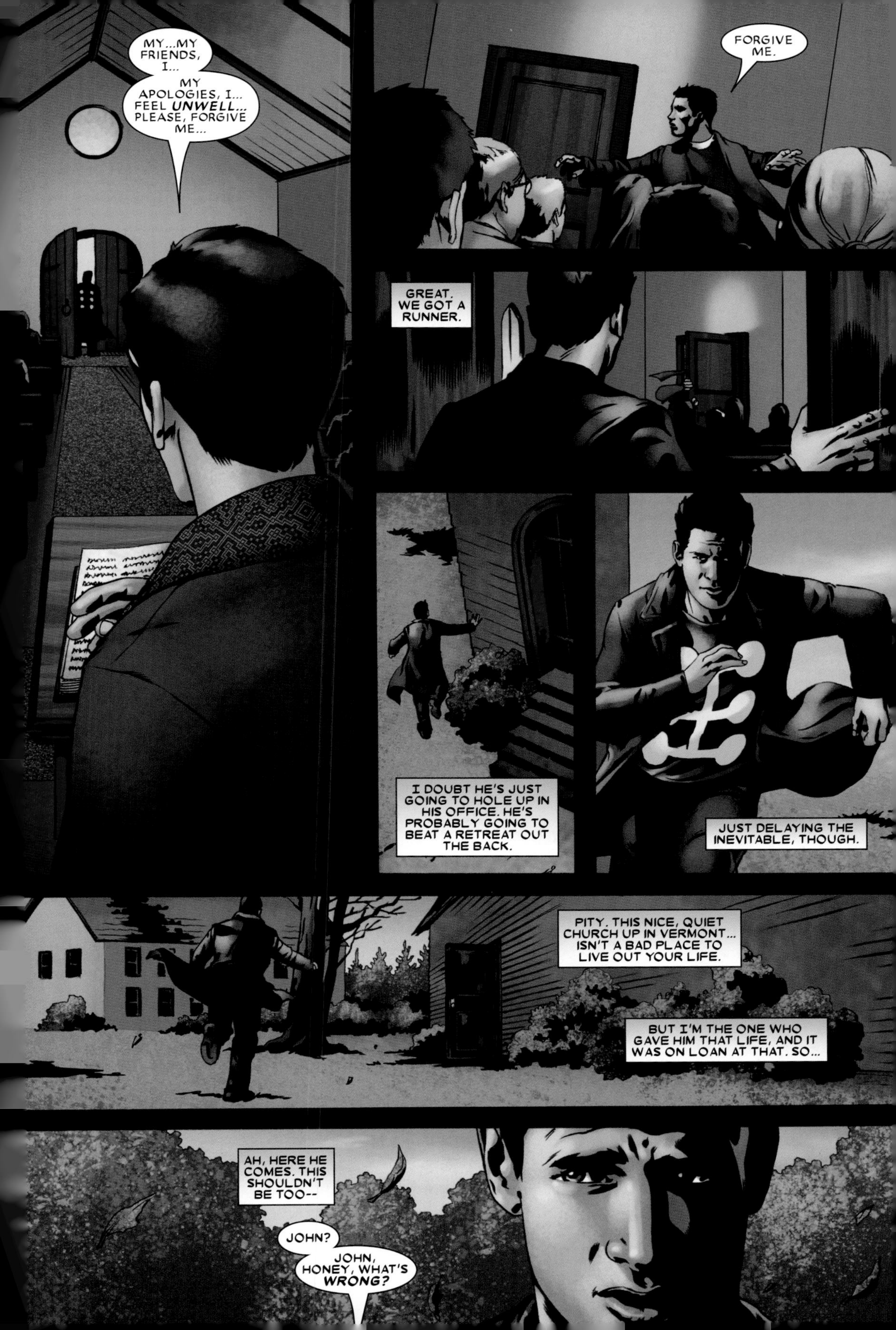
MY...MY FRIENDS, I...
MY APOLOGIES, I... FEEL UNWELL... PLEASE, FORGIVE ME...
FORGIVE ME.
GREAT. WE GOT A RUNNER.
I DOUBT HE'S JUST GOING TO HOLE UP IN HIS OFFICE. HE'S PROBABLY GOING TO BEAT A RETREAT OUT THE BACK.
JUST DELAYING THE INEVITABLE, THOUGH.
PITY. THIS NICE, QUIET CHURCH UP IN VERMONT... ISN'T A BAD PLACE TO LIVE OUT YOUR LIFE.
BUT I'M THE ONE WHO GAVE HIM THAT LIFE, AND IT WAS ON LOAN AT THAT. SO...
AH, HERE HE COMES. THIS SHOULDN'T BE TOO--
JOHN?
JOHN, HONEY, WHAT'S WRONG?

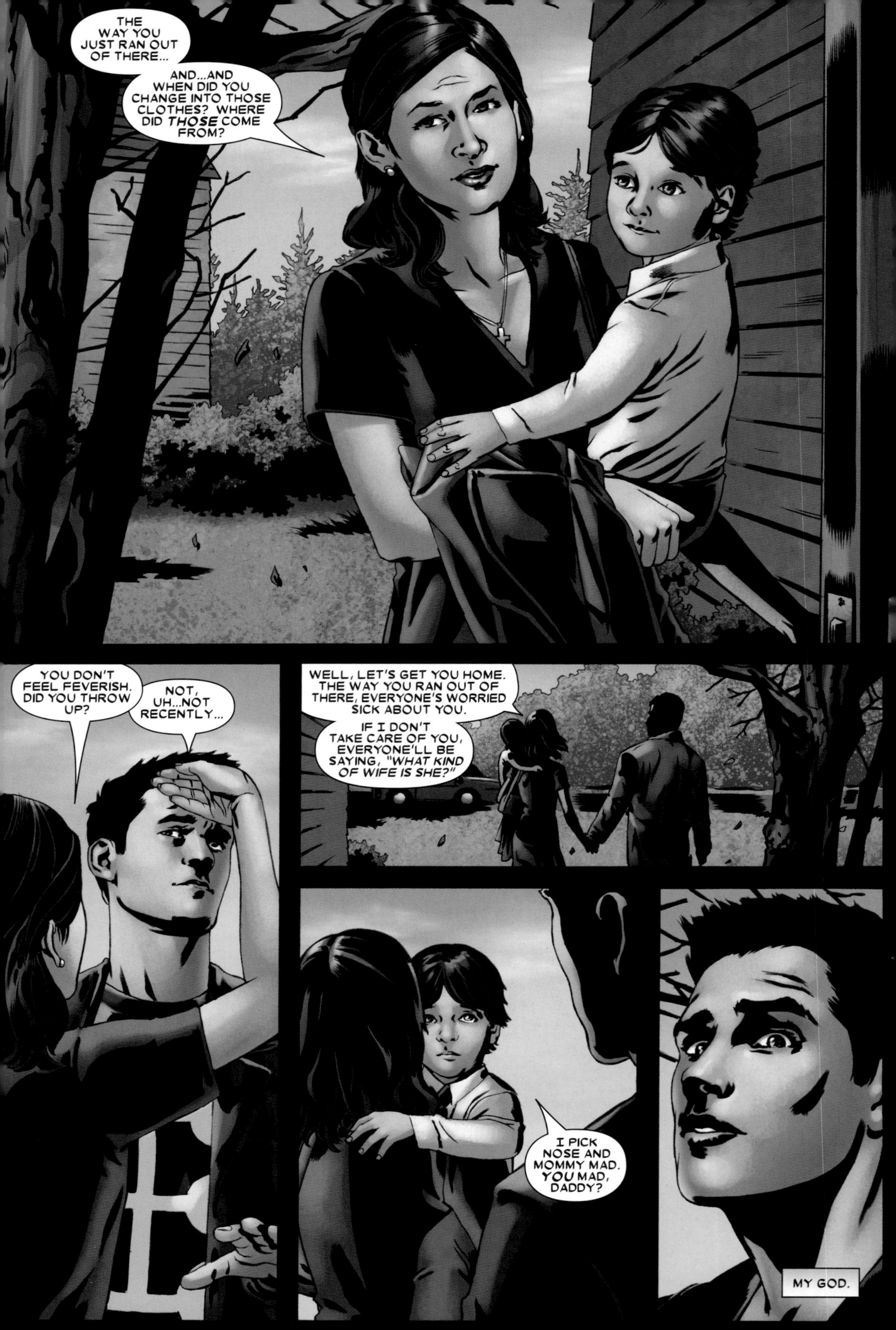
THE WAY YOU JUST RAN OUT OF THERE...
AND...AND WHEN DID YOU CHANGE INTO THOSE CLOTHES? WHERE DID *THOSE* COME FROM?
YOU DON'T FEEL FEVERISH. DID YOU THROW UP?
NOT, UH...NOT RECENTLY...
WELL, LET'S GET YOU HOME. THE WAY YOU RAN OUT OF THERE, EVERYONE'S WORRIED SICK ABOUT YOU.
IF I DON'T TAKE CARE OF YOU, EVERYONE'LL BE SAYING, *"WHAT KIND OF WIFE IS SHE?"*
I PICK NOSE AND MOMMY MAD. *YOU* MAD, DADDY?
MY GOD.

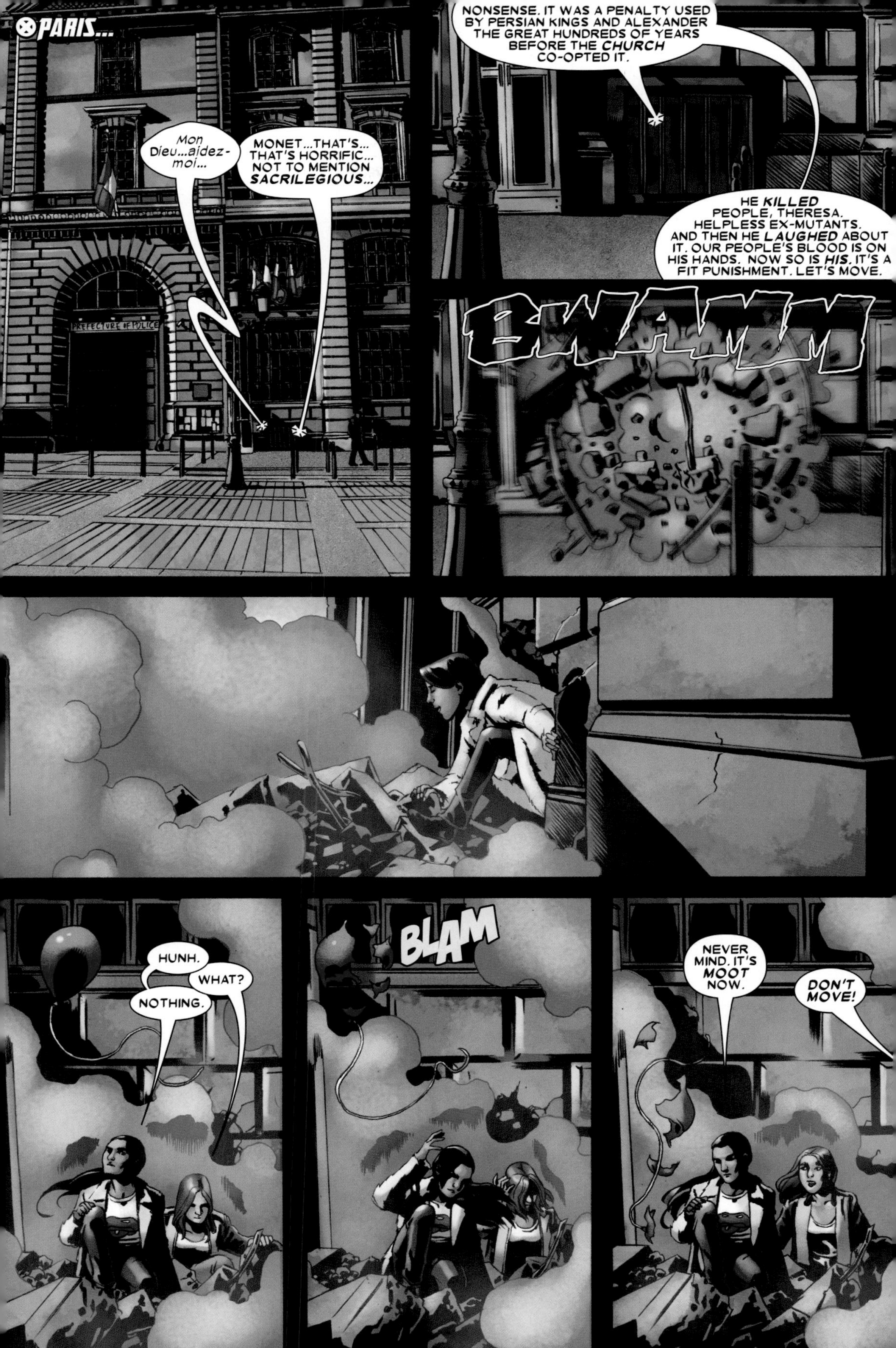
PARIS...
PREFECTURE OF POLICE
Mon Dieu...aidez-moi...
MONET...THAT'S... THAT'S HORRIFIC... NOT TO MENTION SACRILEGIOUS...
NONSENSE. IT WAS A PENALTY USED BY PERSIAN KINGS AND ALEXANDER THE GREAT HUNDREDS OF YEARS BEFORE THE CHURCH CO-OPTED IT.
HE KILLED PEOPLE, THERESA. HELPLESS EX-MUTANTS. AND THEN HE LAUGHED ABOUT IT. OUR PEOPLE'S BLOOD IS ON HIS HANDS. NOW SO IS HIS. IT'S A FIT PUNISHMENT. LET'S MOVE.
BWAMM
HUNH.
WHAT?
NOTHING.
BLAM
NEVER MIND. IT'S MOOT NOW.
DON'T MOVE!

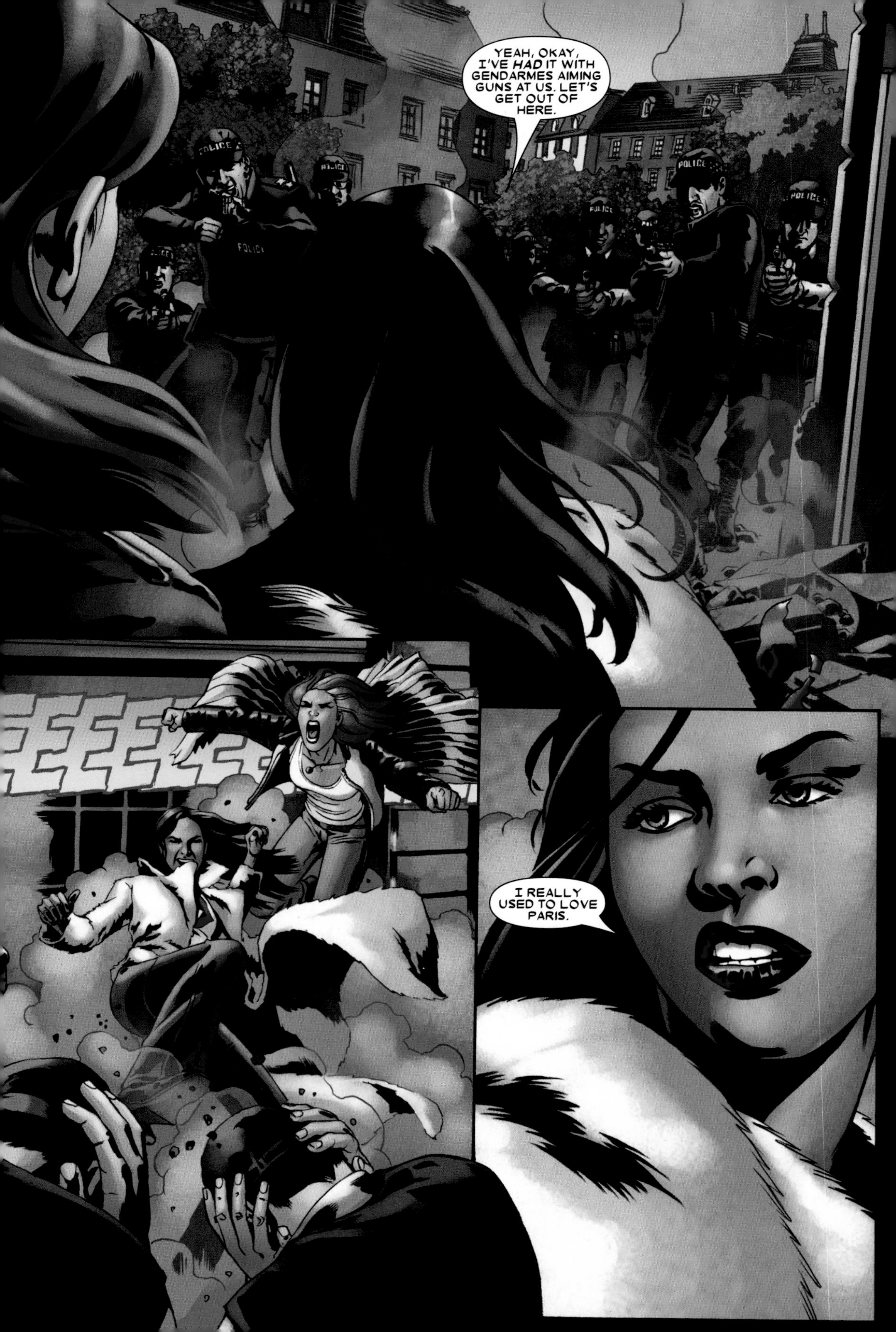
YEAH, OKAY, I'VE HAD IT WITH GENDARMES AIMING GUNS AT US. LET'S GET OUT OF HERE.
I REALLY USED TO LOVE PARIS.

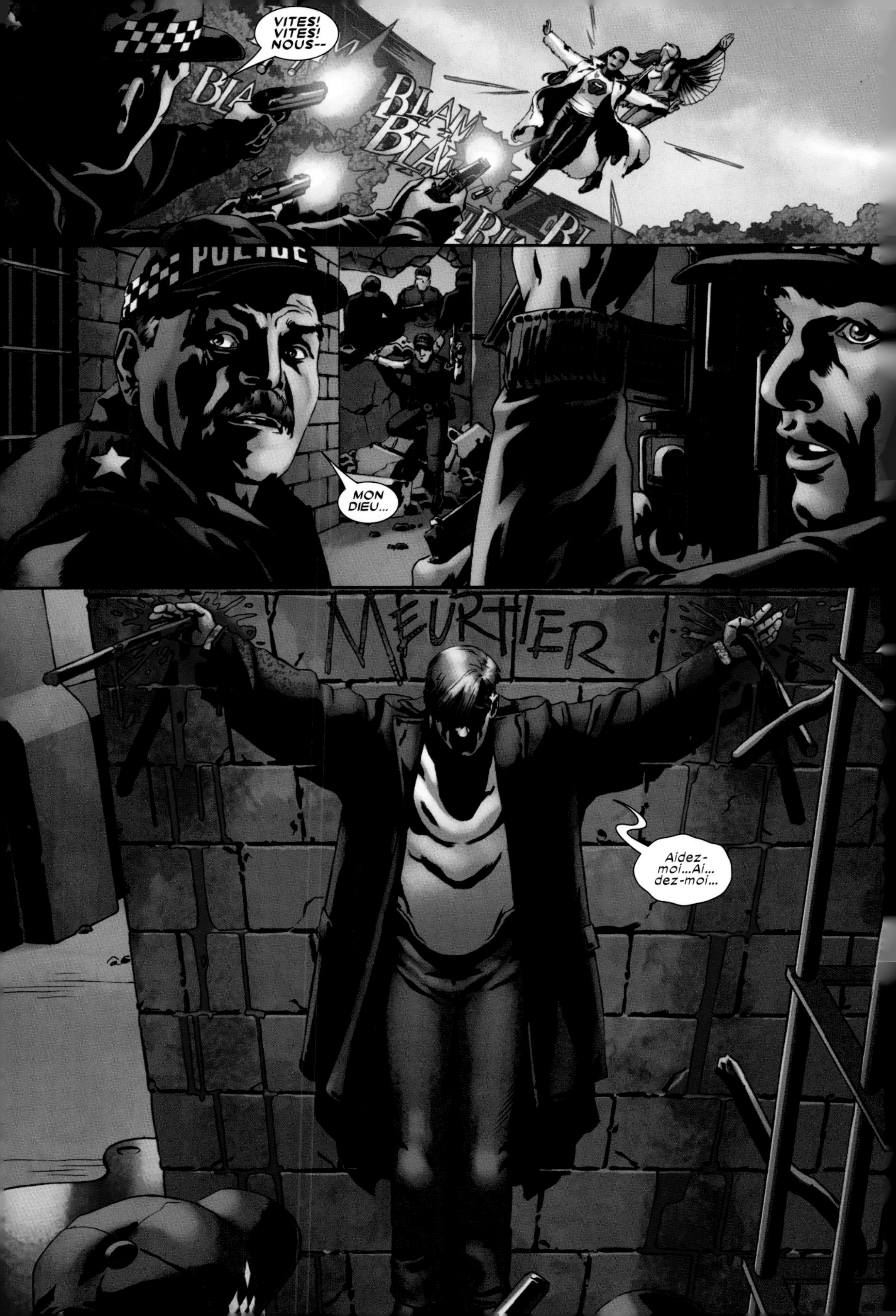
VITES! VITES! NOUS--
BLAM
BLAM BLAM
MON DIEU...
MEURTIER
Aidez-moi...Ai...dez-moi...

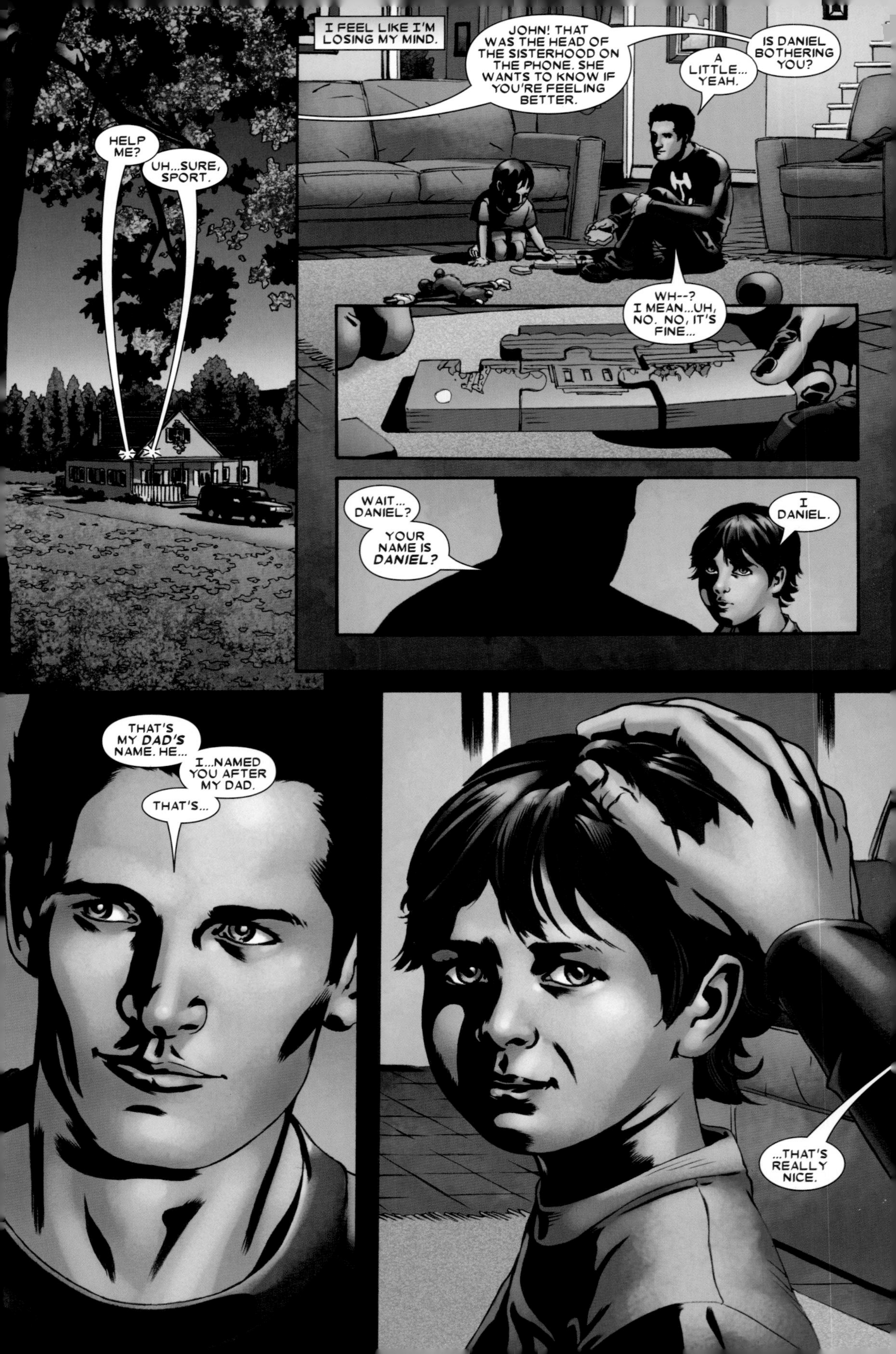
HELP ME?
UH...SURE, SPORT.
I FEEL LIKE I'M LOSING MY MIND.
JOHN! THAT WAS THE HEAD OF THE SISTERHOOD ON THE PHONE. SHE WANTS TO KNOW IF YOU'RE FEELING BETTER.
IS DANIEL BOTHERING YOU?
A LITTLE... YEAH.
WH--? I MEAN...UH, NO. NO, IT'S FINE...
WAIT... DANIEL?
YOUR NAME IS DANIEL?
I DANIEL.
THAT'S MY DAD'S NAME. HE...
I...NAMED YOU AFTER MY DAD.
THAT'S...
...THAT'S REALLY NICE.

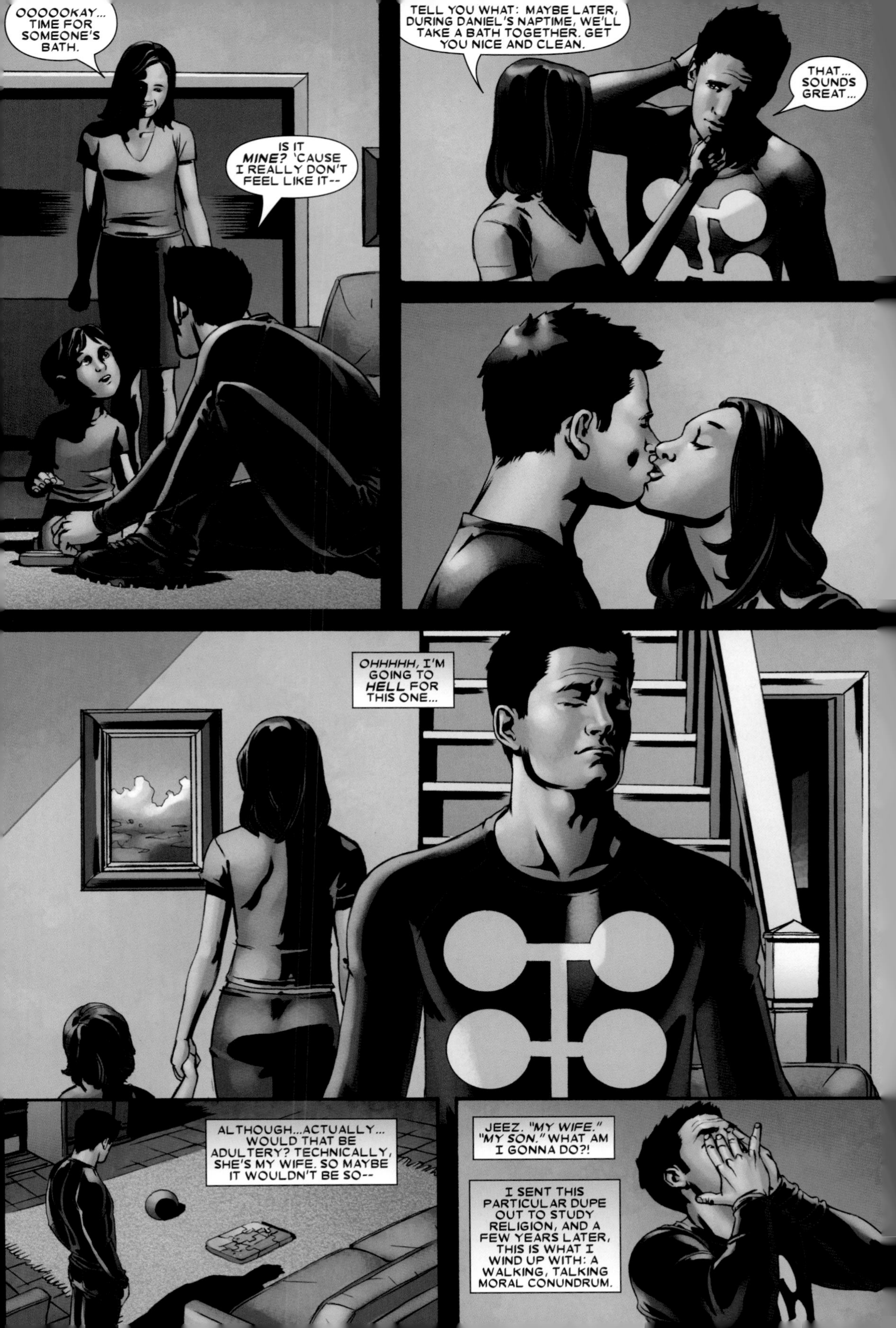
OOOOOKAY... TIME FOR SOMEONE'S BATH.
IS IT *MINE?* 'CAUSE I REALLY DON'T FEEL LIKE IT--
TELL YOU WHAT: MAYBE LATER, DURING DANIEL'S NAPTIME, WE'LL TAKE A BATH TOGETHER. GET YOU NICE AND CLEAN.
THAT... SOUNDS GREAT...
OHHHHH, I'M GOING TO *HELL* FOR THIS ONE...
ALTHOUGH...ACTUALLY... WOULD THAT BE ADULTERY? TECHNICALLY, SHE'S MY WIFE. SO MAYBE IT WOULDN'T BE SO--
JEEZ. *"MY WIFE." "MY SON."* WHAT AM I GONNA DO?!
I SENT THIS PARTICULAR DUPE OUT TO STUDY RELIGION, AND A FEW YEARS LATER, THIS IS WHAT I WIND UP WITH: A WALKING, TALKING MORAL CONUNDRUM.

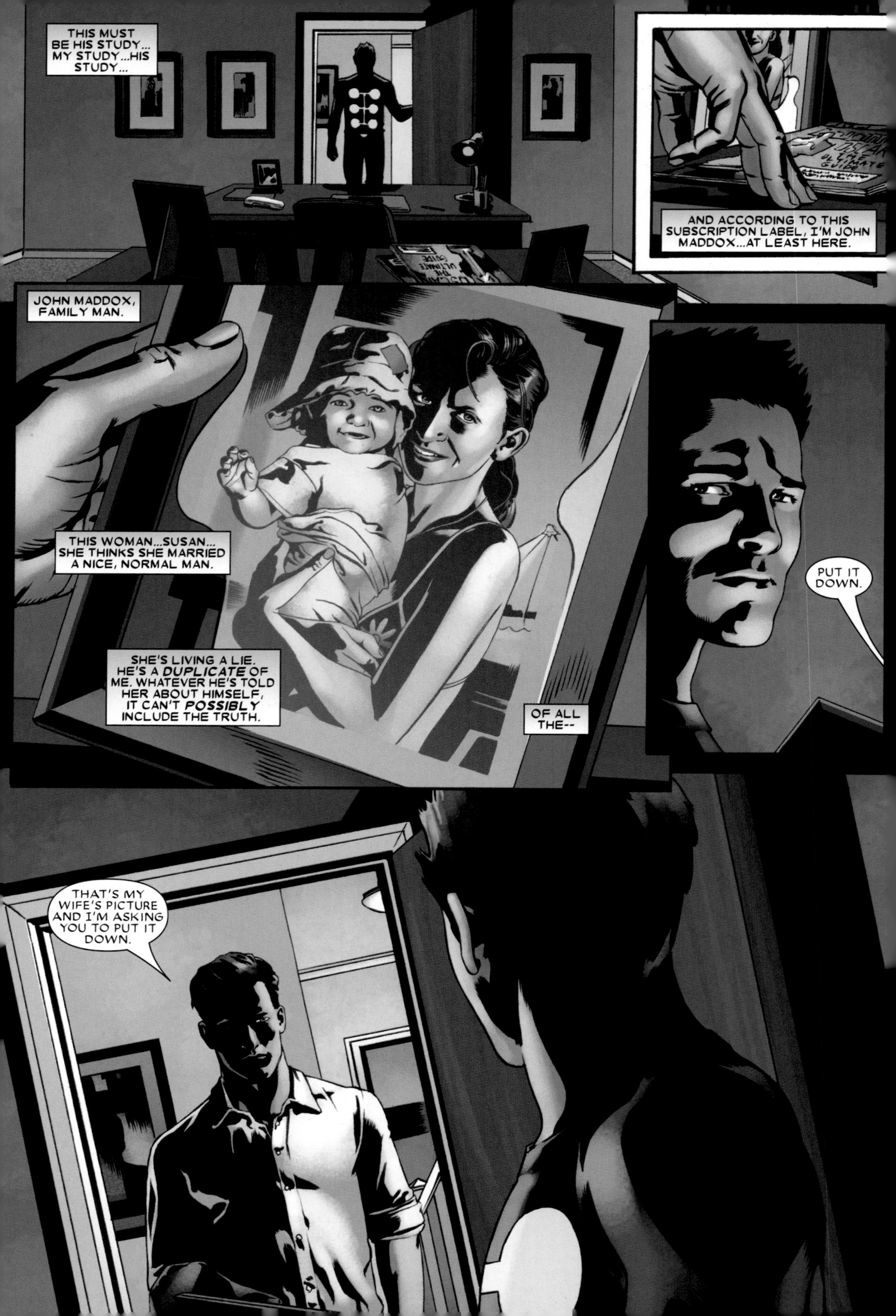
THIS MUST BE HIS STUDY... MY STUDY...HIS STUDY...
AND ACCORDING TO THIS SUBSCRIPTION LABEL, I'M JOHN MADDOX...AT LEAST HERE.
JOHN MADDOX, FAMILY MAN.
THIS WOMAN...SUSAN... SHE THINKS SHE MARRIED A NICE, NORMAL MAN.
SHE'S LIVING A LIE. HE'S A DUPLICATE OF ME. WHATEVER HE'S TOLD HER ABOUT HIMSELF, IT CAN'T POSSIBLY INCLUDE THE TRUTH.
OF ALL THE--
PUT IT DOWN.
THAT'S MY WIFE'S PICTURE AND I'M ASKING YOU TO PUT IT DOWN.

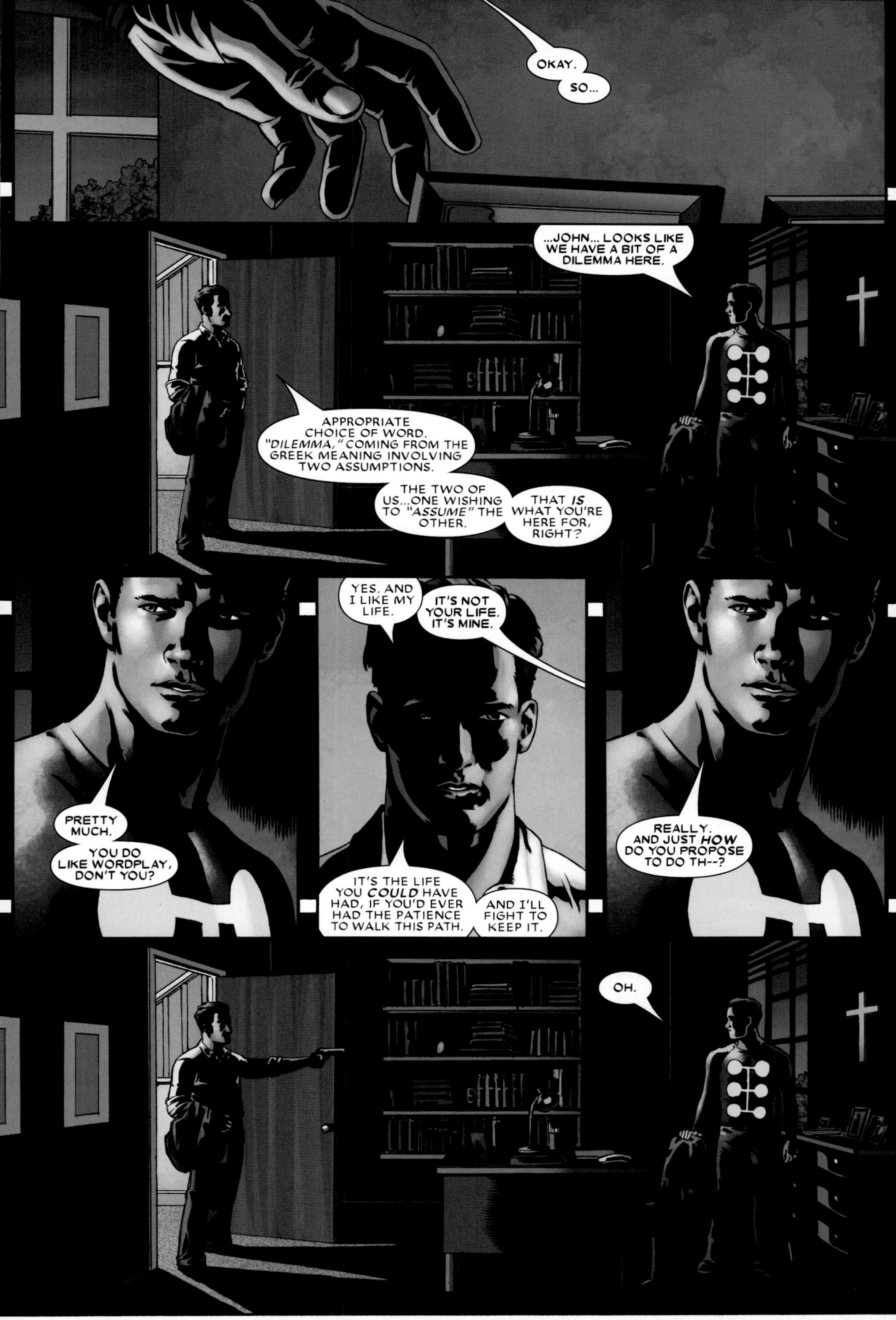
OKAY.
SO...
...JOHN... LOOKS LIKE WE HAVE A BIT OF A DILEMMA HERE.
APPROPRIATE CHOICE OF WORD. "DILEMMA," COMING FROM THE GREEK MEANING INVOLVING TWO ASSUMPTIONS.
THE TWO OF US...ONE WISHING TO "ASSUME" THE OTHER.
THAT IS WHAT YOU'RE HERE FOR, RIGHT?
PRETTY MUCH.
YOU DO LIKE WORDPLAY, DON'T YOU?
YES. AND I LIKE MY LIFE.
IT'S NOT YOUR LIFE. IT'S MINE.
IT'S THE LIFE YOU COULD HAVE HAD, IF YOU'D EVER HAD THE PATIENCE TO WALK THIS PATH.
AND I'LL FIGHT TO KEEP IT.
REALLY. AND JUST HOW DO YOU PROPOSE TO DO TH--?
OH.

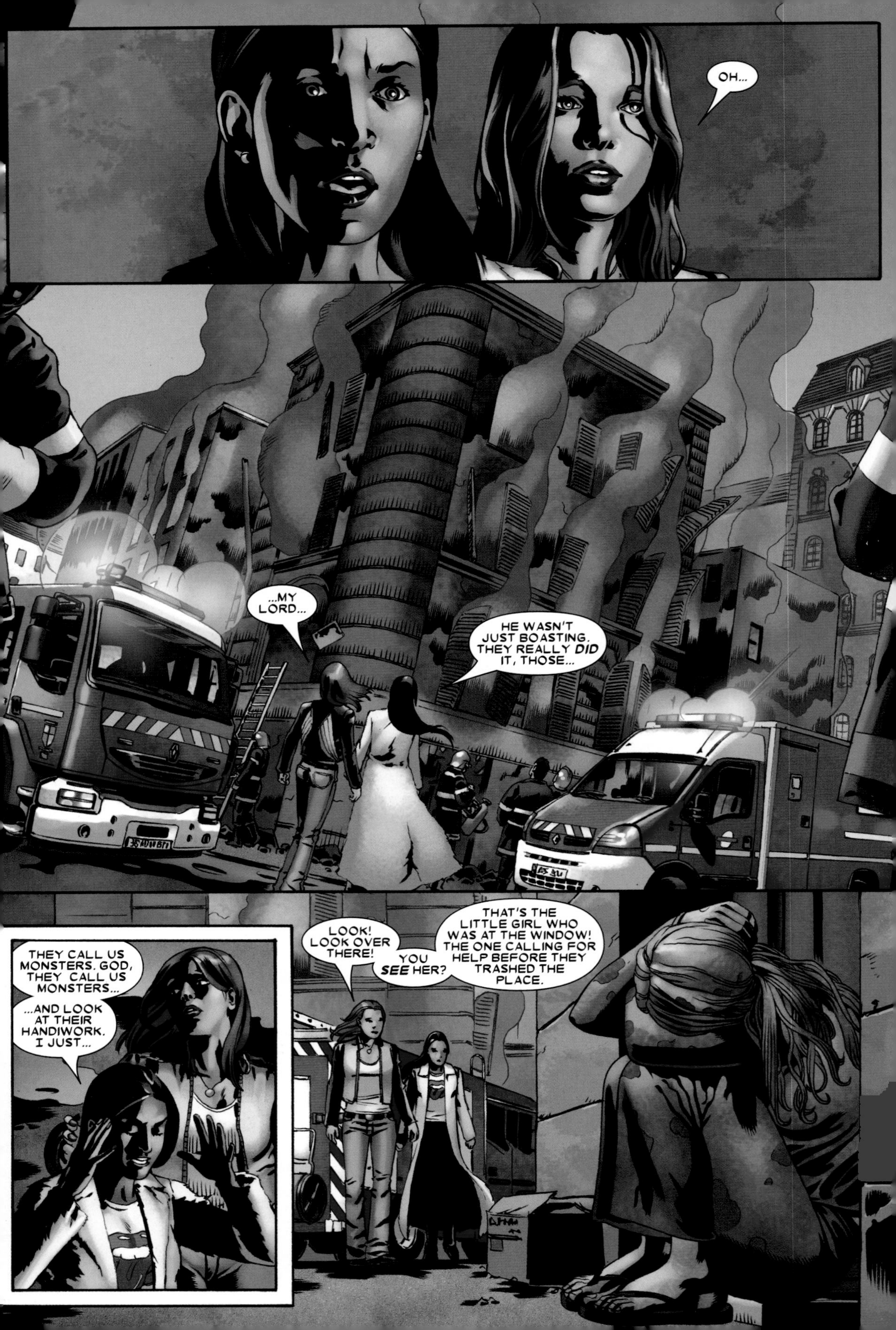
OH...
...MY LORD...
HE WASN'T JUST BOASTING. THEY REALLY DID IT, THOSE...
THEY CALL US MONSTERS. GOD, THEY CALL US MONSTERS...
...AND LOOK AT THEIR HANDIWORK. I JUST...
LOOK! LOOK OVER THERE!
YOU SEE HER?
THAT'S THE LITTLE GIRL WHO WAS AT THE WINDOW! THE ONE CALLING FOR HELP BEFORE THEY TRASHED THE PLACE.

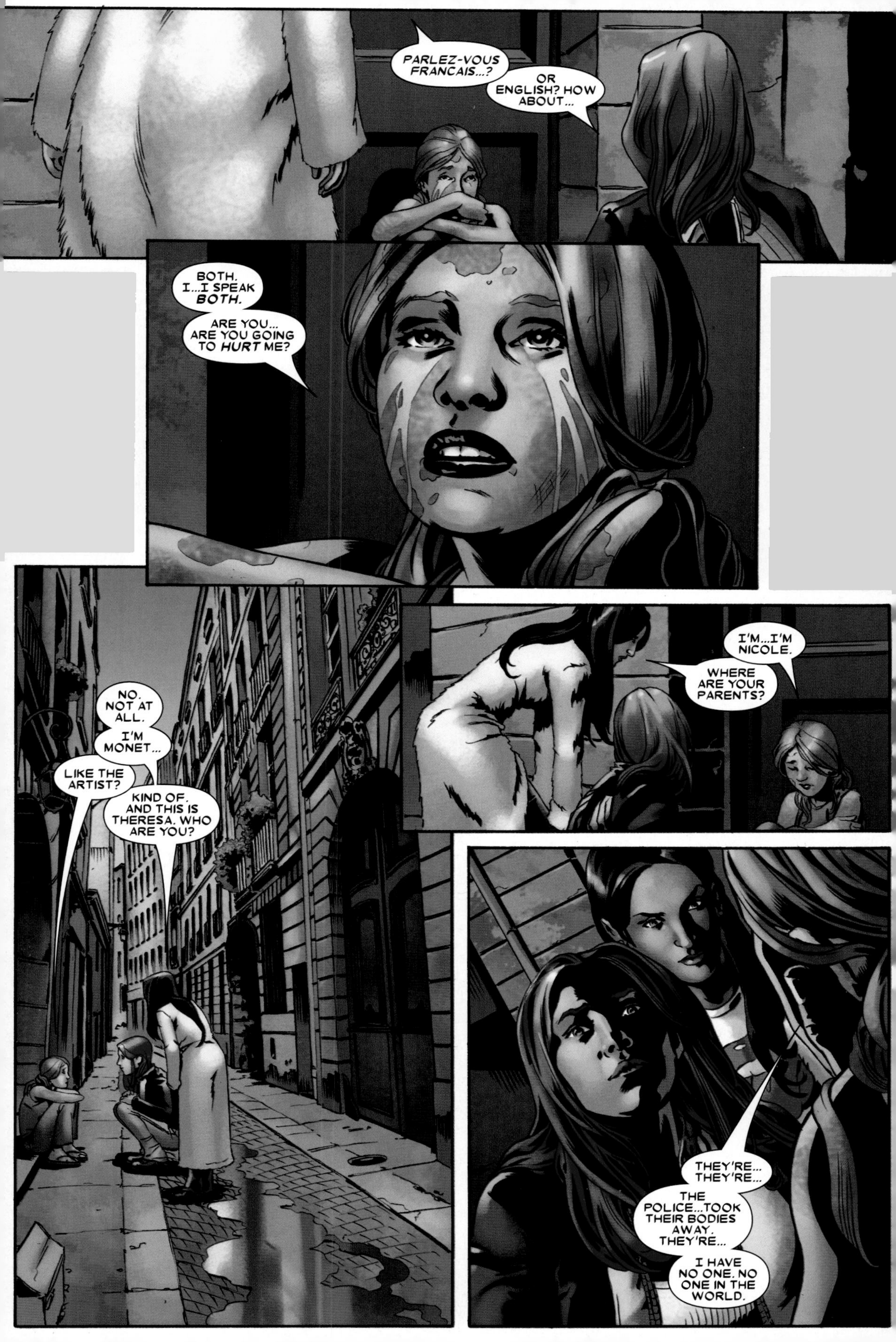
PARLEZ-VOUS FRANCAIS...?
OR ENGLISH? HOW ABOUT...
BOTH. I...I SPEAK BOTH.
ARE YOU... ARE YOU GOING TO HURT ME?
NO. NOT AT ALL.
I'M MONET...
LIKE THE ARTIST?
KIND OF. AND THIS IS THERESA. WHO ARE YOU?
I'M...I'M NICOLE.
WHERE ARE YOUR PARENTS?
THEY'RE... THEY'RE...
THE POLICE...TOOK THEIR BODIES AWAY. THEY'RE...
I HAVE NO ONE. NO ONE IN THE WORLD.

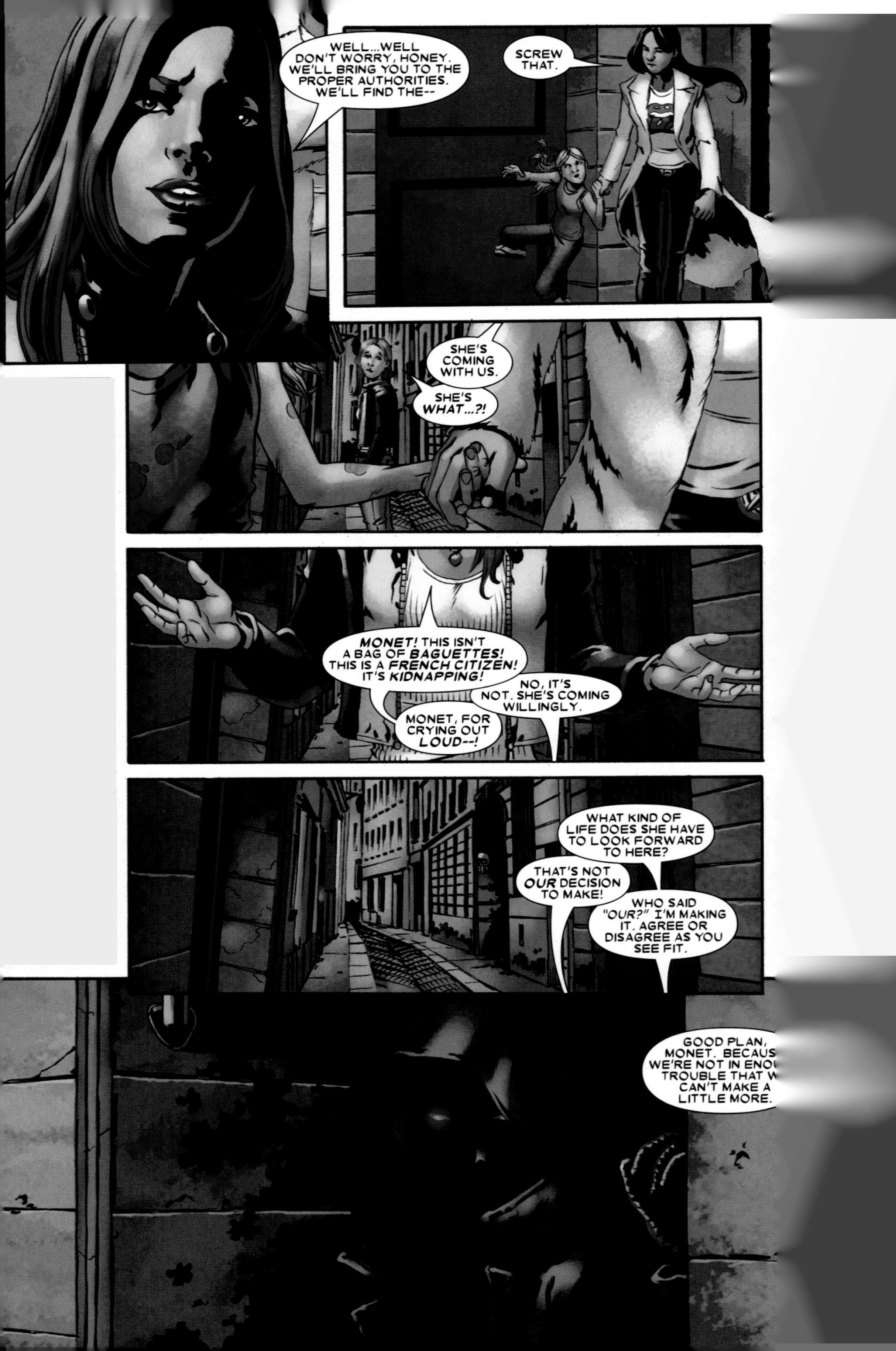

WELL...WELL DON'T WORRY, HONEY. WE'LL BRING YOU TO THE PROPER AUTHORITIES. WE'LL FIND THE--
SCREW THAT.
SHE'S COMING WITH US.
SHE'S WHAT...?!
MONET! THIS ISN'T A BAG OF BAGUETTES! THIS IS A FRENCH CITIZEN! IT'S KIDNAPPING!
NO, IT'S NOT. SHE'S COMING WILLINGLY.
MONET, FOR CRYING OUT LOUD--!
WHAT KIND OF LIFE DOES SHE HAVE TO LOOK FORWARD TO HERE?
THAT'S NOT OUR DECISION TO MAKE!
WHO SAID "OUR?" I'M MAKING IT. AGREE OR DISAGREE AS YOU SEE FIT.
GOOD PLAN, MONET. BECAUS
WE'RE NOT IN ENOU
TROUBLE THAT W
CAN'T MAKE A
LITTLE MORE.

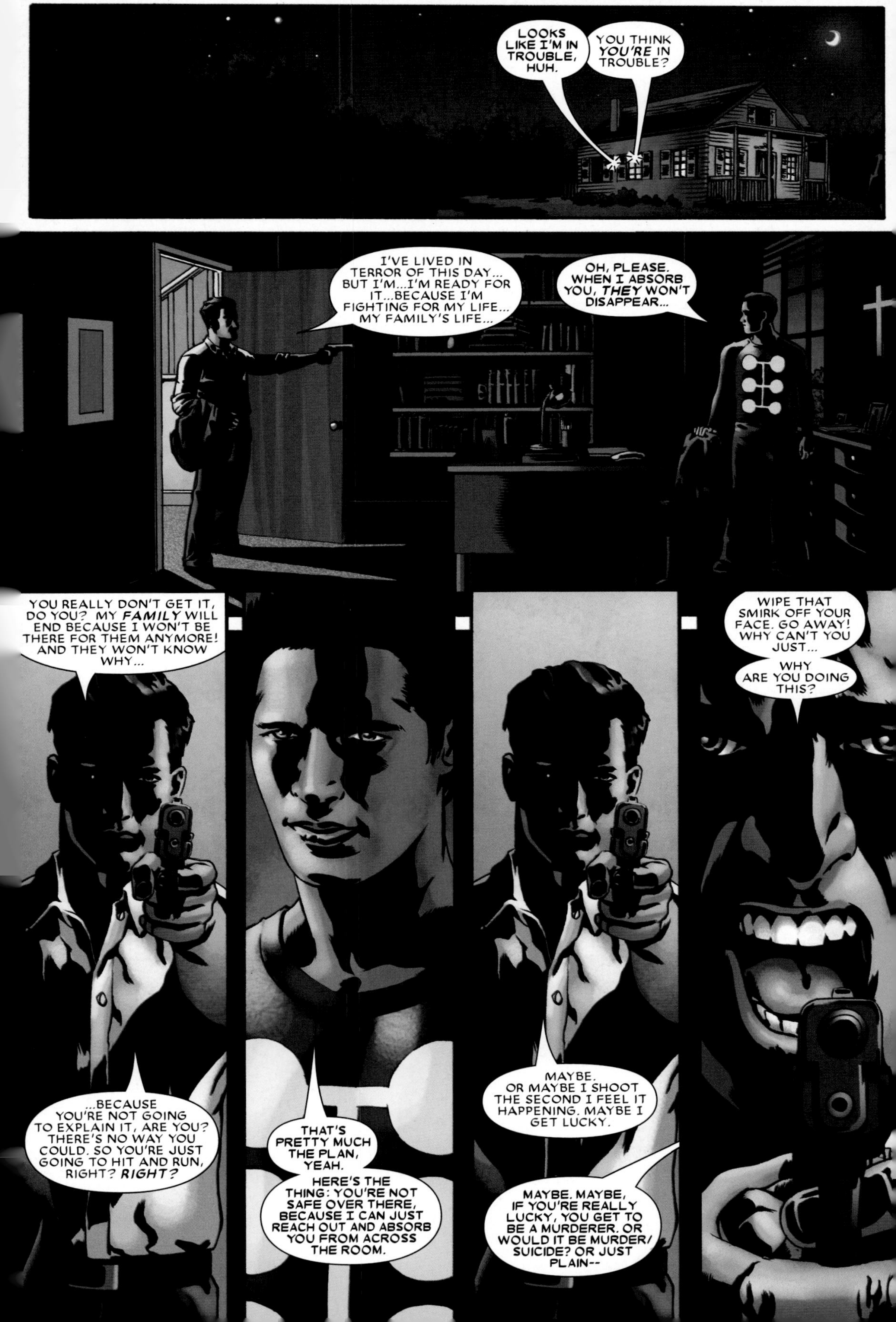

LOOKS LIKE I'M IN TROUBLE, HUH.
YOU THINK *YOU'RE* IN TROUBLE?
I'VE LIVED IN TERROR OF THIS DAY... BUT I'M...I'M READY FOR IT...BECAUSE I'M FIGHTING FOR MY LIFE... MY FAMILY'S LIFE...
OH, PLEASE. WHEN I ABSORB YOU, *THEY* WON'T DISAPPEAR...
YOU REALLY DON'T GET IT, DO YOU? MY *FAMILY* WILL END BECAUSE I WON'T BE THERE FOR THEM ANYMORE! AND THEY WON'T KNOW WHY...
...BECAUSE YOU'RE NOT GOING TO EXPLAIN IT, ARE YOU? THERE'S NO WAY YOU COULD. SO YOU'RE JUST GOING TO HIT AND RUN, RIGHT? ***RIGHT?***
THAT'S PRETTY MUCH THE PLAN, YEAH.
HERE'S THE THING: YOU'RE NOT SAFE OVER THERE, BECAUSE I CAN JUST REACH OUT AND ABSORB YOU FROM ACROSS THE ROOM.
MAYBE. OR MAYBE I SHOOT THE SECOND I FEEL IT HAPPENING. MAYBE I GET LUCKY.
MAYBE. MAYBE, IF YOU'RE REALLY LUCKY, YOU GET TO BE A MURDERER. OR WOULD IT BE MURDER/ SUICIDE? OR JUST PLAIN--
WIPE THAT SMIRK OFF YOUR FACE. GO AWAY! WHY CAN'T YOU JUST...
WHY ARE YOU DOING THIS?

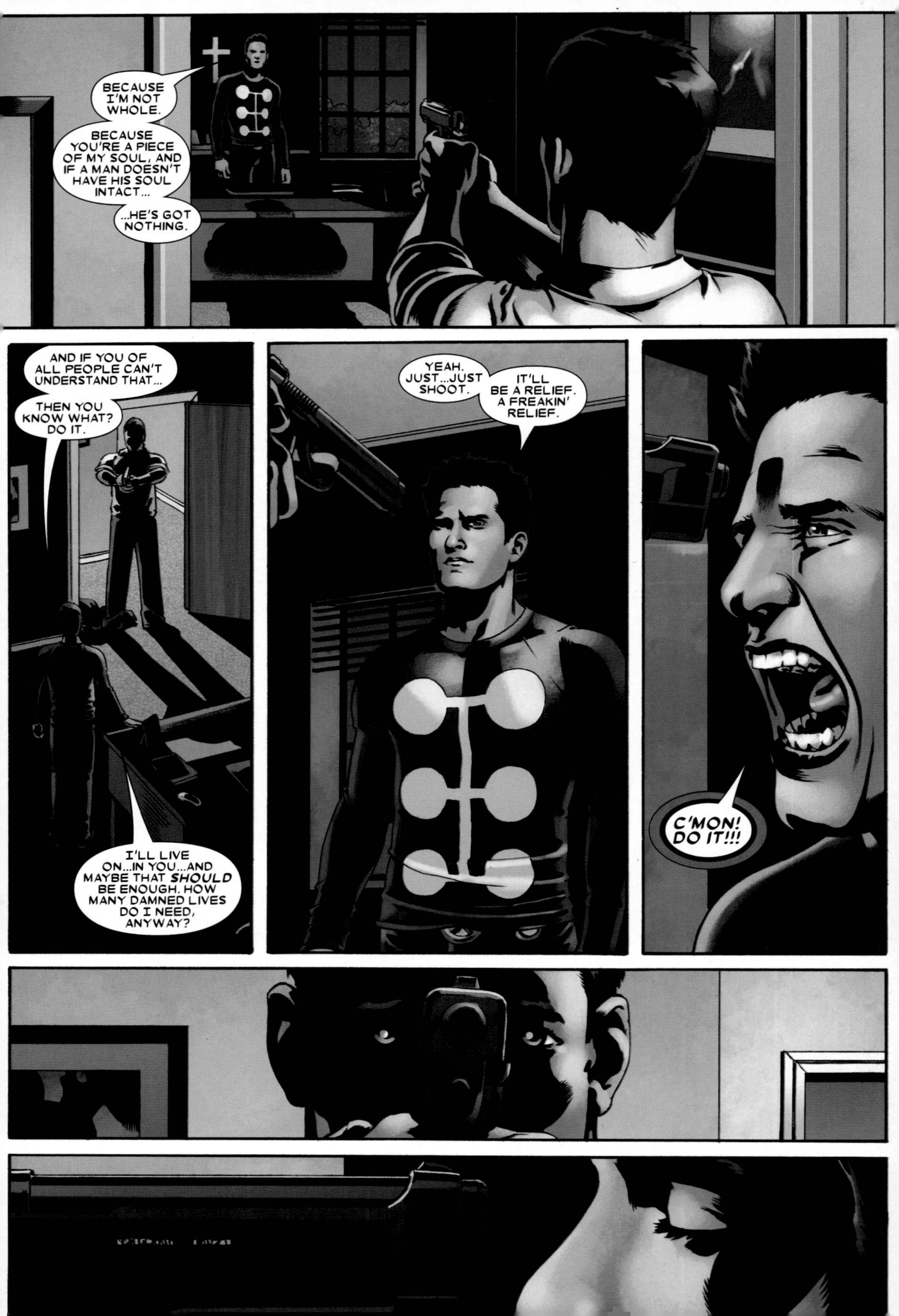
BECAUSE I'M NOT WHOLE.
BECAUSE YOU'RE A PIECE OF MY SOUL, AND IF A MAN DOESN'T HAVE HIS SOUL INTACT...
...HE'S GOT NOTHING.
AND IF YOU OF ALL PEOPLE CAN'T UNDERSTAND THAT...
THEN YOU KNOW WHAT? DO IT.
I'LL LIVE ON...IN YOU...AND MAYBE THAT *SHOULD* BE ENOUGH. HOW MANY DAMNED LIVES DO I NEED, ANYWAY?
YEAH. JUST...JUST SHOOT.
IT'LL BE A RELIEF. A FREAKIN' RELIEF.
C'MON! DO IT!!!

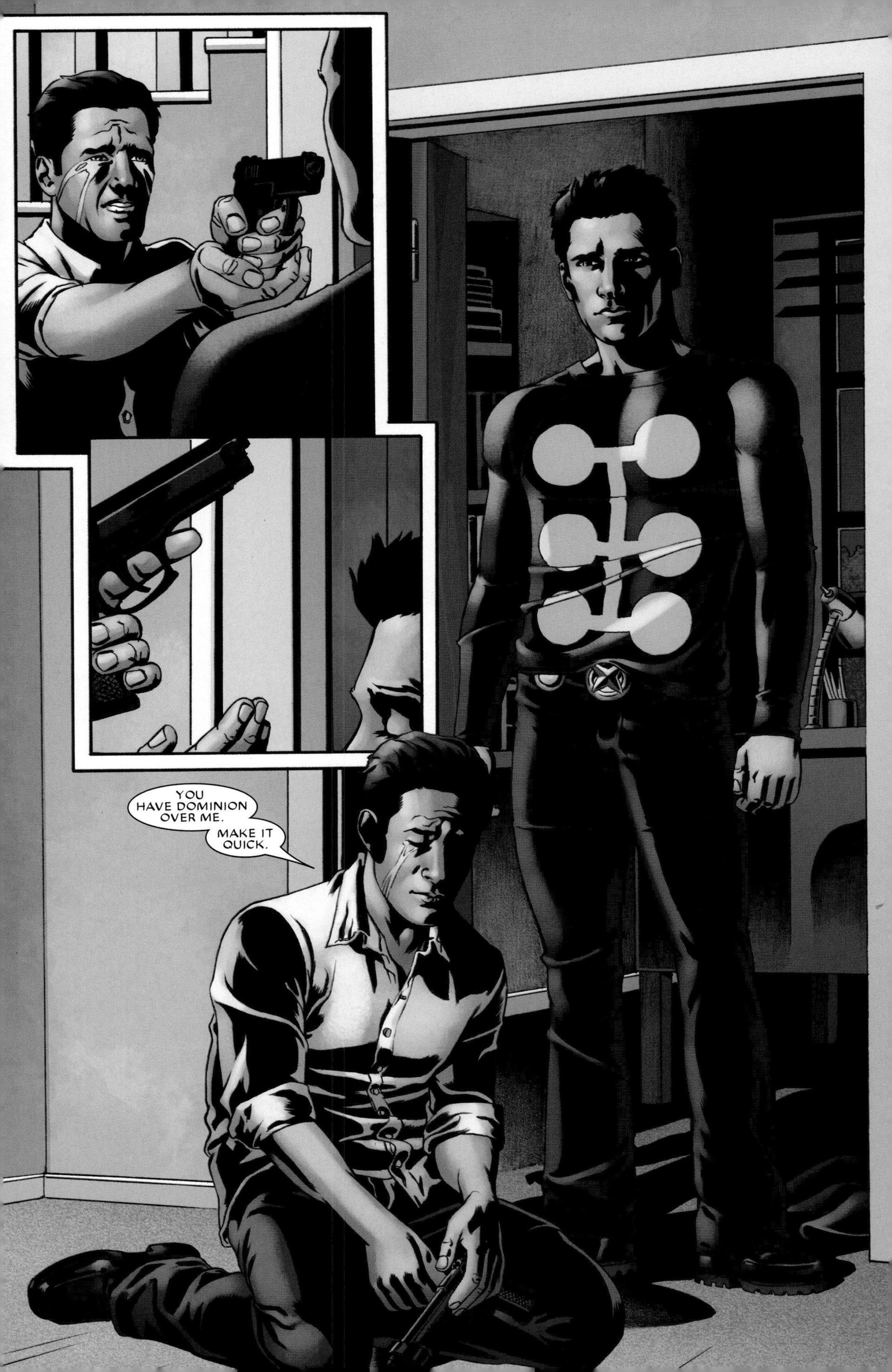
YOU HAVE DOMINION OVER ME.
MAKE IT QUICK.

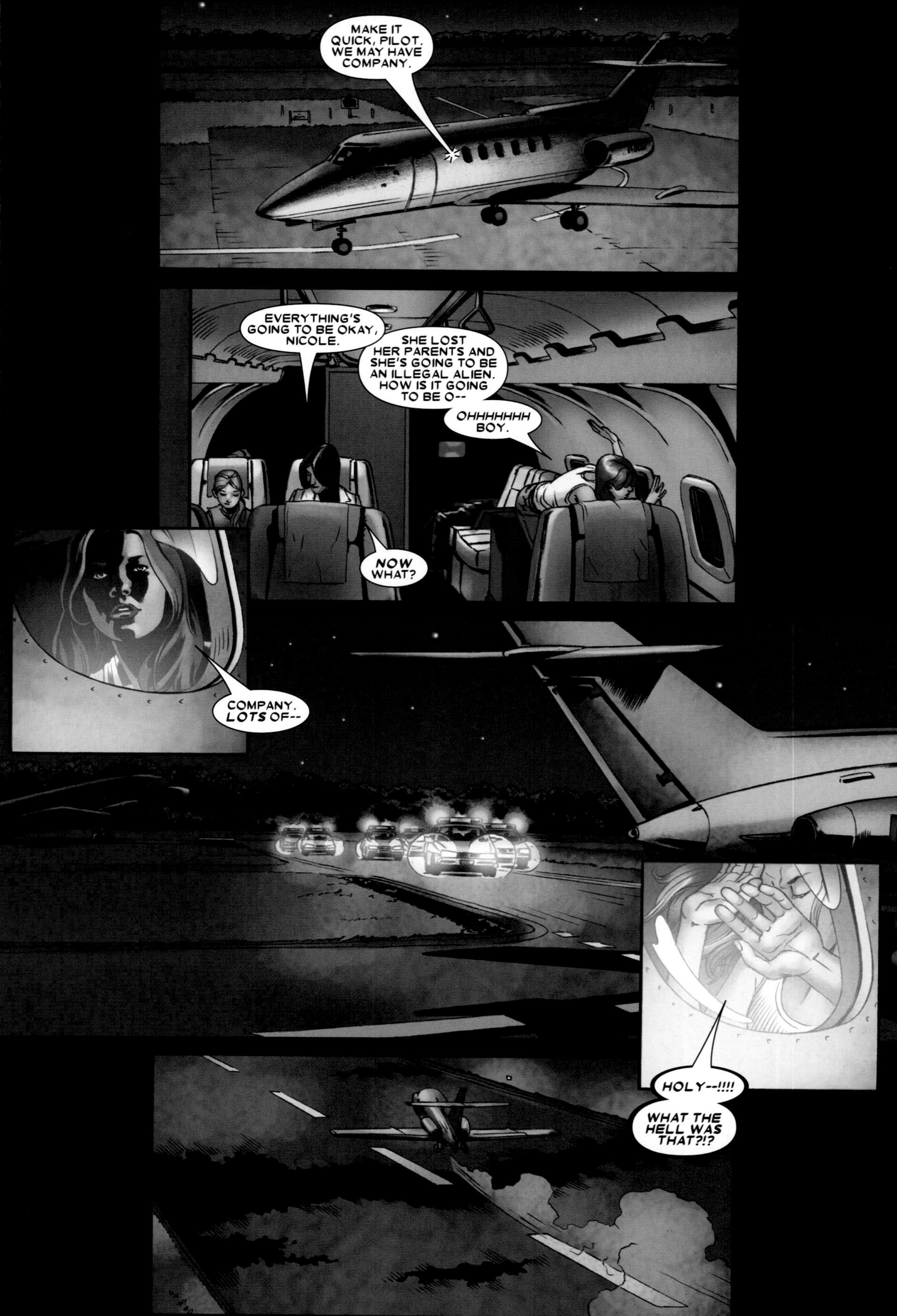
MAKE IT QUICK, PILOT. WE MAY HAVE COMPANY.
EVERYTHING'S GOING TO BE OKAY, NICOLE.
SHE LOST HER PARENTS AND SHE'S GOING TO BE AN ILLEGAL ALIEN. HOW IS IT GOING TO BE O--
OHHHHHHH BOY.
NOW WHAT?
COMPANY. LOTS OF--
HOLY--!!!!
WHAT THE HELL WAS THAT?!?

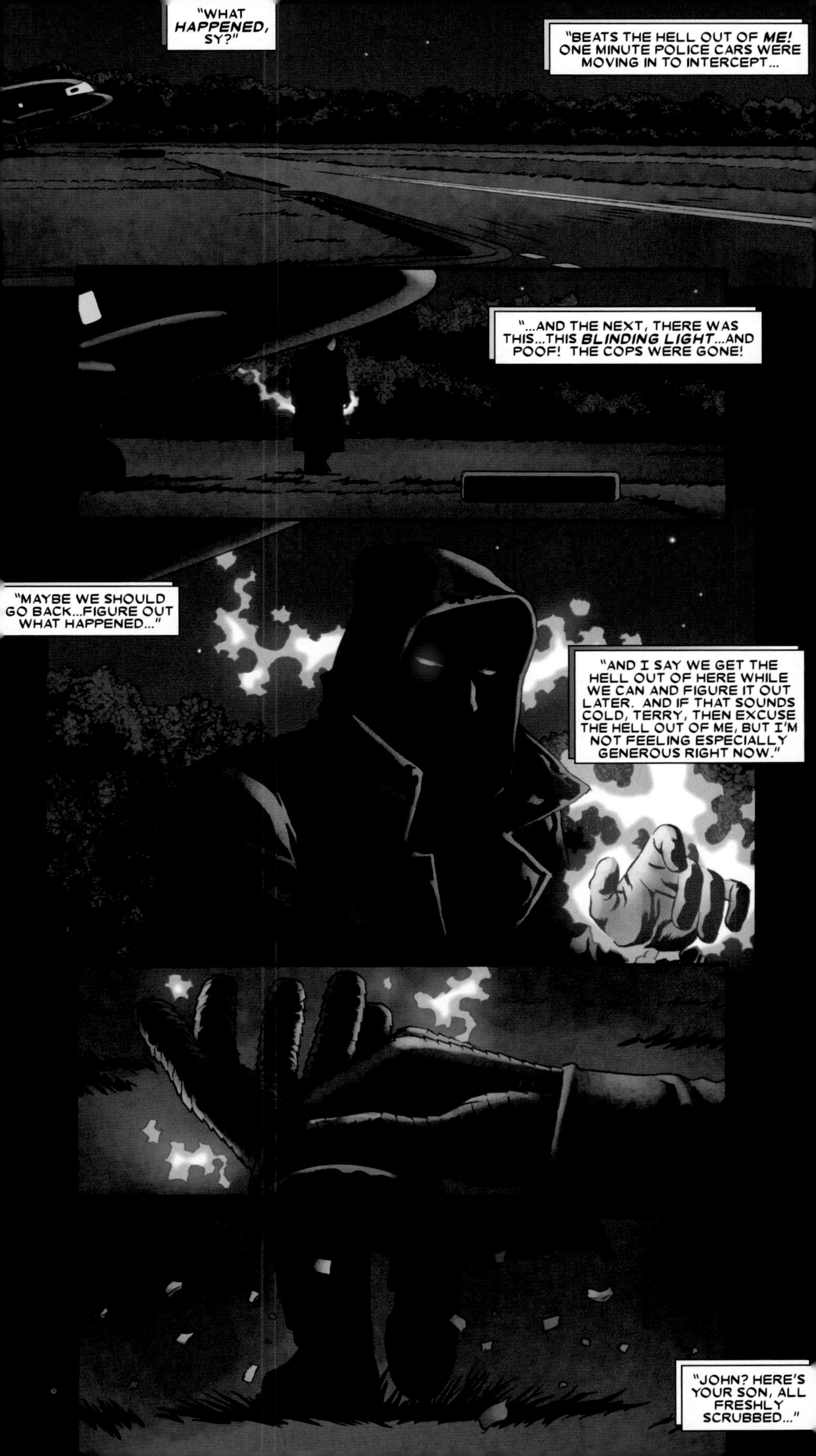
"WHAT *HAPPENED,* SY?"
"BEATS THE HELL OUT OF *ME!* ONE MINUTE POLICE CARS WERE MOVING IN TO INTERCEPT...
"...AND THE NEXT, THERE WAS THIS...THIS *BLINDING LIGHT*...AND POOF! THE COPS WERE GONE!
"MAYBE WE SHOULD GO BACK...FIGURE OUT WHAT HAPPENED..."
"AND I SAY WE GET THE HELL OUT OF HERE WHILE WE CAN AND FIGURE IT OUT LATER. AND IF THAT SOUNDS COLD, TERRY, THEN EXCUSE THE HELL OUT OF ME, BUT I'M NOT FEELING ESPECIALLY GENEROUS RIGHT NOW."
"JOHN? HERE'S YOUR SON, ALL FRESHLY SCRUBBED..."

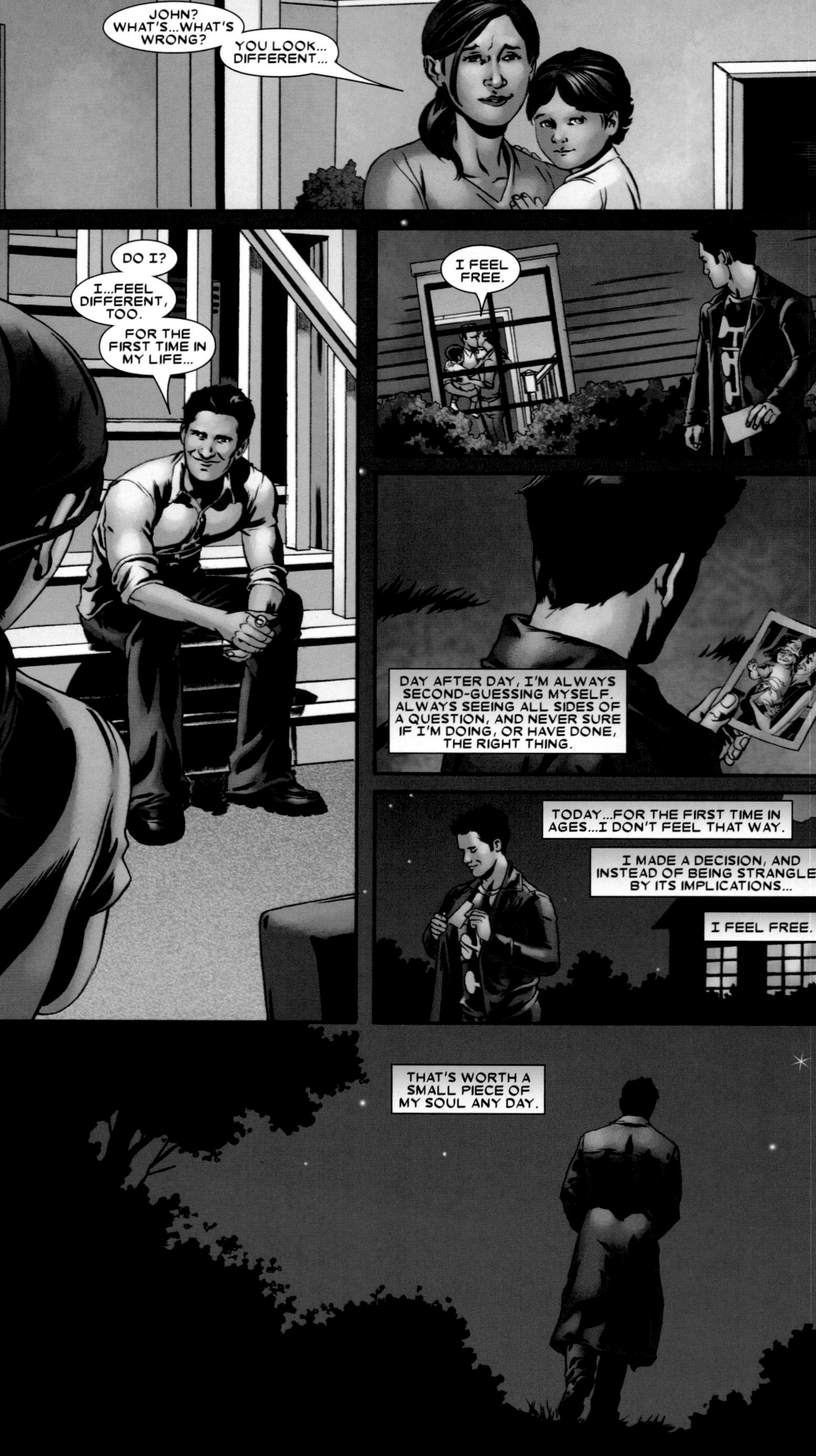
JOHN? WHAT'S...WHAT'S WRONG?
YOU LOOK... DIFFERENT...
DO I?
I...FEEL DIFFERENT, TOO.
FOR THE FIRST TIME IN MY LIFE...
I FEEL FREE.
DAY AFTER DAY, I'M ALWAYS SECOND-GUESSING MYSELF. ALWAYS SEEING ALL SIDES OF A QUESTION, AND NEVER SURE IF I'M DOING, OR HAVE DONE, THE RIGHT THING.
TODAY...FOR THE FIRST TIME IN AGES...I DON'T FEEL THAT WAY.
I MADE A DECISION, AND INSTEAD OF BEING STRANGLE BY ITS IMPLICATIONS...
I FEEL FREE.
THAT'S WORTH A SMALL PIECE OF MY SOUL ANY DAY.

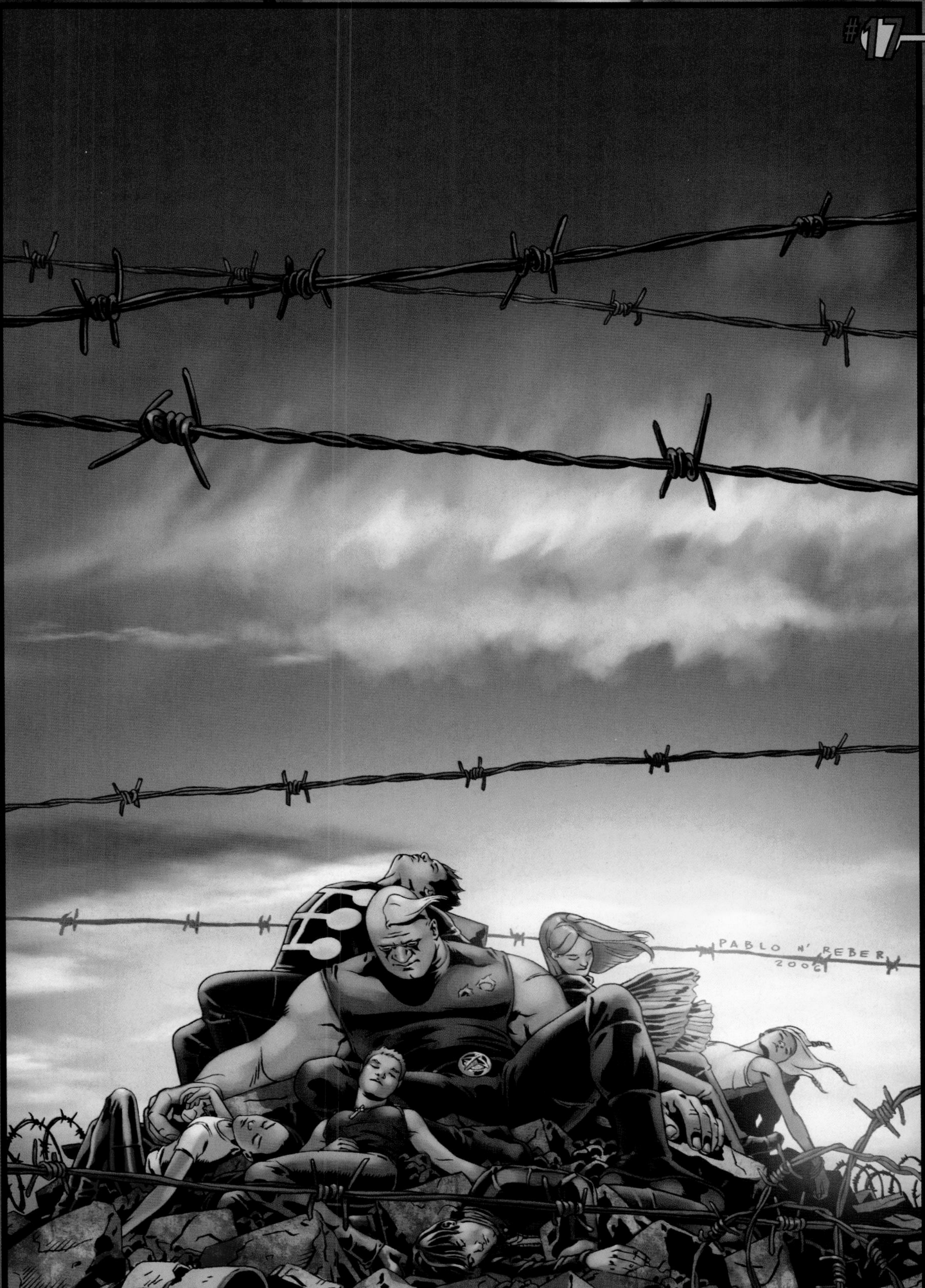
#17
PABLO N' REBER
2006

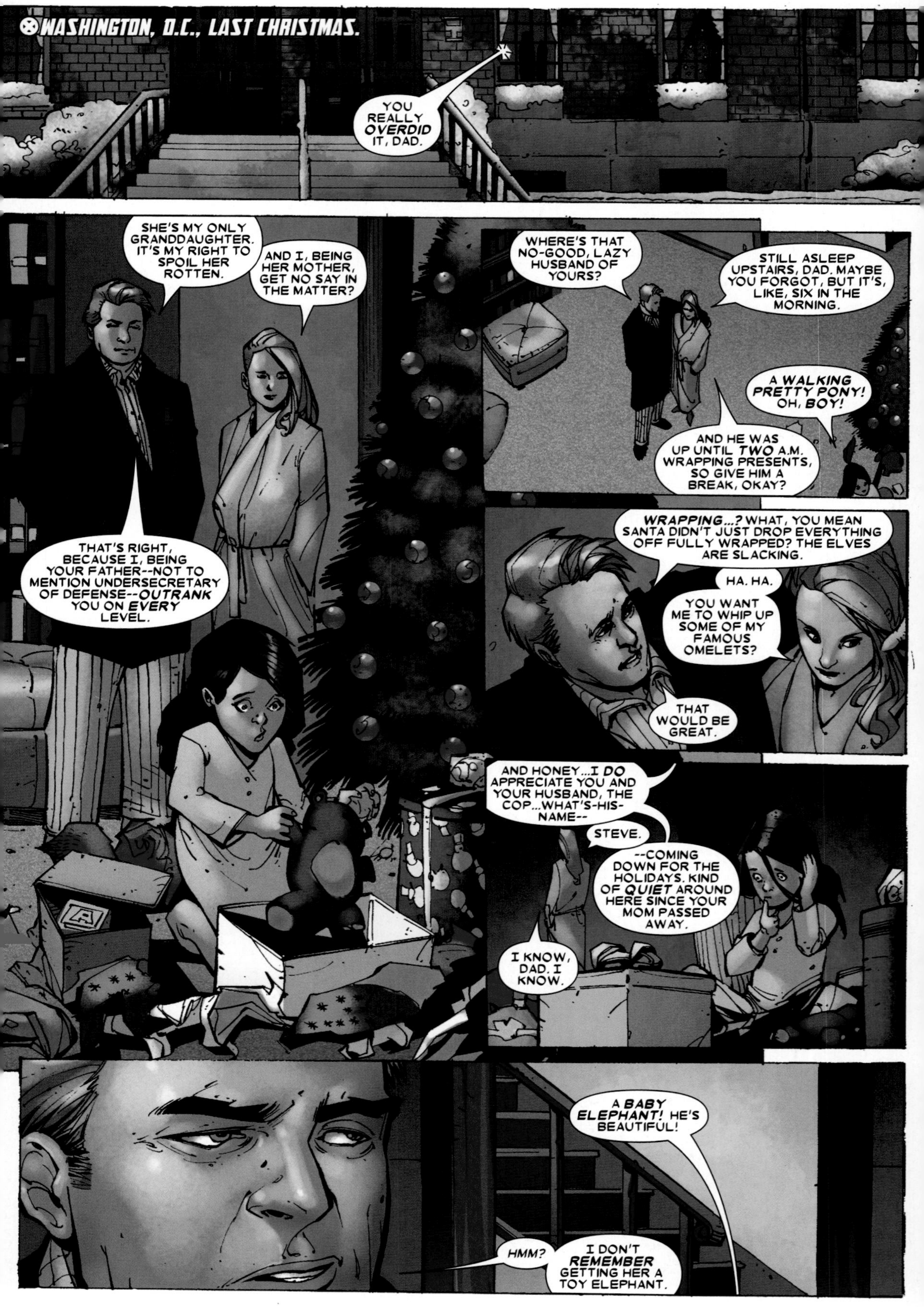
WASHINGTON, D.C., LAST CHRISTMAS.
YOU REALLY *OVERDID* IT, DAD.
SHE'S MY ONLY GRANDDAUGHTER. IT'S MY RIGHT TO SPOIL HER ROTTEN.
AND I, BEING HER MOTHER, GET NO SAY IN THE MATTER?
THAT'S RIGHT, BECAUSE I, BEING YOUR FATHER--NOT TO MENTION UNDERSECRETARY OF DEFENSE--*OUTRANK* YOU ON *EVERY* LEVEL.
WHERE'S THAT NO-GOOD, LAZY HUSBAND OF YOURS?
STILL ASLEEP UPSTAIRS, DAD. MAYBE YOU FORGOT, BUT IT'S, LIKE, SIX IN THE MORNING.
A *WALKING PRETTY PONY!* OH, *BOY!*
AND HE WAS UP UNTIL *TWO* A.M. WRAPPING PRESENTS, SO GIVE HIM A BREAK, OKAY?
WRAPPING...? WHAT, YOU MEAN SANTA DIDN'T JUST DROP EVERYTHING OFF FULLY WRAPPED? THE ELVES ARE SLACKING.
HA. HA.
YOU WANT ME TO WHIP UP SOME OF MY FAMOUS OMELETS?
THAT WOULD BE GREAT.
AND HONEY...I *DO* APPRECIATE YOU AND YOUR HUSBAND, THE COP...WHAT'S-HIS-NAME--
STEVE.
--COMING DOWN FOR THE HOLIDAYS. KIND OF *QUIET* AROUND HERE SINCE YOUR MOM PASSED AWAY.
I KNOW, DAD. I KNOW.
A *BABY ELEPHANT!* HE'S BEAUTIFUL!
HMM?
I DON'T *REMEMBER* GETTING HER A TOY ELEPHANT.

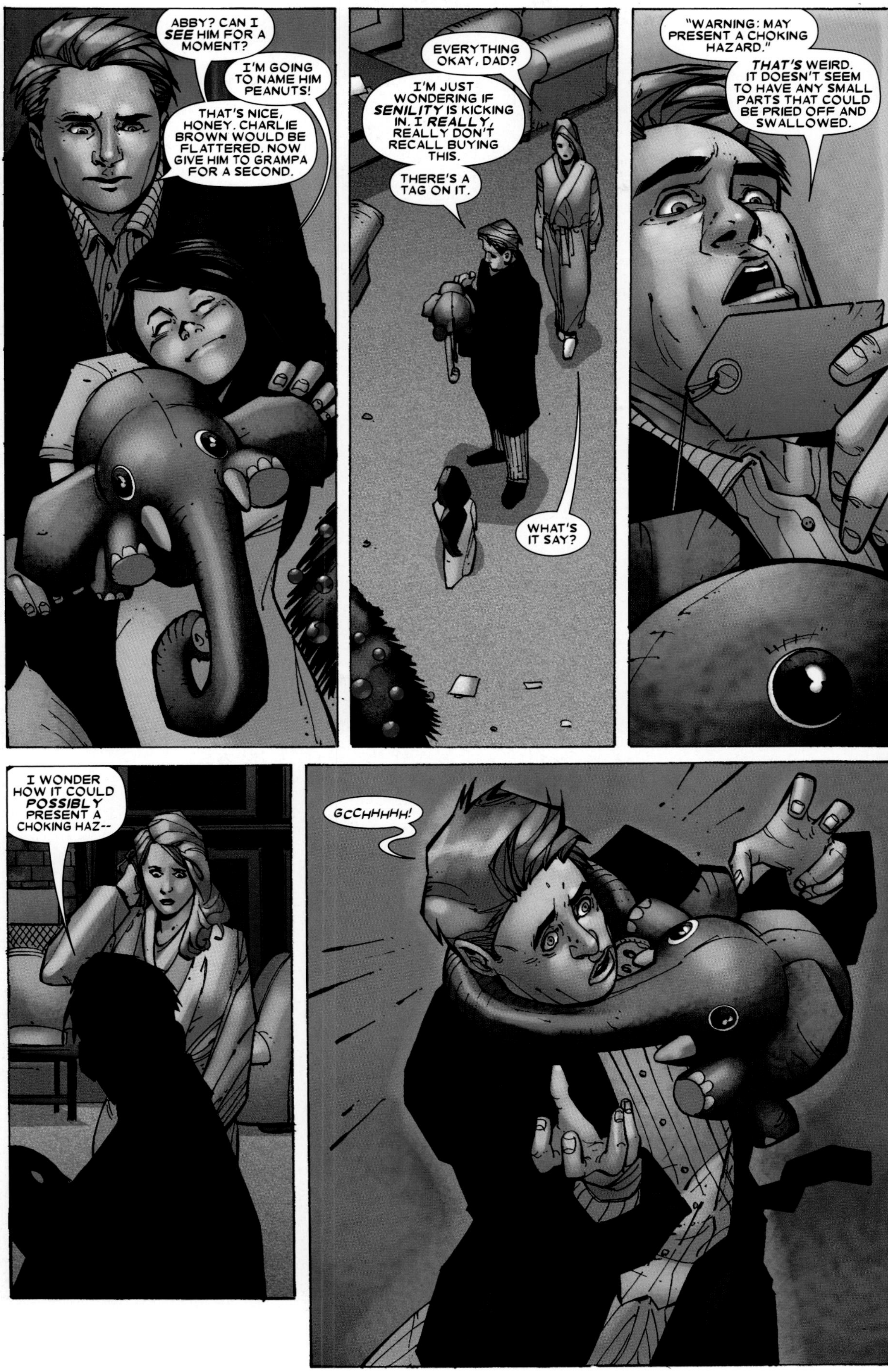
ABBY? CAN I SEE HIM FOR A MOMENT?
I'M GOING TO NAME HIM PEANUTS!
THAT'S NICE, HONEY. CHARLIE BROWN WOULD BE FLATTERED. NOW GIVE HIM TO GRAMPA FOR A SECOND.
EVERYTHING OKAY, DAD?
I'M JUST WONDERING IF SENILITY IS KICKING IN. I REALLY, REALLY DON'T RECALL BUYING THIS.
THERE'S A TAG ON IT.
WHAT'S IT SAY?
"WARNING: MAY PRESENT A CHOKING HAZARD."
THAT'S WEIRD. IT DOESN'T SEEM TO HAVE ANY SMALL PARTS THAT COULD BE PRIED OFF AND SWALLOWED.
I WONDER HOW IT COULD POSSIBLY PRESENT A CHOKING HAZ--
GCCHHHHH!

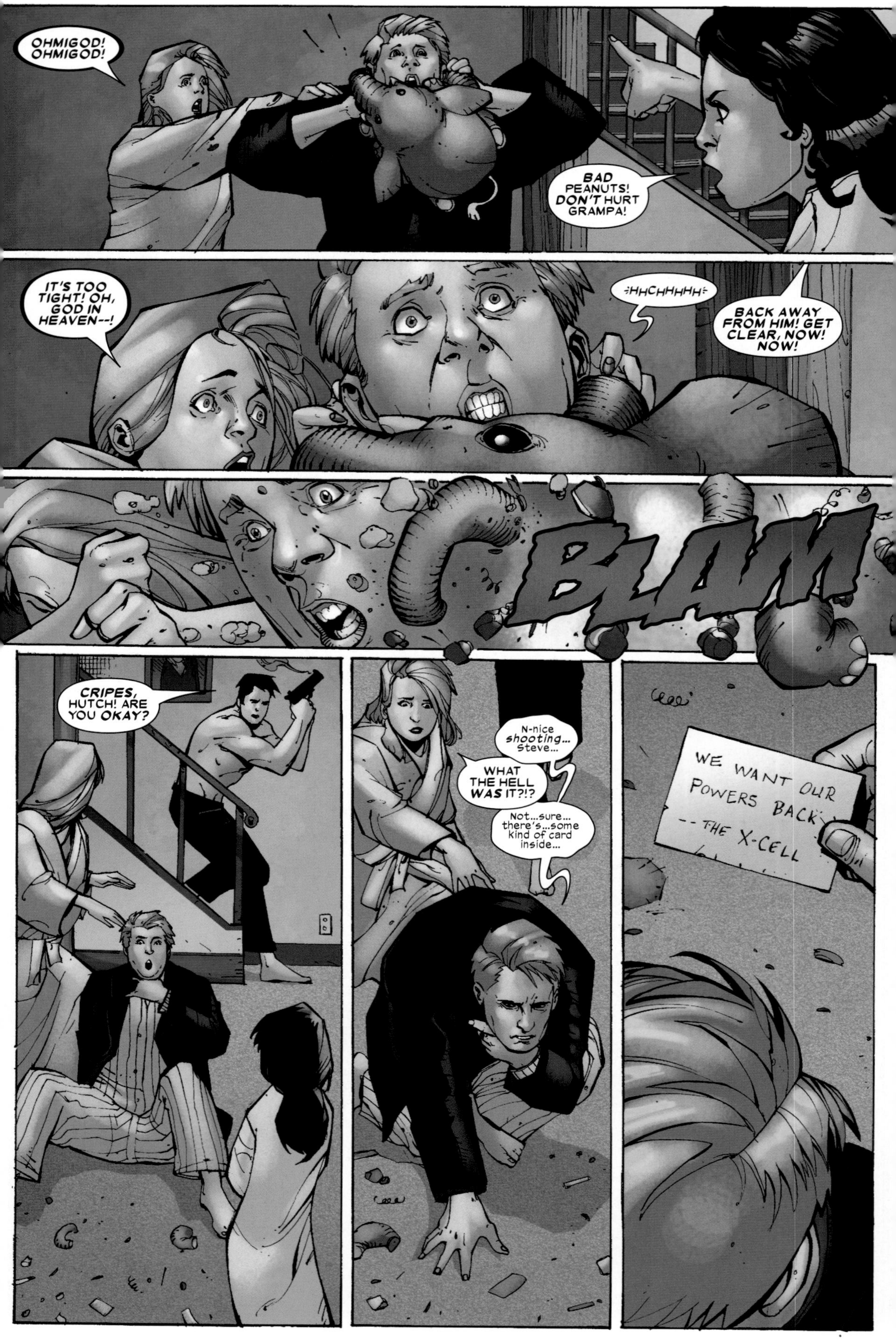
OHMIGOD! OHMIGOD!
BAD PEANUTS! DON'T HURT GRAMPA!
IT'S TOO TIGHT! OH, GOD IN HEAVEN--!
HHCHHHHH
BACK AWAY FROM HIM! GET CLEAR, NOW! NOW!
BLAM
CRIPES, HUTCH! ARE YOU OKAY?
N-nice shooting... Steve...
WHAT THE HELL WAS IT?!?
Not...sure... there's...some kind of card inside...
WE WANT OUR POWERS BACK
--THE X-CELL

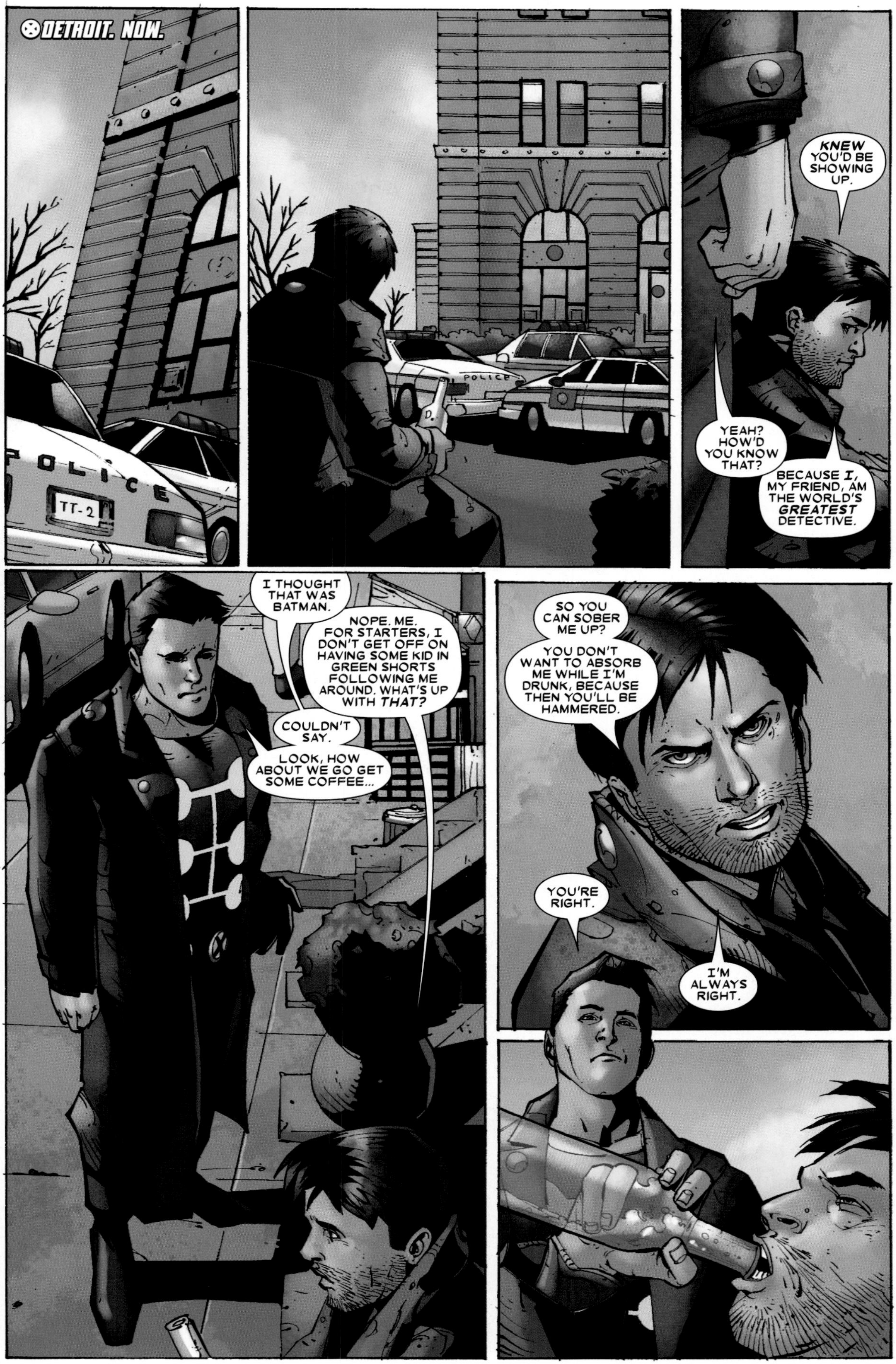
DETROIT. NOW.
KNEW YOU'D BE SHOWING UP.
YEAH? HOW'D YOU KNOW THAT?
BECAUSE I, MY FRIEND, AM THE WORLD'S GREATEST DETECTIVE.
I THOUGHT THAT WAS BATMAN.
NOPE. ME. FOR STARTERS, I DON'T GET OFF ON HAVING SOME KID IN GREEN SHORTS FOLLOWING ME AROUND. WHAT'S UP WITH THAT?
COULDN'T SAY.
LOOK, HOW ABOUT WE GO GET SOME COFFEE...
SO YOU CAN SOBER ME UP?
YOU DON'T WANT TO ABSORB ME WHILE I'M DRUNK, BECAUSE THEN YOU'LL BE HAMMERED.
YOU'RE RIGHT.
I'M ALWAYS RIGHT.

WANT SOME?

NO THANKS. BAD THINGS TEND TO HAPPEN WHEN I DRINK.

LIKE SLEEPING WITH SOMEONE, OR SOMEONES, YOU SHOULDN'T HAVE?

HOW DID YOU KNOW?

WHICH WORD WAS *UNCLEAR?* WORLD'S? GREATEST? OR DETECTIVE?

THAT'S WHAT YOU SENT ME OUT TO *BECOME,* AFTER ALL. AND I DID. CRAMMED A LIFETIME'S WORTH OF LEARNING INTO A FEW YEARS.

AND THEN YOU ABSORB ME AND GET ALL THE KNOWLEDGE. YOU BECOME, IN *REALITY,* THAT WHICH YOU'RE ONLY *PRETENDING* TO BE: A DETECTIVE.

THAT'S THE PLAN.

'CEPT HERE'S THE ONE THING YOU DIDN'T COUNT ON: THE KNOWLEDGE? *THIS* IS WHAT IT DOES TO YOU.

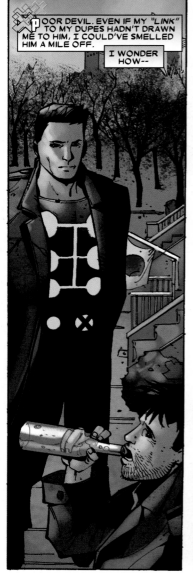

POOR DEVIL. EVEN IF MY *"LINK"* TO MY DUPES HADN'T DRAWN ME TO HIM, I COULD'VE SMELLED HIM A MILE OFF.

I WONDER HOW--

YOU'RE WONDERING HOW MASTERING THE ELEGANT ART OF INVESTIGATION COULD POSSIBLY REDUCE ME TO THIS, HUH?

THINK HARD. PUT IT TOGETHER.

I'LL WAIT.

IT'S NOT THE TECHNIQUES THEMSELVES. YOU *FOUND OUT* SOMETHING. SOMETHING SO UPSETTING THAT YOU'RE TRYING TO DRINK YOURSELF INTO OBLIVION.

THERE Y'GO.

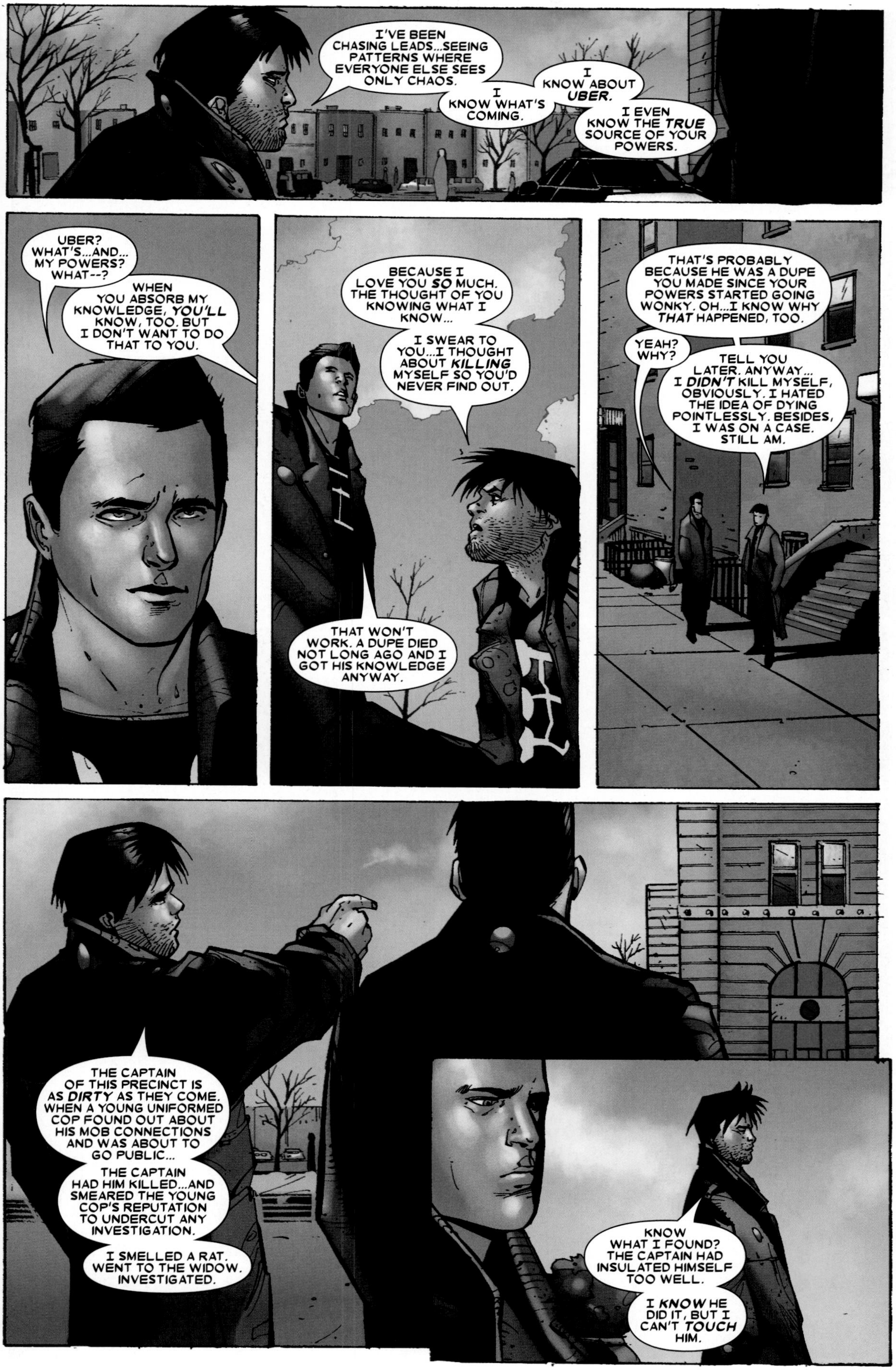
I'VE BEEN CHASING LEADS...SEEING PATTERNS WHERE EVERYONE ELSE SEES ONLY CHAOS.
I KNOW WHAT'S COMING.
I KNOW ABOUT UBER.
I EVEN KNOW THE TRUE SOURCE OF YOUR POWERS.
UBER? WHAT'S...AND... MY POWERS? WHAT--?
WHEN YOU ABSORB MY KNOWLEDGE, YOU'LL KNOW, TOO. BUT I DON'T WANT TO DO THAT TO YOU.
BECAUSE I LOVE YOU SO MUCH. THE THOUGHT OF YOU KNOWING WHAT I KNOW...
I SWEAR TO YOU...I THOUGHT ABOUT KILLING MYSELF SO YOU'D NEVER FIND OUT.
THAT WON'T WORK. A DUPE DIED NOT LONG AGO AND I GOT HIS KNOWLEDGE ANYWAY.
THAT'S PROBABLY BECAUSE HE WAS A DUPE YOU MADE SINCE YOUR POWERS STARTED GOING WONKY. OH...I KNOW WHY THAT HAPPENED, TOO.
YEAH? WHY?
TELL YOU LATER. ANYWAY... I DIDN'T KILL MYSELF, OBVIOUSLY. I HATED THE IDEA OF DYING POINTLESSLY. BESIDES, I WAS ON A CASE. STILL AM.
THE CAPTAIN OF THIS PRECINCT IS AS DIRTY AS THEY COME. WHEN A YOUNG UNIFORMED COP FOUND OUT ABOUT HIS MOB CONNECTIONS AND WAS ABOUT TO GO PUBLIC...
THE CAPTAIN HAD HIM KILLED...AND SMEARED THE YOUNG COP'S REPUTATION TO UNDERCUT ANY INVESTIGATION.
I SMELLED A RAT. WENT TO THE WIDOW. INVESTIGATED.
KNOW WHAT I FOUND? THE CAPTAIN HAD INSULATED HIMSELF TOO WELL.
I KNOW HE DID IT, BUT I CAN'T TOUCH HIM.

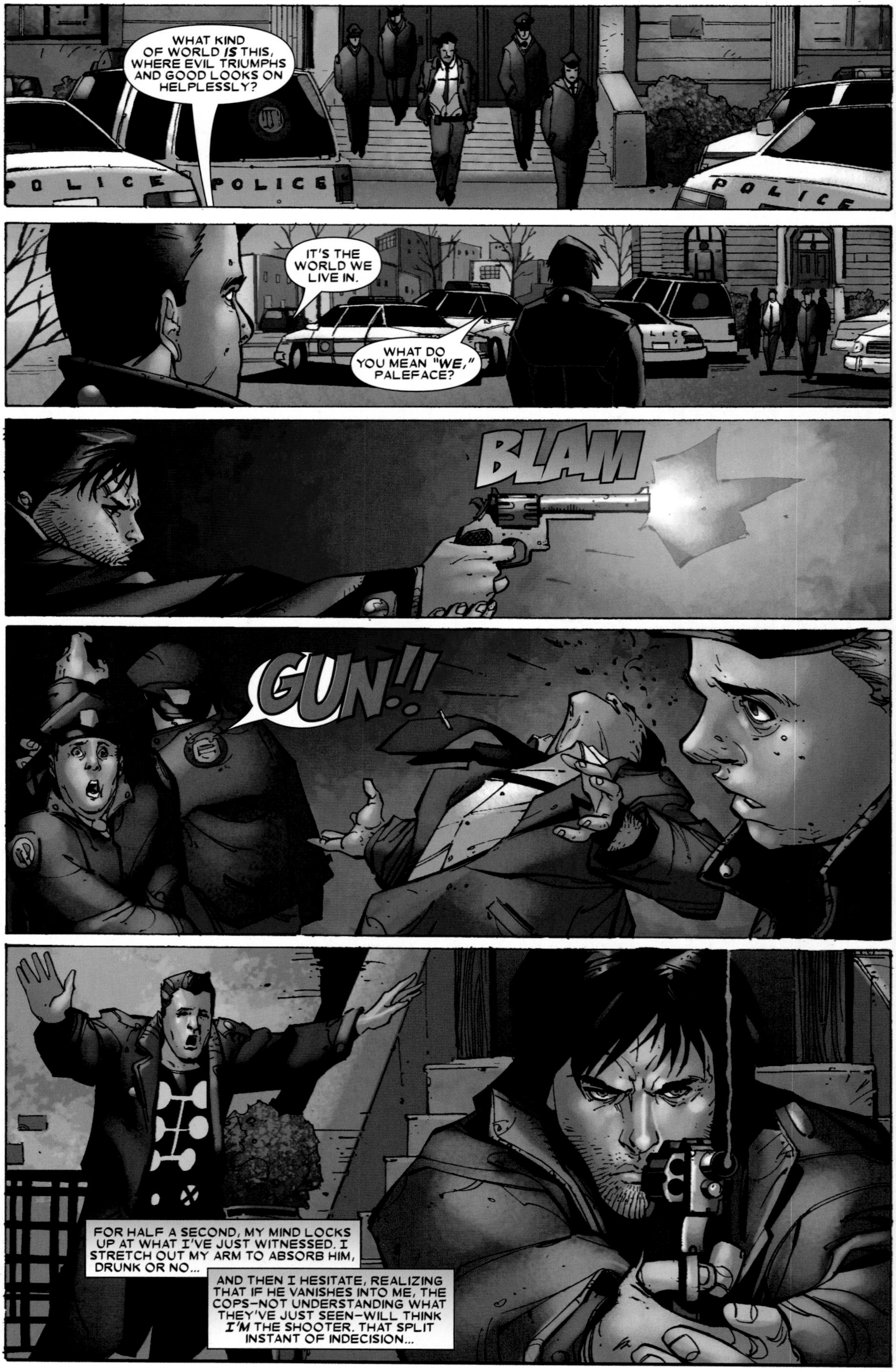
WHAT KIND OF WORLD *IS* THIS, WHERE EVIL TRIUMPHS AND GOOD LOOKS ON HELPLESSLY?
POLICE
POLICE
POLICE
IT'S THE WORLD WE LIVE IN.
WHAT DO YOU MEAN "*WE*," PALEFACE?
BLAM
GUN!!
FOR HALF A SECOND, MY MIND LOCKS UP AT WHAT I'VE JUST WITNESSED. I STRETCH OUT MY ARM TO ABSORB HIM, DRUNK OR NO...
AND THEN I HESITATE, REALIZING THAT IF HE VANISHES INTO ME, THE COPS—NOT UNDERSTANDING WHAT THEY'VE JUST SEEN—WILL THINK *I'M* THE SHOOTER. THAT SPLIT INSTANT OF INDECISION...

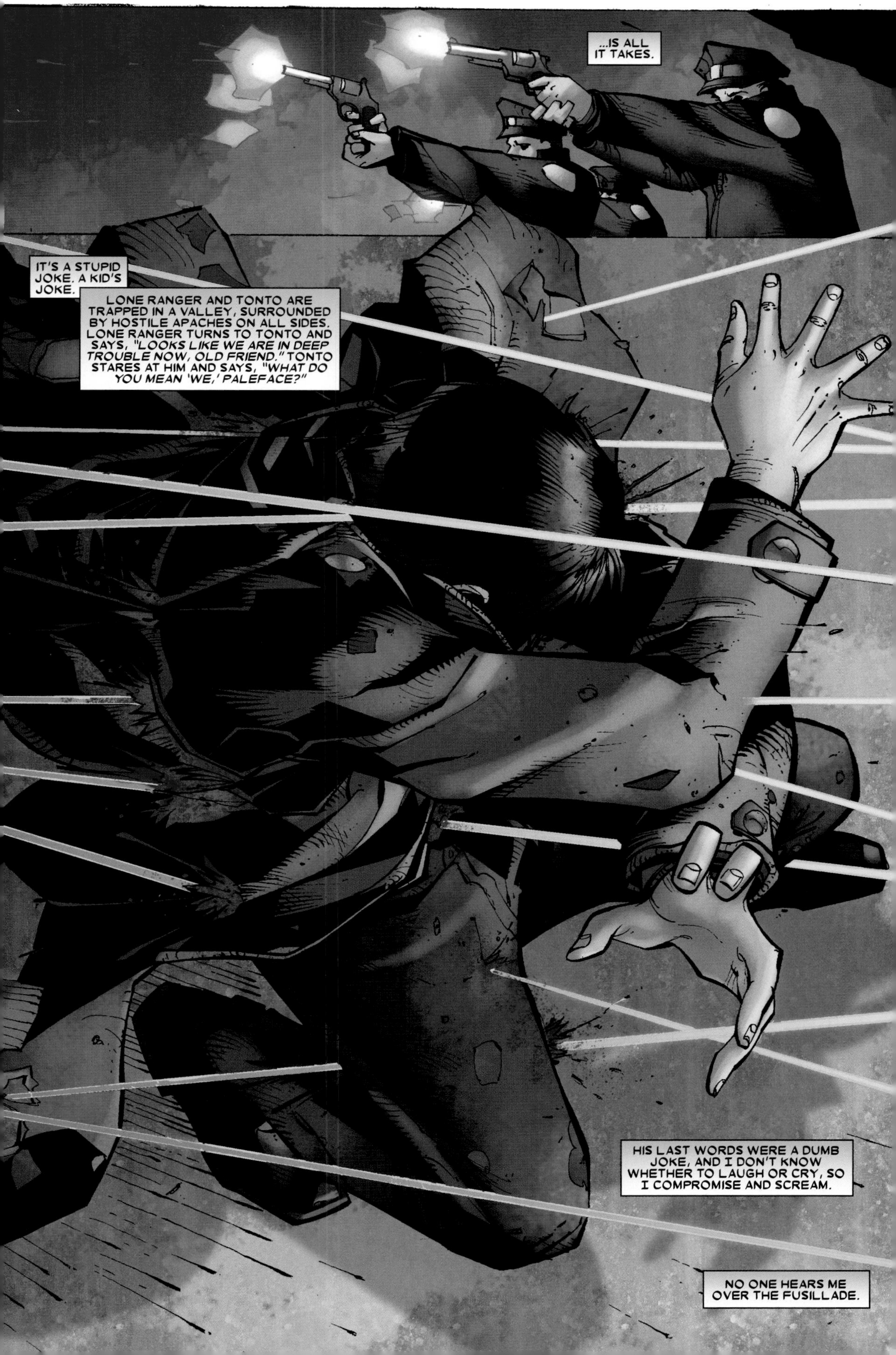
...IS ALL IT TAKES.
IT'S A STUPID JOKE. A KID'S JOKE.
LONE RANGER AND TONTO ARE TRAPPED IN A VALLEY, SURROUNDED BY HOSTILE APACHES ON ALL SIDES. LONE RANGER TURNS TO TONTO AND SAYS, "LOOKS LIKE WE ARE IN DEEP TROUBLE NOW, OLD FRIEND." TONTO STARES AT HIM AND SAYS, "WHAT DO YOU MEAN 'WE,' PALEFACE?"
HIS LAST WORDS WERE A DUMB JOKE, AND I DON'T KNOW WHETHER TO LAUGH OR CRY, SO I COMPROMISE AND SCREAM.
NO ONE HEARS ME OVER THE FUSILLADE.

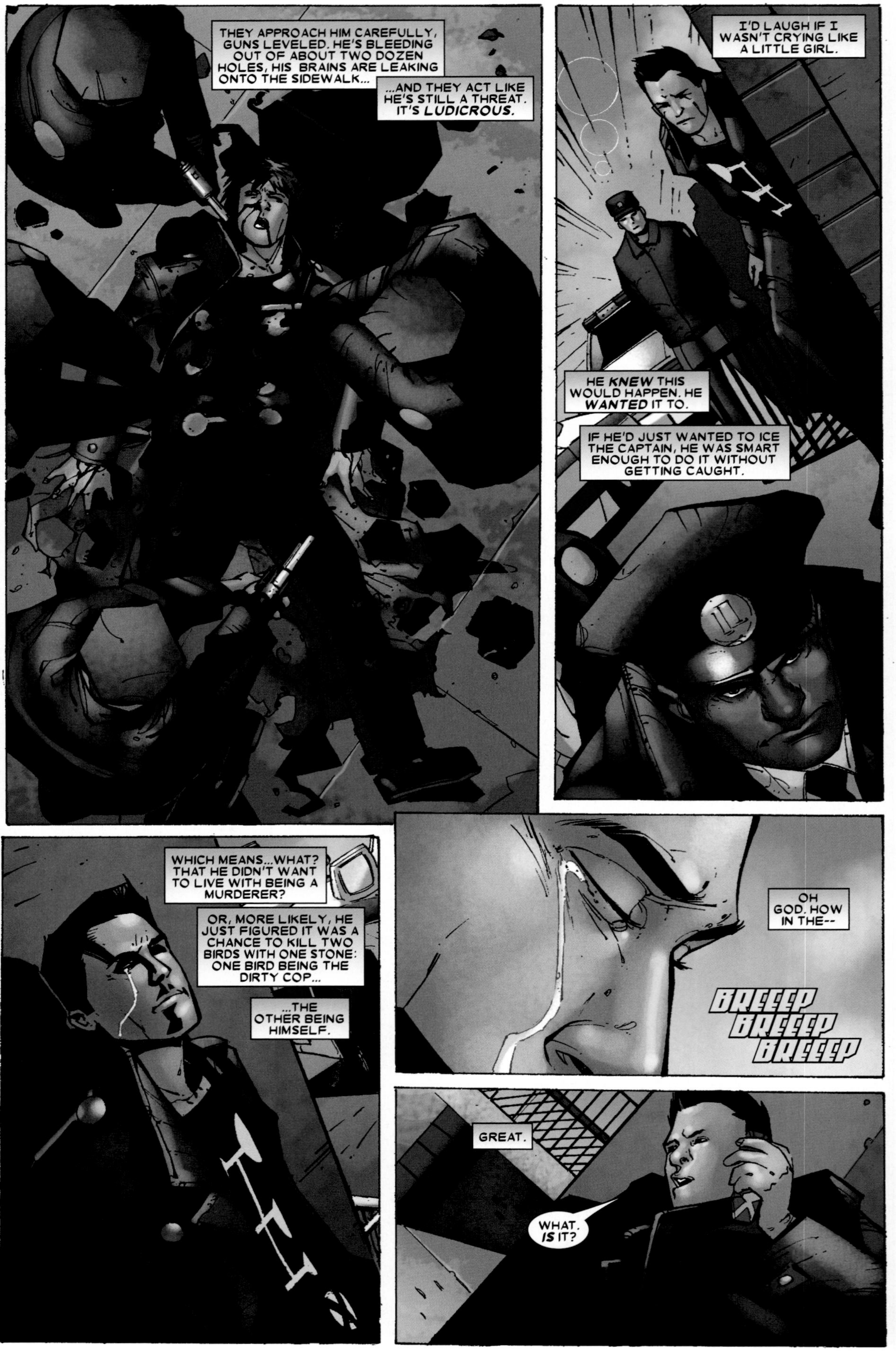
THEY APPROACH HIM CAREFULLY, GUNS LEVELED. HE'S BLEEDING OUT OF ABOUT TWO DOZEN HOLES, HIS BRAINS ARE LEAKING ONTO THE SIDEWALK...
...AND THEY ACT LIKE HE'S STILL A THREAT. IT'S *LUDICROUS.*
I'D LAUGH IF I WASN'T CRYING LIKE A LITTLE GIRL.
HE *KNEW* THIS WOULD HAPPEN. HE *WANTED* IT TO.
IF HE'D JUST WANTED TO ICE THE CAPTAIN, HE WAS SMART ENOUGH TO DO IT WITHOUT GETTING CAUGHT.
WHICH MEANS...WHAT? THAT HE DIDN'T WANT TO LIVE WITH BEING A MURDERER?
OR, MORE LIKELY, HE JUST FIGURED IT WAS A CHANCE TO KILL TWO BIRDS WITH ONE STONE: ONE BIRD BEING THE DIRTY COP...
...THE OTHER BEING HIMSELF.
OH GOD. HOW IN THE--
BREEEP BREEEP BREEEP
GREAT.
WHAT. *IS* IT?

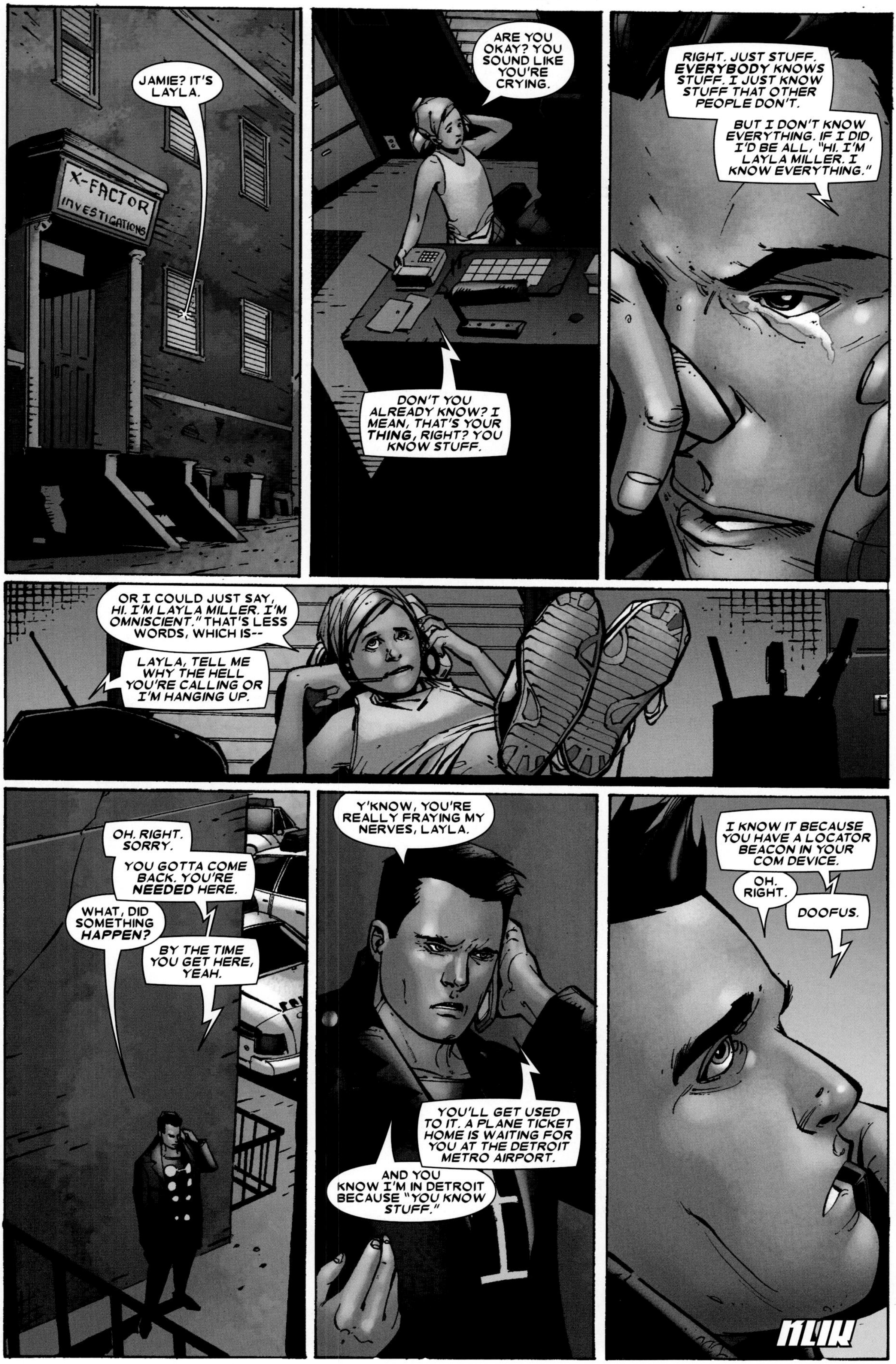
X-FACTOR
INVESTIGATIONS
JAMIE? IT'S LAYLA.
ARE YOU OKAY? YOU SOUND LIKE YOU'RE CRYING.
DON'T YOU ALREADY KNOW? I MEAN, THAT'S YOUR THING, RIGHT? YOU KNOW STUFF.
RIGHT. JUST STUFF. EVERYBODY KNOWS STUFF. I JUST KNOW STUFF THAT OTHER PEOPLE DON'T.
BUT I DON'T KNOW EVERYTHING. IF I DID, I'D BE ALL, "HI. I'M LAYLA MILLER. I KNOW EVERYTHING."
OR I COULD JUST SAY, HI. I'M LAYLA MILLER. I'M OMNISCIENT." THAT'S LESS WORDS, WHICH IS--
LAYLA, TELL ME WHY THE HELL YOU'RE CALLING OR I'M HANGING UP.
OH. RIGHT. SORRY.
YOU GOTTA COME BACK. YOU'RE NEEDED HERE.
WHAT, DID SOMETHING HAPPEN?
BY THE TIME YOU GET HERE, YEAH.
Y'KNOW, YOU'RE REALLY FRAYING MY NERVES, LAYLA.
YOU'LL GET USED TO IT. A PLANE TICKET HOME IS WAITING FOR YOU AT THE DETROIT METRO AIRPORT.
AND YOU KNOW I'M IN DETROIT BECAUSE "YOU KNOW STUFF."
I KNOW IT BECAUSE YOU HAVE A LOCATOR BEACON IN YOUR COM DEVICE.
OH. RIGHT.
DOOFUS.
KLIK

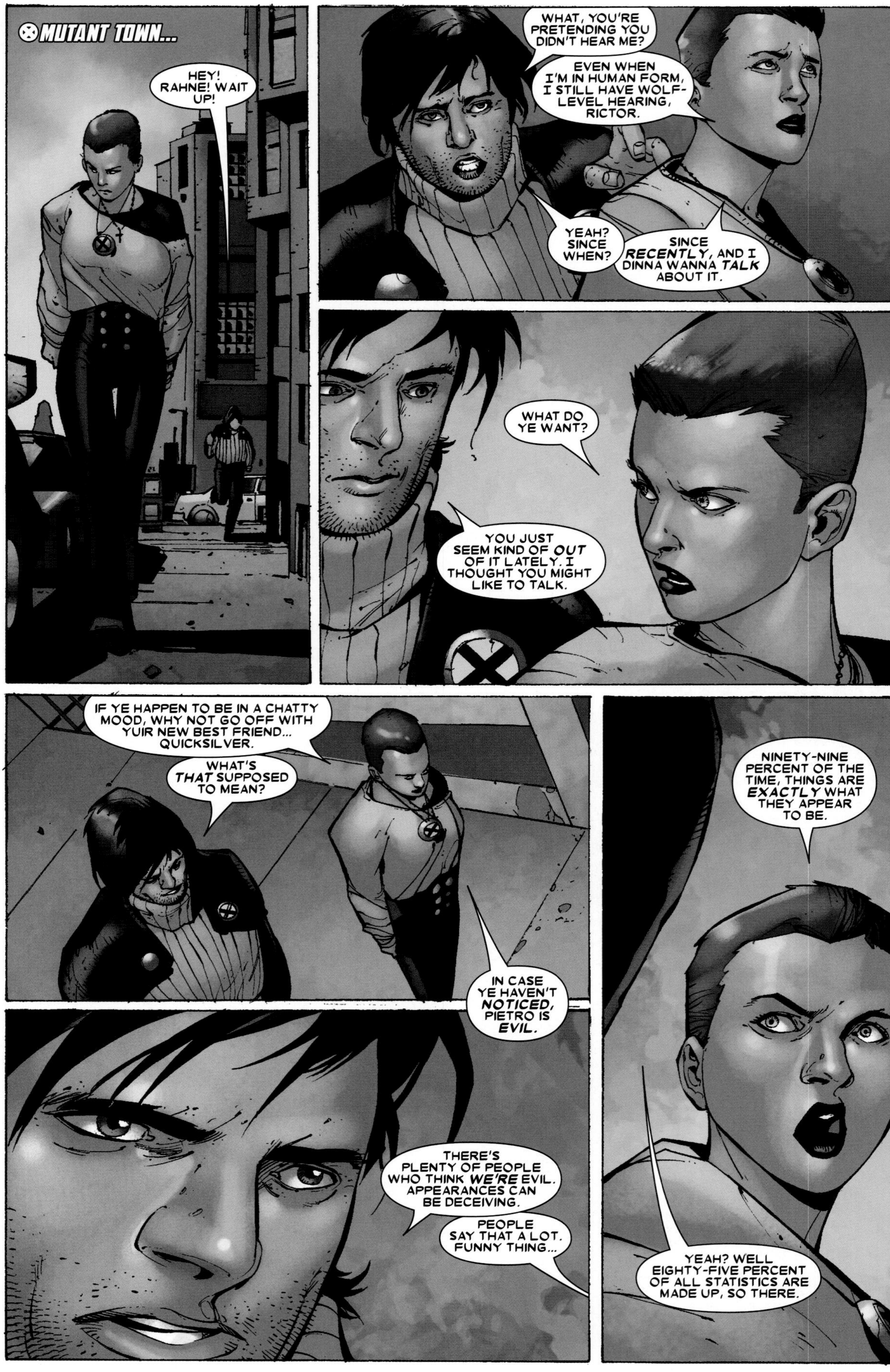
MUTANT TOWN...
HEY! RAHNE! WAIT UP!
WHAT, YOU'RE PRETENDING YOU DIDN'T HEAR ME?
EVEN WHEN I'M IN HUMAN FORM, I STILL HAVE WOLF-LEVEL HEARING, RICTOR.
YEAH? SINCE WHEN?
SINCE RECENTLY, AND I DINNA WANNA TALK ABOUT IT.
WHAT DO YE WANT?
YOU JUST SEEM KIND OF OUT OF IT LATELY. I THOUGHT YOU MIGHT LIKE TO TALK.
IF YE HAPPEN TO BE IN A CHATTY MOOD, WHY NOT GO OFF WITH YUIR NEW BEST FRIEND... QUICKSILVER.
WHAT'S THAT SUPPOSED TO MEAN?
IN CASE YE HAVEN'T NOTICED, PIETRO IS EVIL.
THERE'S PLENTY OF PEOPLE WHO THINK WE'RE EVIL. APPEARANCES CAN BE DECEIVING.
PEOPLE SAY THAT A LOT. FUNNY THING...
NINETY-NINE PERCENT OF THE TIME, THINGS ARE EXACTLY WHAT THEY APPEAR TO BE.
YEAH? WELL EIGHTY-FIVE PERCENT OF ALL STATISTICS ARE MADE UP, SO THERE.

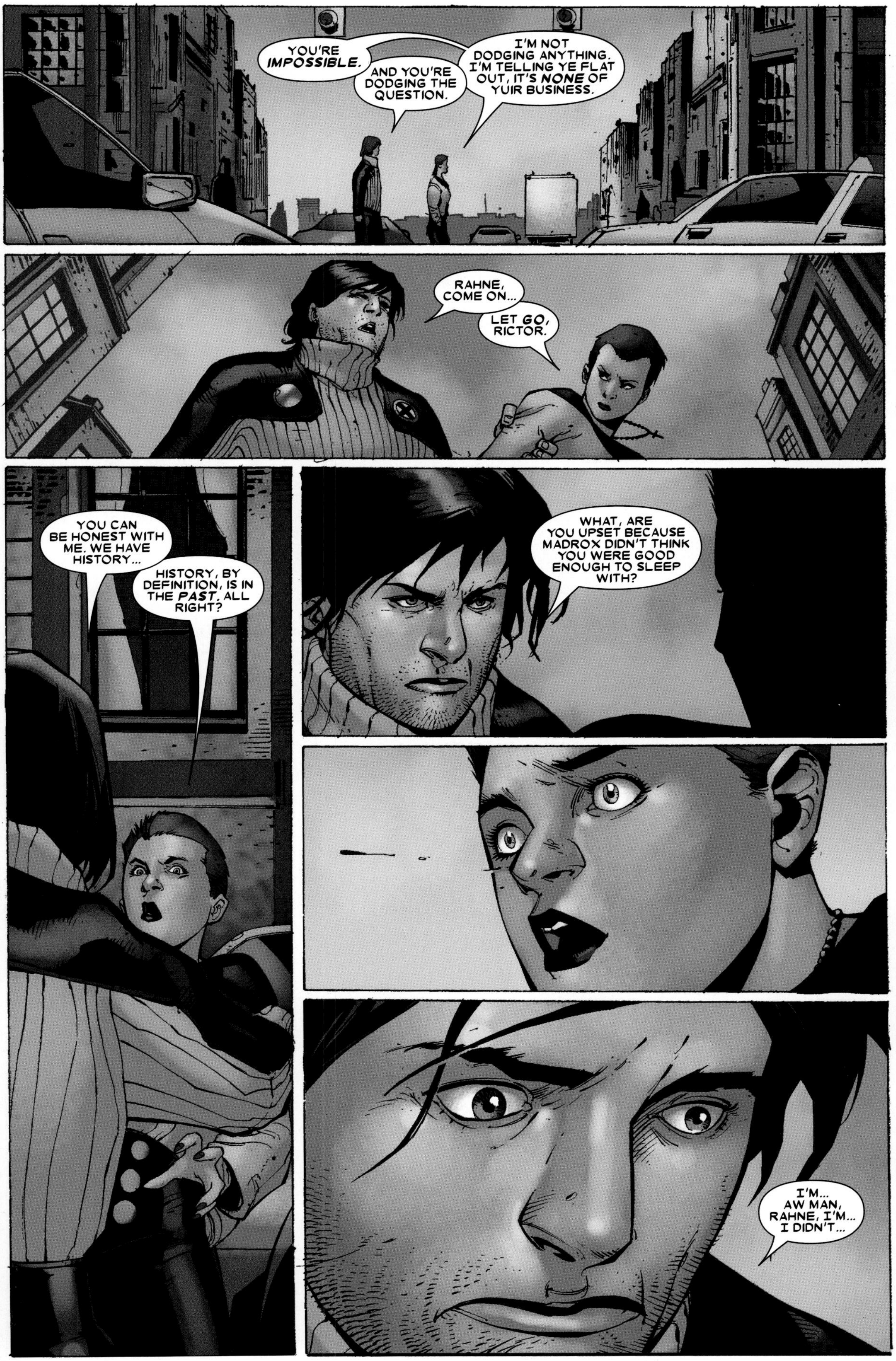
YOU'RE *IMPOSSIBLE.*
AND YOU'RE DODGING THE QUESTION.
I'M NOT DODGING ANYTHING. I'M TELLING YE FLAT OUT, IT'S *NONE* OF YUIR BUSINESS.
RAHNE, COME ON...
LET *GO*, RICTOR.
YOU CAN BE HONEST WITH ME. WE HAVE HISTORY...
HISTORY, BY DEFINITION, IS IN THE *PAST*. ALL RIGHT?
WHAT, ARE YOU UPSET BECAUSE MADROX DIDN'T THINK YOU WERE GOOD ENOUGH TO SLEEP WITH?
I'M... AW MAN, RAHNE, I'M... I DIDN'T...

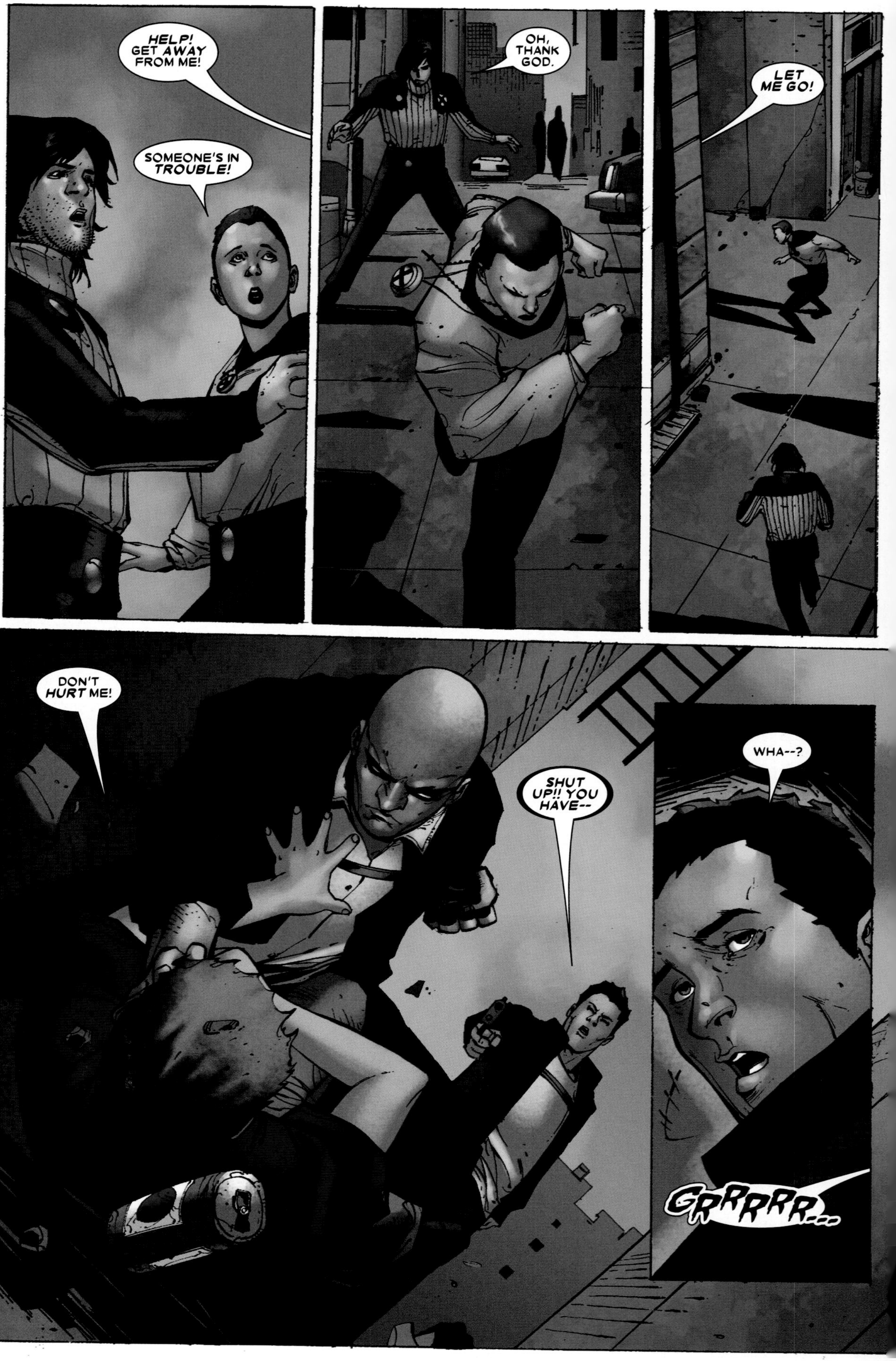
HELP! GET AWAY FROM ME!
SOMEONE'S IN TROUBLE!
OH, THANK GOD.
LET ME GO!
DON'T HURT ME!
SHUT UP!! YOU HAVE--
WHA--?
GRRRRR...

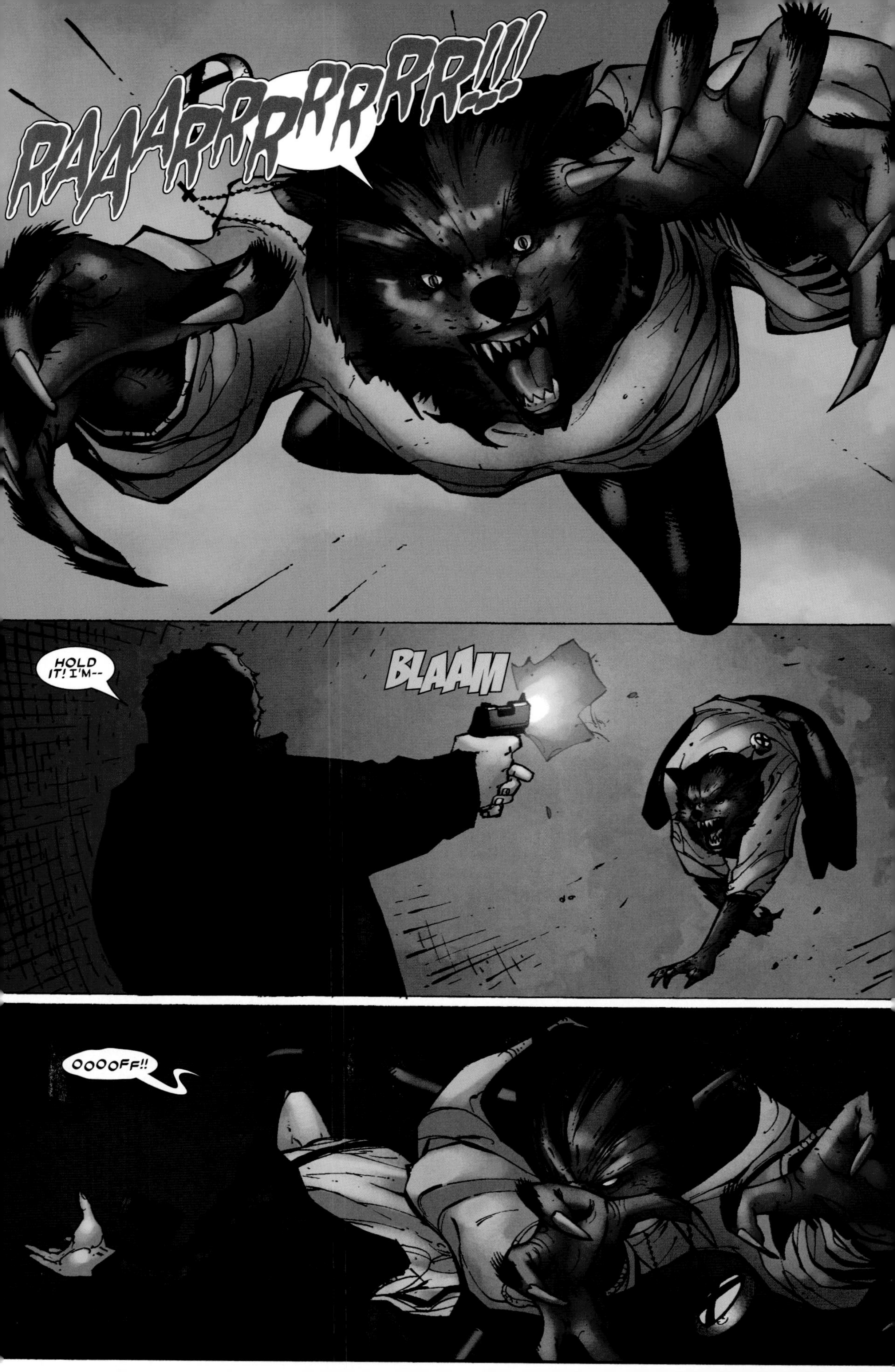
RAAARRRRRRRR!!!
HOLD IT! I'M--
BLAAM
OOOOFF!!

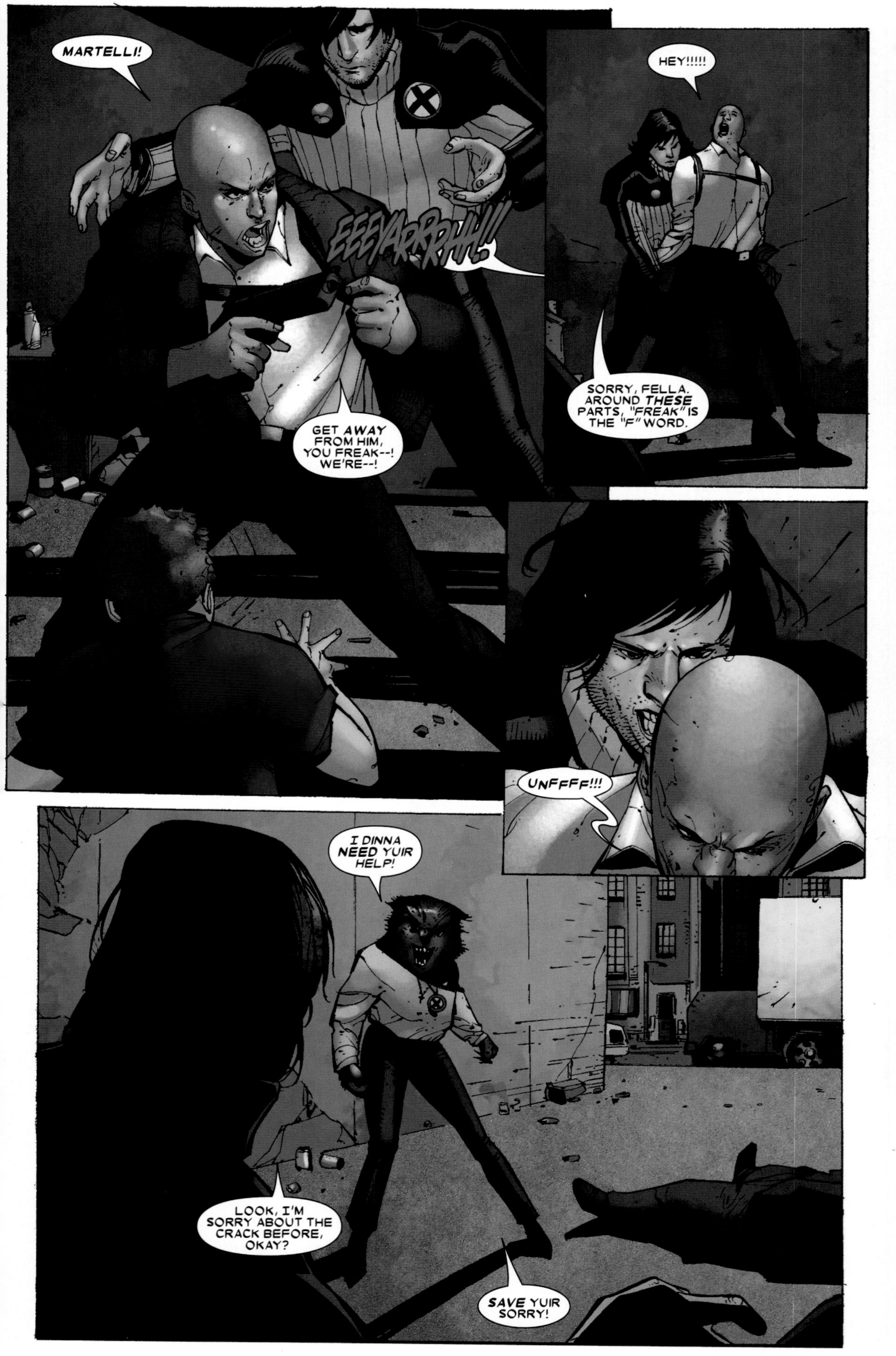

MARTELLI!
EEEYARRRHH!!
GET AWAY FROM HIM, YOU FREAK--! WE'RE--!
HEY!!!!!
SORRY, FELLA. AROUND THESE PARTS, "FREAK" IS THE "F" WORD.
UNFFFF!!!
I DINNA NEED YUIR HELP!
LOOK, I'M SORRY ABOUT THE CRACK BEFORE, OKAY?
SAVE YUIR SORRY!

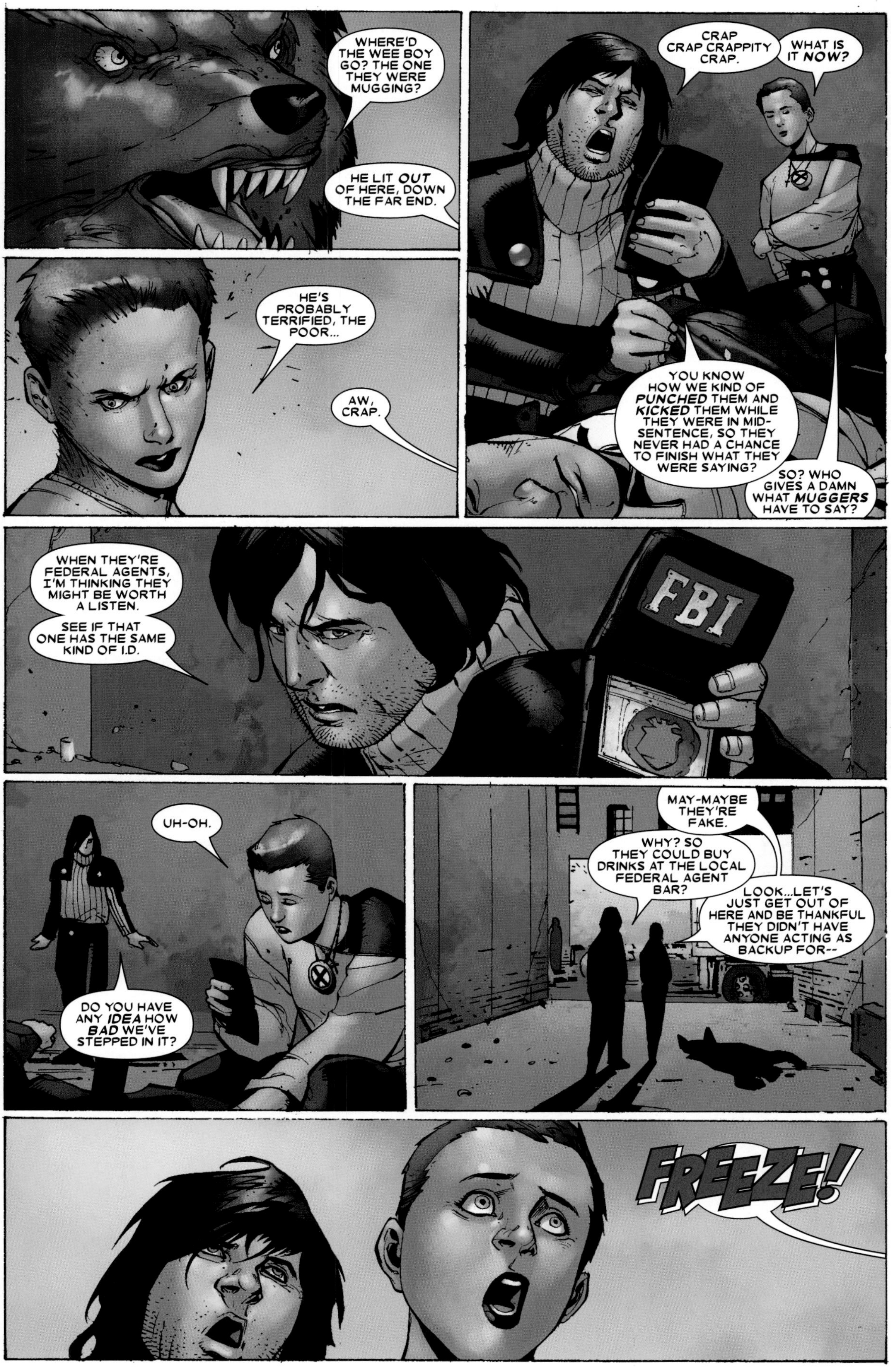
WHERE'D THE WEE BOY GO? THE ONE THEY WERE MUGGING?
HE LIT OUT OF HERE, DOWN THE FAR END.
CRAP CRAP CRAPPITY CRAP.
WHAT IS IT NOW?
HE'S PROBABLY TERRIFIED, THE POOR...
AW, CRAP.
YOU KNOW HOW WE KIND OF PUNCHED THEM AND KICKED THEM WHILE THEY WERE IN MID-SENTENCE, SO THEY NEVER HAD A CHANCE TO FINISH WHAT THEY WERE SAYING?
SO? WHO GIVES A DAMN WHAT MUGGERS HAVE TO SAY?
WHEN THEY'RE FEDERAL AGENTS, I'M THINKING THEY MIGHT BE WORTH A LISTEN.
SEE IF THAT ONE HAS THE SAME KIND OF I.D.
FBI
UH-OH.
DO YOU HAVE ANY IDEA HOW BAD WE'VE STEPPED IN IT?
MAY-MAYBE THEY'RE FAKE.
WHY? SO THEY COULD BUY DRINKS AT THE LOCAL FEDERAL AGENT BAR?
LOOK...LET'S JUST GET OUT OF HERE AND BE THANKFUL THEY DIDN'T HAVE ANYONE ACTING AS BACKUP FOR--
FREEZE!

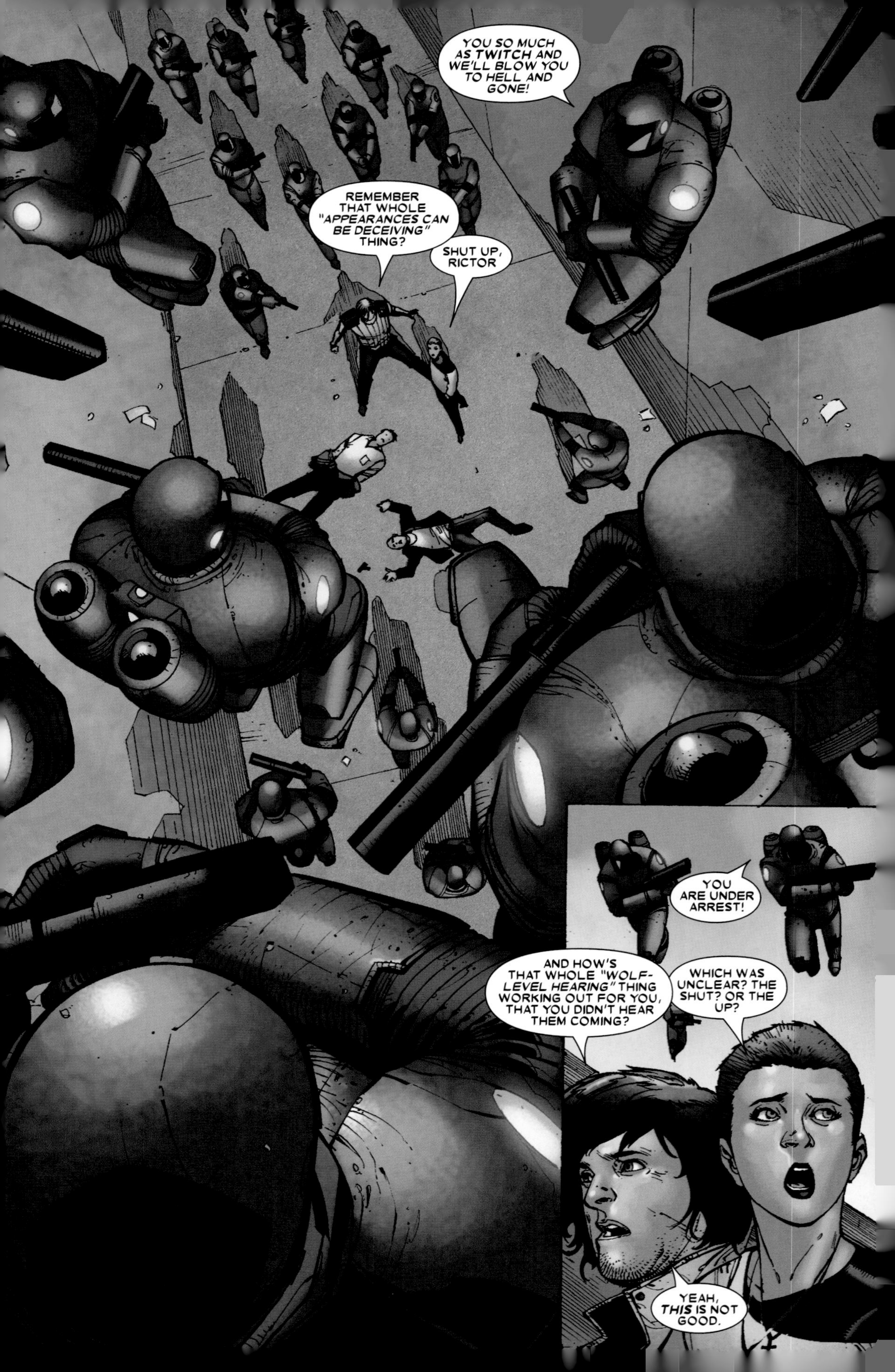
YOU SO MUCH AS TWITCH AND WE'LL BLOW YOU TO HELL AND GONE!
REMEMBER THAT WHOLE "APPEARANCES CAN BE DECEIVING" THING?
SHUT UP, RICTOR
YOU ARE UNDER ARREST!
AND HOW'S THAT WHOLE "WOLF-LEVEL HEARING" THING WORKING OUT FOR YOU, THAT YOU DIDN'T HEAR THEM COMING?
WHICH WAS UNCLEAR? THE SHUT? OR THE UP?
YEAH, THIS IS NOT GOOD.

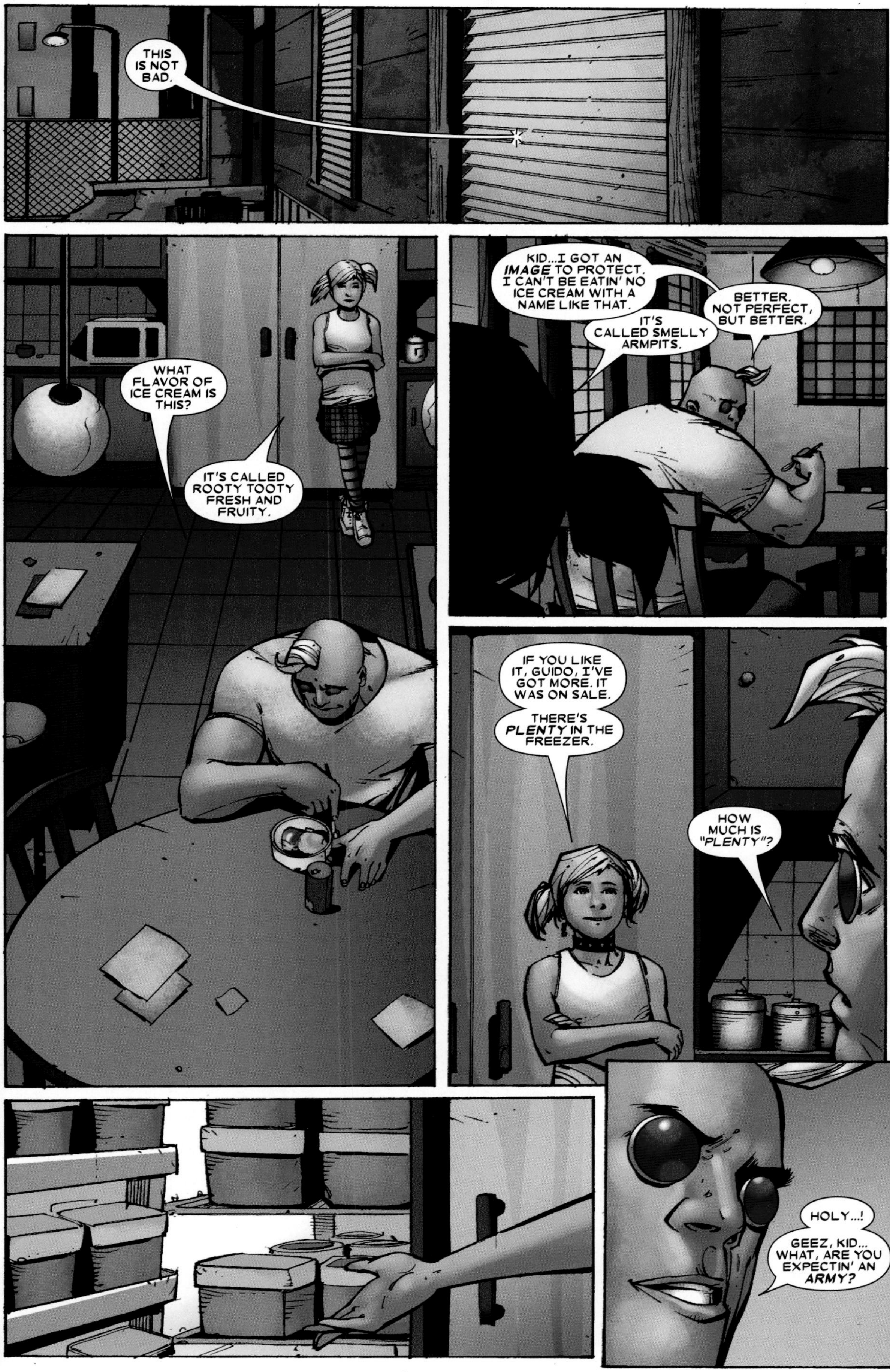
THIS IS NOT BAD.
WHAT FLAVOR OF ICE CREAM IS THIS?
IT'S CALLED ROOTY TOOTY FRESH AND FRUITY.
KID...I GOT AN *IMAGE* TO PROTECT. I CAN'T BE EATIN' NO ICE CREAM WITH A NAME LIKE THAT.
IT'S CALLED SMELLY ARMPITS.
BETTER. NOT PERFECT, BUT BETTER.
IF YOU LIKE IT, GUIDO, I'VE GOT MORE. IT WAS ON SALE.
THERE'S *PLENTY* IN THE FREEZER.
HOW MUCH IS "*PLENTY*"?
HOLY...!
GEEZ, KID... WHAT, ARE YOU EXPECTIN' AN *ARMY*?

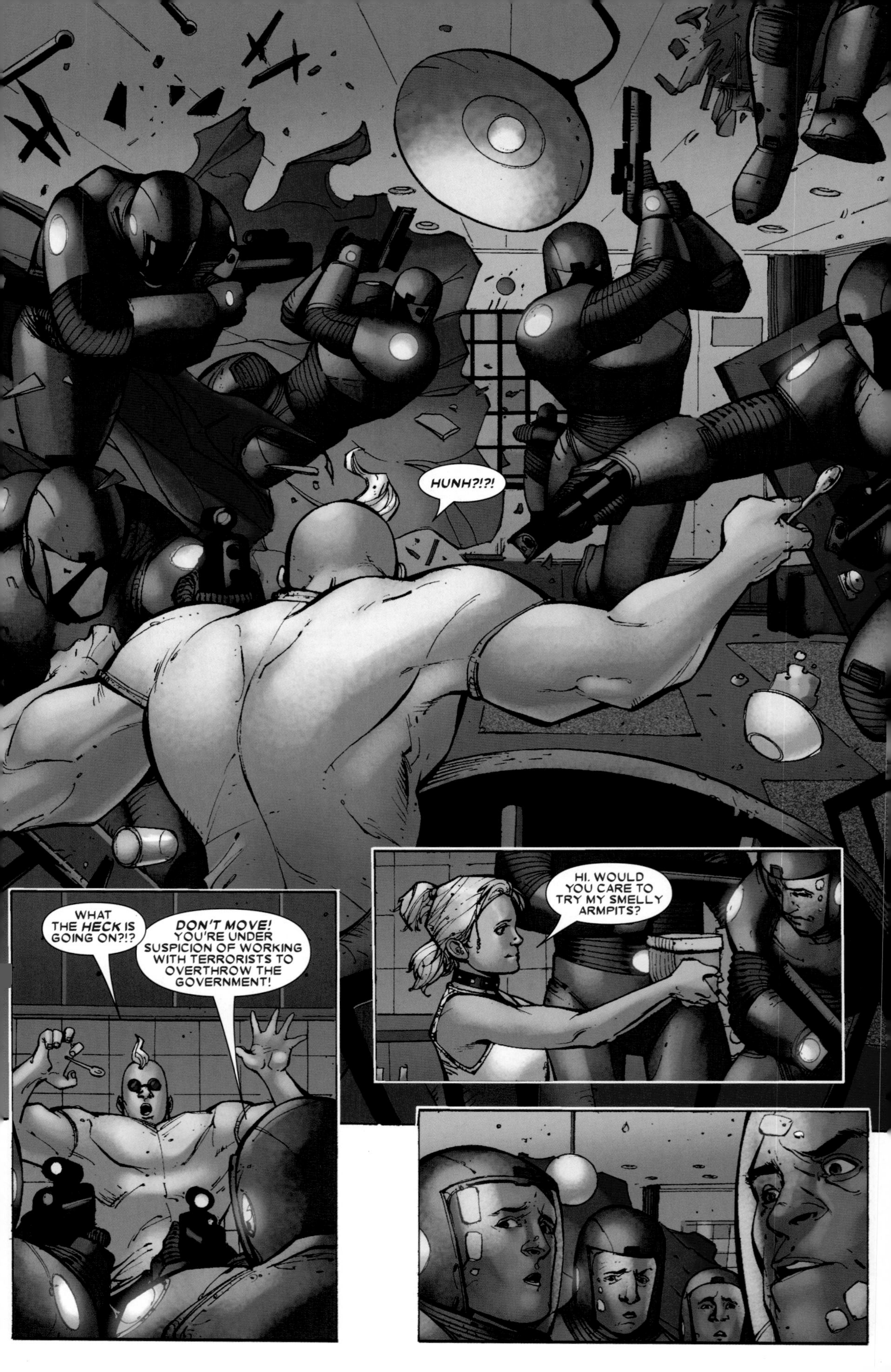
HUNH?!?!
WHAT THE HECK IS GOING ON?!?
DON'T MOVE! YOU'RE UNDER SUSPICION OF WORKING WITH TERRORISTS TO OVERTHROW THE GOVERNMENT!
HI. WOULD YOU CARE TO TRY MY SMELLY ARMPITS?

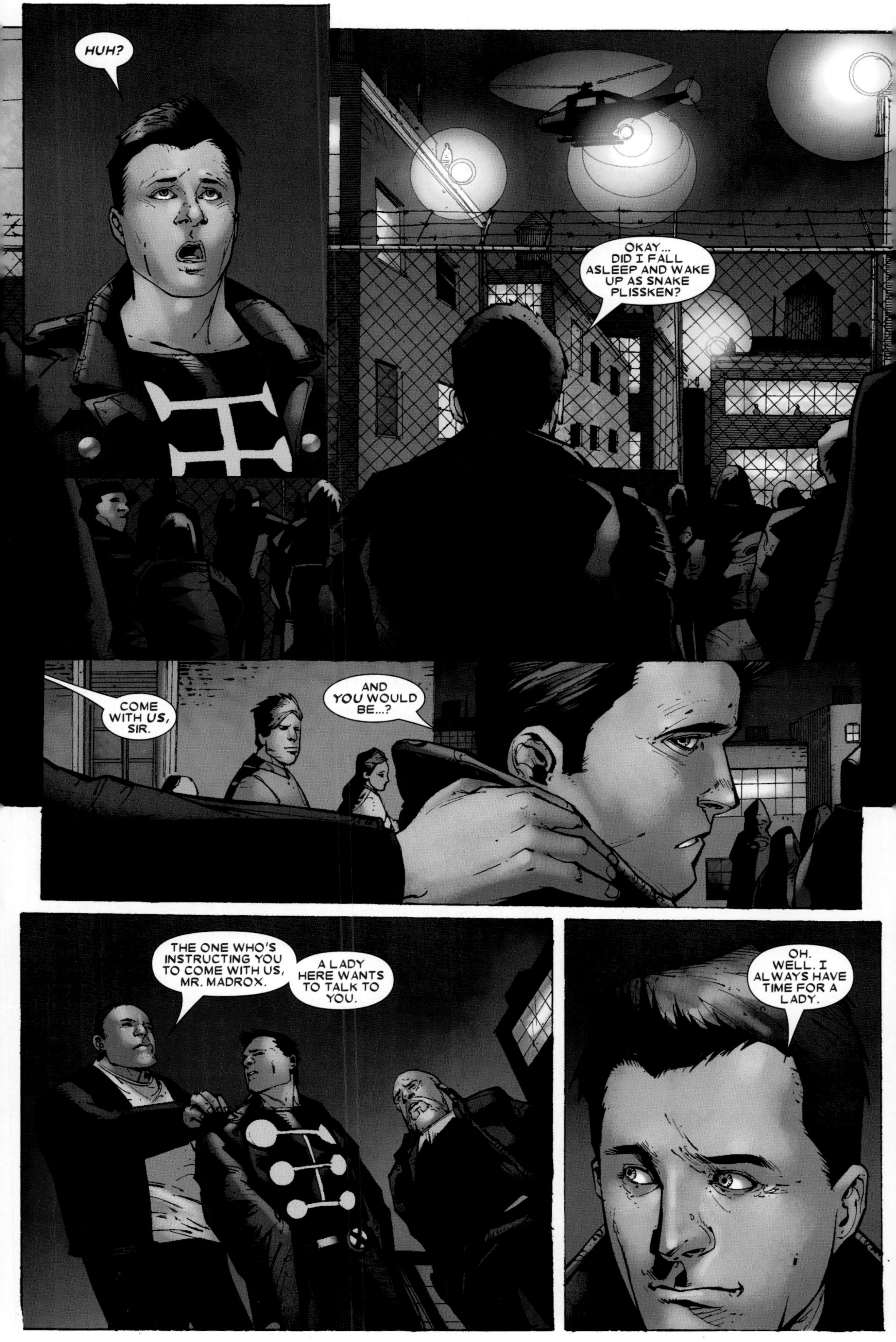
HUH?
OKAY... DID I FALL ASLEEP AND WAKE UP AS SNAKE PLISSKEN?
COME WITH US, SIR.
AND YOU WOULD BE...?
THE ONE WHO'S INSTRUCTING YOU TO COME WITH US, MR. MADROX.
A LADY HERE WANTS TO TALK TO YOU.
OH. WELL. I ALWAYS HAVE TIME FOR A LADY.

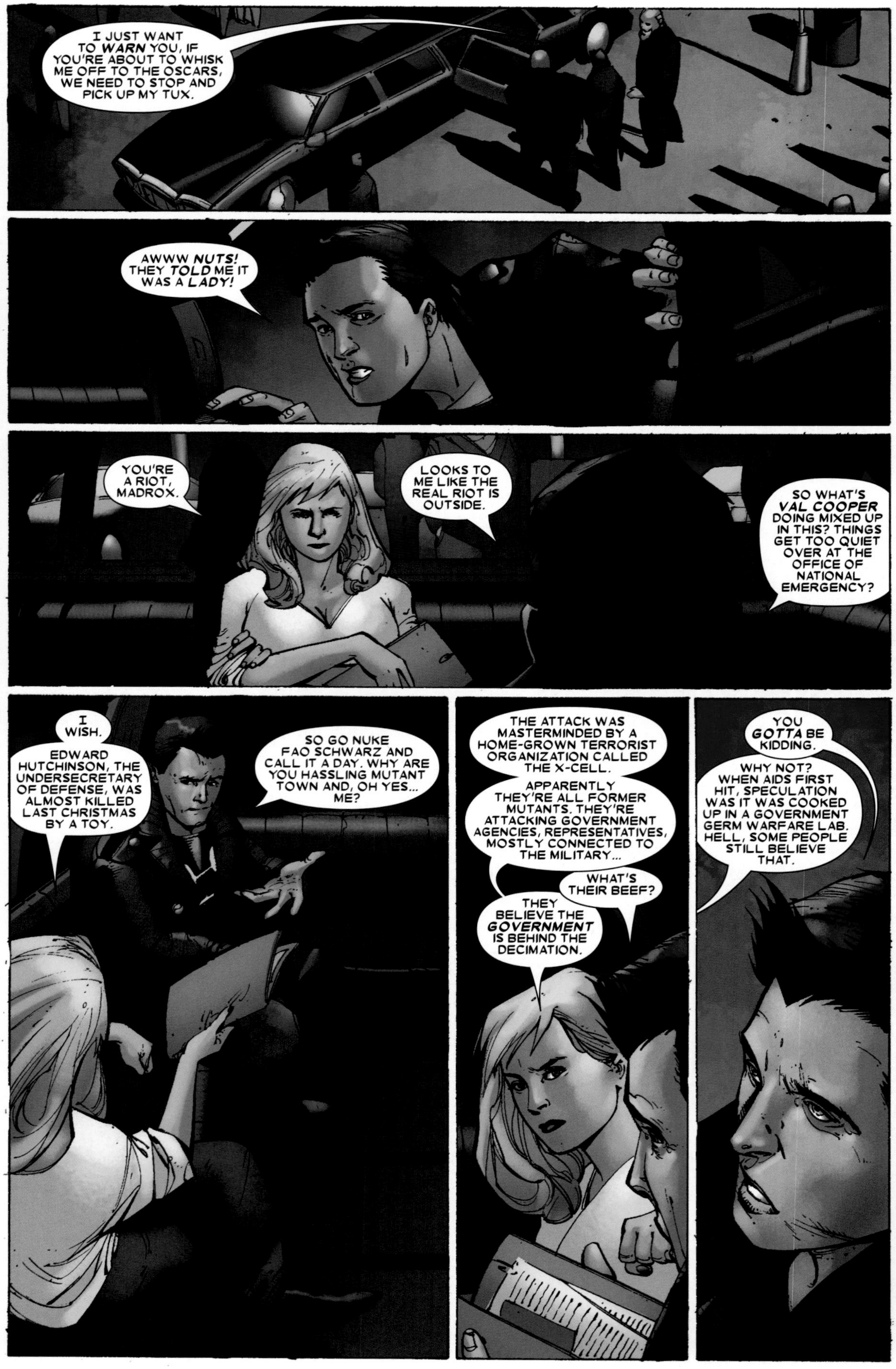
I JUST WANT TO WARN YOU, IF YOU'RE ABOUT TO WHISK ME OFF TO THE OSCARS, WE NEED TO STOP AND PICK UP MY TUX.
AWWW NUTS! THEY TOLD ME IT WAS A LADY!
YOU'RE A RIOT, MADROX.
LOOKS TO ME LIKE THE REAL RIOT IS OUTSIDE.
SO WHAT'S VAL COOPER DOING MIXED UP IN THIS? THINGS GET TOO QUIET OVER AT THE OFFICE OF NATIONAL EMERGENCY?
I WISH.
EDWARD HUTCHINSON, THE UNDERSECRETARY OF DEFENSE, WAS ALMOST KILLED LAST CHRISTMAS BY A TOY.
SO GO NUKE FAO SCHWARZ AND CALL IT A DAY. WHY ARE YOU HASSLING MUTANT TOWN AND, OH YES... ME?
THE ATTACK WAS MASTERMINDED BY A HOME-GROWN TERRORIST ORGANIZATION CALLED THE X-CELL.
APPARENTLY THEY'RE ALL FORMER MUTANTS. THEY'RE ATTACKING GOVERNMENT AGENCIES, REPRESENTATIVES, MOSTLY CONNECTED TO THE MILITARY...
WHAT'S THEIR BEEF?
THEY BELIEVE THE GOVERNMENT IS BEHIND THE DECIMATION.
YOU GOTTA BE KIDDING.
WHY NOT? WHEN AIDS FIRST HIT, SPECULATION WAS IT WAS COOKED UP IN A GOVERNMENT GERM WARFARE LAB. HELL, SOME PEOPLE STILL BELIEVE THAT.

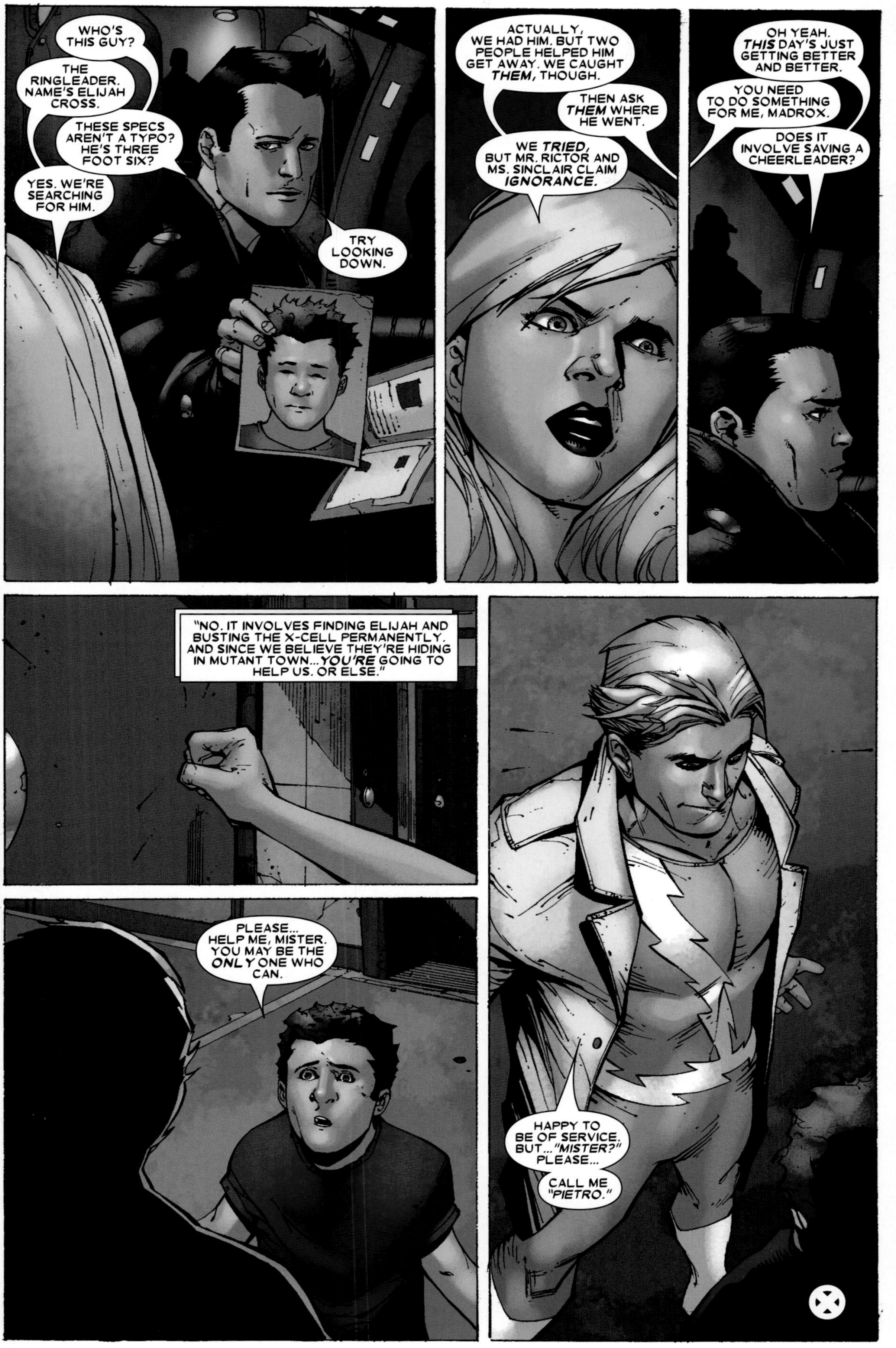
WHO'S THIS GUY?
THE RINGLEADER. NAME'S ELIJAH CROSS.
THESE SPECS AREN'T A TYPO? HE'S THREE FOOT SIX?
YES. WE'RE SEARCHING FOR HIM.
TRY LOOKING DOWN.
ACTUALLY, WE HAD HIM. BUT TWO PEOPLE HELPED HIM GET AWAY. WE CAUGHT *THEM*, THOUGH.
THEN ASK *THEM* WHERE HE WENT.
WE *TRIED*, BUT MR. RICTOR AND MS. SINCLAIR CLAIM *IGNORANCE*.
OH YEAH. *THIS* DAY'S JUST GETTING BETTER AND BETTER.
YOU NEED TO DO SOMETHING FOR ME, MADROX.
DOES IT INVOLVE SAVING A CHEERLEADER?
"NO. IT INVOLVES FINDING ELIJAH AND BUSTING THE X-CELL PERMANENTLY. AND SINCE WE BELIEVE THEY'RE HIDING IN MUTANT TOWN... *YOU'RE* GOING TO HELP US. OR ELSE."
PLEASE... HELP ME, MISTER. YOU MAY BE THE *ONLY* ONE WHO CAN.
HAPPY TO BE OF SERVICE. BUT... *"MISTER?"* PLEASE...
CALL ME *"PIETRO."*

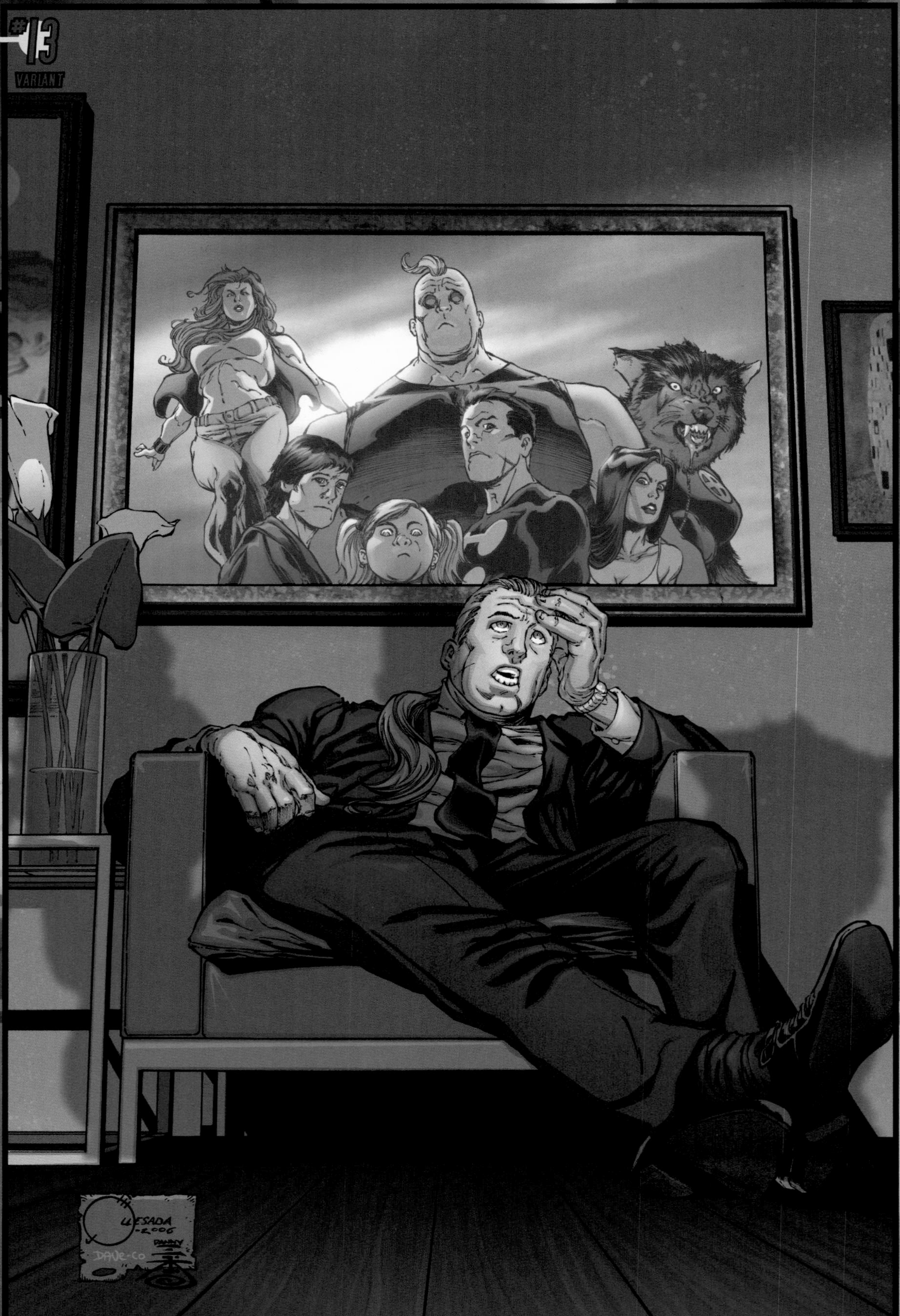
#13
VARIANT
QUESADA
2006
DANNY
DAVE-CO